CRIMSON HEART:
LET ME TELL YOU MY STORY

BY MAL M. MOORE

WITH STEVE TOWNSEND

Published by The Mal and Charlotte Moore
Crimson Heart Foundation
Crimsonheartfoundation.com
Officially Licensed by the University of Alabama
First published 2014
Revised edition printed 2016

In keeping with Mal's wishes, this book is published by The Mal and Charlotte Moore Crimson Heart Foundation. All proceeds of this and future projects of the Foundation will go to support various charities and entities that were near to Mal and Charlotte's heart. The Foundation is organized as a 501(c)3 charitable entity. For additional information concerning The Mal and Charlotte Moore Foundation go to www.crimsonheartfoundation.com.

ISBN: 978-0-692-78275-0
Library of Congress Control Number: 2014914863
Photo on the Front Cover by Kent Gidley
Photos on Rear Cover provided by University of Alabama Athletics and
Paul W. Bryant Museum

CONTENTS

TRIBUTE

MY FATHER'S FINAL GIFT

BY HEATHER MOORE COOK

I am still not certain that I have accepted that my first love, my daddy, is no longer with us. This past year has been the toughest of my life. When one loses someone they love so dearly, it helps to know others feel your pain and that they too feel the loss.

To say I am not alone in my grief would be an understatement. I do believe Daddy, Coach Moore or Mal, however you knew him, was one of the most beloved figures in college athletics. His legacy, what he accomplished professionally, the lessons he taught, and his charismatic personality will stand the test of time.

The outpouring of love for my father from the people of Alabama has been overwhelming and his impact did not stop at our borders. I have heard from people all over this country and different parts of the world about how much they loved and admired my father.

I could easily write my own book of stories growing up as a coach's kid, and how I would love to share what all I have received in hand written letters, long phone conversations, and "I want you to know" moments. There was no doubt my father was a special man, but until his death, I did not realize the magnitude of how many lives that he personally touched and enriched for the better.

Daddy was a man's man, a relentless competitor, a player's coach, a coach's AD, a friend's most sincere confidant, a charmer with quite the wit, and the best damn story teller around! Daddy was a success at everything he did and his secret weapon was his heart.

My father was raised in a God fearing home and knew nothing but love and hard work growing up. When my parents became engaged, Mama Moore told my mother, "Mal will be good to you because he knows no other way." My parents had been happily married for 22 years when my mother started her long and devastating 20-year battle with Alzheimer's.

Daddy truly took to heart his wedding vows and lovingly took care of Mother until the day she died. Now that I am grown and have experienced adult life, how I marvel at the strength of character, the devotion and the sheer toughness my father showed stepping away from coaching, the only career that he had ever known and loved, at only 53 years of age, to care for his sweet Charlotte.

What he endured daily was heartbreaking. If anyone came to Dad with a similar story, he was there for them no matter how long they needed to talk or if they needed some grace to be shown. The personal letters we have received from former players, coaches, and the community on how my father comforted them is unbelievable. Jenny Mainz, Alabama's women's tennis coach, gave a beautiful interview this spring on how she would always be grateful to my father for his unwavering support for her, when she too, was going through a similar situation with her family.

To know my father cared and understood, gave people strength. If you had been touched by my father at some point in time, then he was your friend for life and you could always count on him to be there, in the best of times and the worst.

Luckily for my father, he was born a Moore and if you are born into our clan, there are two things you just naturally know how to do: give a good hug and have a heck of a good time...and old Mal was an expert at both!

Gene Stallings, an assistant of Coach Bryant's when Daddy was a player, once said in a staff meeting, "Everywhere I go, I see Mal Moore!" And, I don't think he was talking about the library. Enjoying life was never a problem for my father. If Daddy wasn't dancing in the kitchen with Mama, then he was dancing with me and he knew the words to just about every song to boot.

I honestly don't think there was a bird hunt Daddy turned down until the very end, when he was just too weak. Hunting was his passion. Boy, how he loved to hit the outdoors with his dear old buddies Paul, Goat, Angus, Jim, Price, Kirk, Ronny and his brother, Frank. My cousins, Randy and Chuck, had to report in on all of their hunting excursions or they were in trouble.

Daddy had a lot to learn in life, like we all do, but no one could laugh at himself better than he could. For most of us, there are situations we would like to soon forget. Mal would turn an embarrassing experience into a story that would have a room full of people laughing including himself. He could make anyone feel at ease and he didn't care what your stake in life was, he befriended everyone.

As you read the book, you will soon discover there was a reason Coach Bryant was sending Dad and his dear friend, Dude Hennessey, to recruit the best. If you ask Nick Saban, Jay Seawell, our current back to back national champion men's golf coach, or Executive Associate Athletic Director Ronny Robertson, they will all tell you, they had no intention of coming to Alabama until they sat down with Coach Moore. George Husack, Alabama's men's tennis coach and Daddy's last coaching hire, told me of his experience when he sat down with my father.

George said Daddy started by saying he wasn't going to talk salary, what he wanted to know was if after seeing Alabama's beautiful campus, the facilities and meeting some of her people, "could he fall in love with the University and give her all he had?"

Coach Husack said he had never had anyone present a school that way and he was hooked. I think I heard from every coach that if they had a huge recruit visiting they were bugging his administrative aide Judy Tanner to see Dad. "Coach Moore could seal the deal," was the common theme. No one loved the University of Alabama more, so when Daddy spoke true love flowed from his heart.

One thing is a fact, Coach Moore loved his players/athletes and would do anything for them and their families, and it did not matter if they were currently playing or had graduated thirty plus years ago. Daddy was always trying to reunite teams and recognizing players when they needed to be remembered. He had their utmost respect as a coach.

When Major Ogilvie, one of our great halfbacks, was inducted into the Alabama Sports Hall of Fame this past May, he thanked Daddy for being the great man that he was. Major said it was obvious to the players how much faith, respect and confidence Coach Bryant had in Mal as a coach and as a person, and how much all the past players appreciated what Daddy had done with improving our athletic facilities and guiding our athletic program.

I have stacks of letters from former players telling me how much they admired and love my father. Allen Pinkett, the outstanding Notre Dame and NFL tailback, autographed a picture to Daddy, "Simply, the best coach I've ever had. Also a great man who instilled in me the value of loyalty and pride. I will never forget you coach."

Richard Todd, one of Daddy's great Alabama quarterbacks and an 11-year veteran of the NFL, wrote, "Your dad was a mountain top above any of my other coaches because he really cared about you as a person and not only as a player. If I would have been a coach your father would have been the only one I would have wanted to emulate."

A letter I received from Kevin Smith, a Notre Dame quarterback and an old friend, summed up something that I heard from so many people that worked for Dad. He wrote, "As a coach he had the unique ability to make you want to give your best effort without yelling or screaming. He carried himself with a quiet dignity that set him apart from the other coaches. My Notre Dame teammates all thought Coach Moore was special."

It is without question, my father was a great football coach and teacher. I know this for the simple fact, Coach Bryant could have had anybody he wanted and he slowly groomed my father to be one of his most trusted men. I read something years ago that said, if Emory Bellard was the "Father of the Wishbone," then Mal Moore was the "Wishbone Wizard."

My father's offenses in the 1970s were legendary and he was a hot ticket at coaches' clinics during that decade. He had several head coaching offers during that time. One that he strongly considered was the Fresno State job.

Coach Bryant convinced Mal to turn the job down and told him better things were in store for him if he stayed. Honestly, there was only one head job Daddy ever wanted and that was to be the head coach of the Crimson Tide. That dream never was fulfilled, but Coach Bryant was right in the end and better things were in store for Dad.

It was during this time, that Daddy was gaining all the experience that he would need and would use to become one of the strongest and most successful athletic directors in the country. Coach Moore's last full year as athletic director, 2012, the University of Alabama had the most national championships in the NCAA that year with FOUR: football, gymnastics, softball and women's golf. (And if Texas had not made a 20-foot birdie on the 18th green, we might have had a fifth, in men's golf. Alabama had to wait one more year for that championship.) This did not happen by chance. It was leadership that created the environment and set the standards to be champions.

In the old days, most athletic directors were coaches. I am sad to say Daddy was one of a dying breed. Any coach will tell you, unless you have coached and recruited, you have no idea what all is involved and the pressures you feel.

My father knew first-hand what a coach's life is like, how the profession can affect your family, how hard it is to recruit and at a school like Alabama, the immense pressure you feel to not just win, but to win championships. He backed all of his coaches with everything he had and was always straight up with them on how they stood.

Mitch Gaspard, Alabama's baseball coach, told me one day that Daddy had such a wealth of experience that there wasn't a player problem that you could not come to him about. Coach Moore had encountered just about everything in his career and he was happy to lend advice on what had worked for him.

Due to the fact Daddy had played and coached on so many championship teams, he knew first-hand what the intensity level and commitment had to be from a coaching staff and team to reach the ultimate goal. Daddy also knew it was not an overnight deal to win a championship and that it took time and many variables are involved.

One of the most important necessities is your facilities. When Daddy took over in 1999, Alabama was probably close to the bottom of the SEC in this area. What is so astonishing about what my father was able to accomplish was the amount of money the athletic department raised and the detailed vision my father had and sold to just about every Crimson Tide supporter he met...and he didn't do it when we were winning, he orchestrated this when we were down and out and on probation!

This is the result of an almost fifty year relationship with the Alabama faithful: athletes, alumni, employees, and fans. Everyone knew how much my father loved the University and if you could ever trust someone, it would be Mal Moore. As

Daddy used to say about the completed facilities "The table is set for great things to come."

Johnny Plott, a family friend, told me not long after Daddy passed away, "Heather, your Daddy could assemble a group of 10 or 12 very prominent business men that are all used to getting their way; and in the meeting, none of us would get what we wanted, but no one would have their feathers ruffled and Mal would be advancing the ball forward. He had some kind of magic over people and there will never be another one quite like him."

I have to agree with Johnny. I do not think I will ever know another soul as strong, as loving and as selfless as my father. As soon as it became apparent to Daddy, that the fight for his life, if given the chance, was going to be a very long and drawn out ordeal, he put the retirement wheels in motion.

I personally tried to stop him because I have always known in my heart that as soon as Daddy retired from the athletic world, I would lose him within a month, just like Coach Bryant. Daddy was so loved and cherished by the University, they were willing to wait for his return, but my father told me in the most certain and strong voice that I had no idea what it was like to run that athletic department and it could not be without a strong leader for a day.

With the help of Dr. Judy Bonner, Dr. Robert Witt and the Board of Trustees, he made sure it was all done very quickly and quietly so that the new athletic director was in place and ready to roll without missing a beat. Coach Bill Battle, was a teammate of my father, a long time personal friend of his, and a very accomplished business man in his own right. Coach Battle will do a fantastic job.

The last of Daddy's many gifts he has given over his whole career is this book. My husband, Steve, read it ahead of me, and due to the fact, that my Steve absolutely loved my Dad, he was slightly disappointed because Daddy never took credit for anything, but that we all know, is the Mal way.

As I read the book, I cried and I laughed. I found myself staring out the window after many stories. Whatever story I was reading, I would relive that time period and all the added details I knew and all the emotions that my father had invested. I cannot tell you how many times we would talk on the phone and he would say, "Let me go sweet Heather, I have a lot on my mind."

He worried about that department and its people like he did his own home and family. At the University's Memorial Service for Daddy, Dr. Witt mentions that a trainer had once told him if you really listen to Mal's stories, he is usually trying to tell you something. Later on, Coach Saban spoke and gave a perfect example of a story Daddy once told that helped him in coaching Mark Ingram, our Heisman Trophy winner.

Well, this book is filled with those types of stories. I feel that a young athlete especially one that would like to go into coaching could read this book at three different stages of his/her career, as a player, a young coach and as a seasoned veteran and walk away learning something. Some of the stories he did not have to tell, but he did it for the deep love and admiration for the athletes and coaches he left behind.

I hope you enjoy the book as much as I did. Daddy did not like to play political games, but he was always a "team player." Now he wanted his teams or his boys to know a few of the behind the scenes details. How I wish Daddy could have lived to have finished all of his stories and to have polished up the book, but this is pure Mal and I could hear his voice as I turned the pages.

In coming to a close, everyone knew Daddy had a million guy buddies, but I want to personally thank the strong women that played a key role in his life and that always provided that hug Daddy always seemed to need.

When we were at Duke Hospital, I affectionately termed us, Mal's Gals. Tricia Stone, one of my Dad's dearest friends and favorite sidekick: Judy Tanner, his personal assistant (Daddy use to say, "What a boy from Dozier and a good ole girl from Opp, can do."); Mary Reyner, who my father so enjoyed and loved his last couple of years; and Mama Moore's fun but strong daughters, Donna Mason, Jean Long, Martha Morris and Amber Yoe, along with Daddy's strongest shield and supporter, my mother, Charlotte.

These ladies shared endless hugs and a million laughs. Our precious memories are our greatest treasures. No one ever loved or was more proud of their father, than I am. I will miss Daddy every day for the rest of my life, he was just that special.

I found a letter sent to my father after a team reunion. I am sharing a couple of paragraphs because the content speaks volumes:

Mal, we as former players owe you a lot-for you have kept the door open for all of us and kept the past alive in every aspect of Alabama Football. I have always said that if you do not recognize the past you cannot celebrate the present or the future. I have been involved in many Universities and no one recognizes the former players and makes them a part of the program like you do. Thank you for doing so.

Going through what we did-and it was pure survival at times with many not being able to endure-we were probably the crazy ones that did survive. But the funny thing-it was not the most talented-not the biggest or the strongest but it was the ones that had the toughest minds that would not give up. I really believed Coach Bryant pushed us to the limits-just to see how far he could push us during a game to win it down the stretch- he knew we would not ever give up no matter how hard it was.

As you enjoy this book, you will see Alabama through the eyes of a man who was surrounded by "champions" his whole life...as a player, as a coach and as their leader.

I have done a lot of reflecting this past year and I know one thing, greatness is molded over time. It is built brick by brick and passed down from one generation to the next. Coaches and their players are forever entwined as the lessons of the past are carried into the future and if you are not tough-minded, you will never make it.

Ponder these last few thoughts on my father's storied career:

The legendary, Knute Rockne coached Frank Thomas at Notre Dame, who in turn, coached Paul W. Bryant at Alabama. These three men won 12 national championships combined and my father was always keenly aware of the two schools' strong ties. Coach Bryant coached and mentored my father for 24 of the 25 five years he was at the Capstone. Upon leaving his alma mater, my father went to Notre Dame for three years and then coached in the NFL for four.

My father longed for the pageantry and traditions of college ball and he felt the most rewards coaching and molding young athletes. Coach Gene Stallings brought Daddy back home to Alabama as his head assistant and offensive coordinator. Daddy would never leave Alabama again.

Years later, as athletic director, Daddy was armed with the knowledge of the difference between coaching in the pros versus working at the collegiate level. Now equipped with freshly renovated, state of the art athletic facilities, and representing the Crimson Tide, one of the country's most storied athletic programs, my father was able to persuade Nick Saban to make his final coaching move. Coach Saban has four national titles, three of them at Alabama and his story isn't finished by a long shot.

My father was never a starter as a player nor a head coach, but that never stopped him from pursuing greatness. Due to his failing health, my father retired one week before he passed away. He left a championship record that included 16 national titles, including 10 in football. As athletic director, Alabama also won three gymnastics, one softball, one women's golf and finally men's golf a month after he passed away.

Daddy's 10th football title and the last championship victory he would see was against, no other, than the Fighting Irish of Notre Dame. Ironically, Coach Bryant and my father had coached against Notre Dame four times and could never beat them. This win would be Alabama's 15th national title in football. Daddy's Alabama jersey number was #15.

Just recently, Bill Battle pointed out to Kent Gidley, Alabama's photographer, that in the morning light Daddy's name reflects from the football building onto the black marble slab above the large silver script A on the Sarah Patterson Championship Plaza. A plaza designed by my father to showcase all of Alabama's championship teams and their outstanding coaches.

Coincidences maybe, but if you ask me, these are all signs that there was a master plan for my father's life that needed to have great triumphs and great sorrows. Without a doubt, Coach Moore was the bridge that connected Alabama's glorious past to the present and insured that her winning ways would continue for generations to come. However, more importantly, my father was used to mentor so many, both young and old, as an example of how a selfless life should be lived. As you read, discover what one can accomplish when you never give up and your guiding forces are trust, love, and loyalty. No one was more cherished by the masses or more loved at home, than my father, Mal Mathad Moore.

With all my love and admiration,

Heather Moore Cook

FOREWORD

BY NICK SABAN

Mal Moore was a very special man, a true Southern gentleman, a devoted family man and most importantly to me, my friend.

When Mal came to Miami to try to persuade me to take the Alabama job, I called Terry after I had my player meetings and told her that I didn't think I wanted to meet with him. I was going to stay with the Dolphins. She informed me then that Mal had already been to the house, and they had visited and she had invited him back to dinner that night.

It was one of the most important turning points in my professional career. Mal's pleasant way, his simple manner and his obvious love for the University of Alabama helped make a most difficult decision for me easier. Here was a man whose genuineness, honesty and integrity were important to me and when Terry and I were meeting privately to make our decision, those qualities helped me decide to coach the Crimson Tide.

Mal's sense of humor was another trait that I always admired. That night in Miami when Terry and I were discussing the Alabama job, Mal went in another room with my representative Jimmy Sexton. Jimmy asked Mal what he was going to do if I turned the job down. Mal laughed and said, "I'm sure not going back to Tuscaloosa. I'll just get the pilot to take me to Cuba where it's probably safer for me."

Working alongside Mal only strengthened me personally. Here was the most selfless man I'd ever known. He had no hidden agendas, never held a grudge, and never disrespected a single soul. I never heard him say a bad word about anyone and I sure never heard anyone say that Mal Moore treated them unfairly.

When I needed something for the football program, I'd go to Mal and he'd tell me, "Let's talk." And, then he would get it done.

During my six years with Mal, he was always at our dressing room door when a game ended, and he was always the happiest person there when we had been successful and won. He would shake hands and congratulate every player and every coach. A lot of people knew that, but what they didn't know was he was there when we lost as well.

Every Sunday morning after we'd lose a game, he would come by my office and we'd share some private time together and he always had the unique quality of making me feel better despite the way the game had turned out the day before. I think Mal just had that ability to make everyone feel a little better and be a better person.

My happiest moment for Mal was when he won the John Toner Award, given annually to the nation's best athletic director. I saw him before the dinner, and he had tears in his eyes and he thanked me for changing his life.

I told Mal that he had it wrong. Mal Moore had changed my life. He made me a better coach, a better person, a better team man. For all he accomplished in athletics, to me his lasting tribute is the care and loyalty he had to his wife Charlotte. His quiet dedication to her is the thing I respected most about Mal. His loyalty to her is, in my opinion, his greatest achievement.

Mal never forgot his roots and the values he learned as a child. His honesty and integrity will forever be a part of his legacy at the University of Alabama. I just appreciate the time I got to spend with Mal and see how happy he was after we won a National Championship. I am just honored to have been a part of helping him achieve his goal of returning the Crimson Tide to prominence. I am more honored to have been his friend.

Nick Saban
Head Football Coach, University of Alabama

PROLOGUE

In February 2013, after experiencing a persistent and nagging cough throughout the fall of 2012, Mal Moore was finally convinced by his close friend, confidant and Senior Associate Athletic Director Ronny Robertson to consult with Dr. Allen Yeilding in Birmingham to determine the cause of his malady.

The diagnosis wasn't good. A visit to pulmonary specialist confirmed that the 73-year-old patriarch of Alabama athletics was suffering from idiopathic pulmonary fibrosis. Without a lung transplant, the prognosis for recovery was disheartening at best.

A day after his doctor visit, Mal and I had our weekly taping session about his memoirs at the Bryant Museum, but unlike our numerous other meetings over the years, he didn't greet me with his usual smile. He told me that he had received the prognosis he, like any of us, would dread. He believed he was in the early stages of his disease, but he knew he had to make plans to exit the stage of Crimson Tide sports.

My friendship with Mal dated back to his days as an assistant coach for the legendary Paul Bryant. Our friendship became ever closer when Mal returned to Tuscaloosa with Gene Stallings in January 1990, and was forever sealed in 1993 when he left his beloved position of coaching and joined the administrative team under then-Athletic Director Hootie Ingram.

I didn't need to offer Mal my help or consolation that day. I knew what he expected me to do. His attorney and friend, Kirk Wood, contacted me and we began helping Mal formulate his exit strategy.

He planned to retire at the end of the 2013 football season, with the second alternative being leaving at the end of the fiscal year that July. Both plans called for Mal to continue serving the institution he loved as Athletic Director Emeritus, a position in which he could contribute to the University at the direction of the President and the Board.

Under a cloak of secrecy, Mal worked on his retirement plans. Once he was satisfied with the plan, he met with Dr. Judy Bonner, Paul Bryant Jr., and then with the chancellor of the University System, Dr. Robert Witt, to make them aware of his health issue and to seek their guidance and approval.

Sadly, it didn't require much medical expertise to recognize that Mal was failing quickly. The realization that he might not make either of his deadline dates was sobering.

Our final meeting in the Bryant Museum came on Thursday, March 7. He had difficulty walking through those doors that day and he told me after our meeting he wanted to make sure I stayed on top of two projects: finishing his memoirs and the completion of the display with all of his bowl watches and championship rings in the building that bears his name.

He stressed he wanted the book to be his memories and his view of what transpired, not those of others remembering what had happened during his long and illustrious career as an athlete, coach and administrator. His final day in his office, Friday, March 8, was marked by triumph and sorrow.

Despite his failing health, Mal was extremely pleased with the completion of the new weight facility adjacent to his office. His loyal assistant, Judy Tanner, who was also acutely aware of his health issues, arranged for Mal to imprint his hands in wet cement outside his office in a patio area that overlooked the practice fields where he had labored for so many years.

Photographer Kent Gidley was there to capture the moment, and Kirk Wood was also there finishing some necessary legal business in regards to his imminent retirement.

After placing his hands in the cement, Mal had to have help from all three to stand back up and help him back into his office. As he was settling back in his chair, one of the construction workers on the building mistook the handprint as a prank and he smoothed over the area, forever erasing that one final moment Mal spent as the department head.

The moment had passed. The concrete hardened too quickly on a cold afternoon and Mal was just not able to repeat the ceremony. The inadvertent act of the worker though hardly diminishes the memories of his accomplishments or his unyielding loyalty to the Crimson Tide.

Before leaving his office for the final time, Mal asked his administrative assistant Judy Tanner to visit with him, and he read her one of his favorite poems, Crossing the Bar, by Alfred Tennyson.

Mal entered Brookwood Hospital in Birmingham Sunday, March 10 and was transported to the Duke Medical Center in Durham the following Wednesday.

During my last visit with Mal on March 28 at the Duke Medical Center, he shooed some others out of the room and reiterated his wishes to me about completing his display and his book. I promised him I'd get it done in the fashion he wanted.

Sadly, we had many more yarns and details of other events to cover, but we never had that opportunity to complete them. They were moments forever lost, just like the paved-over handprints near his old office. So the following pages are a compilation of stories that were important to Mal, told in Mal's own words. These are Mal's Memories from the truly crimson heart of Mal M. Moore.

Steve Townsend
University of Alabama

INTRODUCTION

L ooking out on the football practice fields from my office window in late November 2006, I felt the weight of the entire Alabama football world on my shoulders. Out there on those deserted fields were lingering memories of championships won and disappointments endured on a roller coaster ride the Crimson Tide had experienced for much of the past decade.

I knew the history and tradition of the University's football program rested squarely on my shoulders. Frankly, it was hard not to think about it, because virtually every friend I had kept reminding me that the future of Alabama football would be determined by my decisions in the upcoming weeks. Perhaps that's an overstatement, but I can assure you I was resolved to make the right decision for the sake of my school.

Going through another coaching change was neither something I had planned, nor something I wanted to do. The easiest thing, I had learned from first-hand experience was for critics to say, "You should have hired this one or that one." Only the privileged few who know all the inside information really understand all the variables involved in hiring a coach. There is just a lot of information that cannot be shared with even the most ardent supporters.

I didn't need telephone calls, faxes or e-mails to know this hire would be the most critical one for the Crimson Tide since Paul Bryant was hired away from Texas A&M in December 1957. Even though I had many people offering help and suggestions, in many ways I faced the loneliest and most excruciating five or six weeks in my professional career.

You know, a lot of memories raced through my mind, starting with my days growing up in Dozier, Alabama, and all the years I had spent in athletics. Most of those years had been spent as part of the Crimson Tide, and so many with my mentor and coach, Paul Bryant. I had learned through my family and through Coach Bryant about the will to win, and to do it with class and dignity.

I wasn't going to waver in my resolve to re-establish Alabama as a pre-eminent football program; and I knew it would take every one of those life experiences, some good and some not so good, to hire the very best person to uplift the sagging hopes of our players and fans.

As the sun set on Tuscaloosa, I thought of the future. But I didn't forget my past either, from those days growing up in Dozier to all those years I spent as a player, a coach and then an administrator at the school I loved with all my heart.

Those memories strengthened me that day to persevere and bring pride back to the Crimson Tide. These are my memories, so let me tell you my story . . .

1

GROWING UP IN DOZIER: THOSE WORLD WAR II MEMORIES

U nless you were born in the pre-World War II time frame like I was, I doubt if you can really relate to the small-town, farming lifestyle in which most of us lived back in the 1930s and 1940s. I was born December 19, 1939 to Dempsey Clark Moore and Fannie Bozeman Moore on a farm about seven miles from Dozier, a small spot on the map in Crenshaw County, Alabama.

That was the first year of the now-defunct Blue-Gray All-Star Football Classic in Montgomery. My mother happened to be reading the newspaper, saw the Blue team had a player named Mal and she obviously liked it.

I was born near Limbs Crossroads where one of my first memories was attending Limbs Baptist Church. My father and mother claimed to have coerced me into going by reminding me I liked listening to the hymns, though I really don't recall that. As the years passed by, I know I always loved hearing all those church hymns from my childhood.

I tell you what I do remember was that on the back wall behind the pulpit, written in a big semi-circle in gold letters was the phrase, "In God We Trust." My mom would always tell me to remember those words.

The little country church also had these old kerosene lamps to light up the building; just like our house. By the time I was nine however, we had a house with electricity, something I found quite amazing. Just flip a switch and there was light.

Sunday afternoons were my favorite time of the week. All of our family would come home for the weekend, and as a young child, there was a comfort being surrounded with such a loving congregation of folks.

If I had to tell people something about me that would probably surprise them the most is that I always loved poetry, though I was never much of a writer and I never penned a poem in my life. I always thought a poet could describe in a short paragraph, the true feelings of one's spirits. On those Sundays, after my family and friends had dispersed and headed home, I always felt the poems, "A Psalm of Life" and "The Day Is Done." expressed my feelings.

The words that forever flow from my soul when I thought about those days were from "The Day is Done" by Henry Wadsworth Longfellow:

I see the lights of the village
Gleam through the rain and the mist,
And a feeling of sadness comes o'er me
That my soul cannot resist:

A feeling of sadness and longing,
That is not akin to pain,
And resembles sorrow only
As the mist resembles the rain. – Henry Wadsworth Longfellow

I always found comfort in poetry. I enjoyed reading and reciting poems to my wife, Charlotte and my daughter, Heather and later to my two grandchildren, Anna Lee and Cannon Cook. My family is the cornerstone of my life, and I wouldn't trade my parents, siblings, wife, daughter, son-in-law and grandchildren for any in the world.

You should never forget where you come from, and growing up in Dozier, Alabama, to me was about as good as it could really get. Growing up there made me who I am and prepared me for the challenges I'd face along the way.

I was the sixth of seven children. My oldest siblings, twins Douglas and Donna were followed by Jean, Frank and Martha before I came along. I was born in the front bedroom of our old farmhouse. My youngest sister, Amber, became the first of the Moore children to be born in a hospital.

Back in those days, every small town seemed to have a country doctor who would make the rounds and help out families in the community. Dr. Parker helped deliver me, so I had early medical attention, though many children in the area came into the world with the help of a midwife.

Of course, I don't remember it, other than listening to my parents sometimes talk about it, but the United States was just easing out of the Great Depression that had commenced 10 years before I was born. My folks struggled just like everyone else, but they had their farm and helped out their neighbors as much as possible by sharing their crops and milk from the cows.

During my early years, the highlight of my day was running to the mailbox, hoping we'd gotten a letter, even better, a package of some sort. Around lunchtime, I'd hear the sound of the old mail truck approaching the dirt road near our house.

I'd race the 50 yards or so to meet the mailman, who'd tease me every day about being his most faithful customer, as I was always there to greet him regardless of the weather conditions. He was always there, just like the old creed said, whether, rain, snow or sleet, and I was always there to greet him as well.

Our nearest neighbors lived about two miles away, so before I entered school I had to do quite a bit of self-entertaining during the day. One of the most exciting times came when Rural Electric Association started stringing lines, bringing electricity into the county.

I'd spend hours watching the men work, putting up poles and climbing them to hang the wires. Whenever my dad would unravel a sack of mule feed, I'd grab the strings and save them, to make myself a belt to emulate the men who climbed up those poles with their big leather belts.

I never could figure out how to make spikes for my shoes, but I'd use my self-made, sack-stringed belts and buckle them around trees in the yard to shinny up them just like the REA workers. Then I'd tie more string from tree to tree and hang old flashlight batteries on them to make them look like the transformers on the electrical lines. It was all in fun, but it sure kept me busy for an entire summer.

Probably our most important appliance in the house back then was a battery-powered radio. Our family radio would provide entertainment during those years, but during the war, it was the source of news about what was taking place on the major fronts of the world.

My oldest brother Douglas enlisted in the United States Navy immediately after the attack on Pearl Harbor in 1941, and I don't even remember seeing him since I was only two years-old at the time of the assault.

Our closest neighbors, Earl and Euni Bryan, would come to our house, listen to news broadcasts with us, and drink coffee with my parents. I didn't understand the gravity of the war and its impact, including the welfare of my brother Douglas, who had probably never been out of Crenshaw County his entire life before marching off to war. He was assigned to the USS Portland, a heavy cruiser that was involved in quite a few naval battles.

I remember how faithfully my mother would write him and how everyone prayed for his and others safe return from both European and Pacific Theaters. During December, 1944, around my fifth birthday, our community was rocked with the news that one of our own, Bruzell Hogg, had been killed by the Germans in one of the last major battles in Europe, the Battle of the Bulge.

Everyone felt the immense pain of the Hogg Family. My father dressed me up and took me to the military funeral that featured a 21-gun salute to our fallen soldier. Patriotism became awfully important to me on that sad winter's day.

In August of 1945, the mill's whistle started pealing and didn't stop. There was jubilation, for the war was finally over, and my oldest brother would be returning home, much to the happiness of the Moore family.

My mother was out milking the cows and I was outside playing near the old dirt road that wound down from our house to the log cabin where Earl and Euni Bryan lived. It was getting late in the day, and I could hear this truck roaring down the road and see the dust flying up from its tires.

The truck started braking when it got past our property and backed up a little bit, and then pulled over to where my mother was milking the last cow of the day. A passenger got out and asked, "How are you doing, Mrs. Moore?"

I was watching all this, not really grasping it. My mother told the man that she was doing fine but I could tell she was as puzzled by the entire scene as I was. Then this man in his full Navy uniform got out of the middle of the cab of the truck, and I heard my mother scream and start crying.

I knew then that my brother had come home. That's the first time I ever remember seeing him. Douglas had caught a train from the West Coast all the way to Dozier, where the two men picked him up and delivered him home. It was a surreal moment; one that I would never forget.

2

RADIO SHOWS, BANK ROBBERY AND THE WASHING MACHINE

I t's truly amazing that what was so intriguing to me as a child would certainly seem mundane with today's young folks. We never owned a television the entire time I was growing up, and we had to use our imagination to create our own games and entertainment.

Our family used to love to gather around the piano and sing hymns and other popular songs of that time period. My father loved to sing, my sister Donna had a beautiful voice, sister Jean could sing alto, and sister Martha played the piano. I think about those family gatherings and how wonderful those moments were to all of us.

One thing I didn't look forward to was going to school for the first time. It's pretty laughable now, but it wasn't on that first day of elementary school in Dozier. My mother and father had to almost drag me there, howling all the way. Like I said, our closest neighbors lived two miles away and the only children I really knew were my older siblings. I'd never been away from them and this was a whole new experience being around other children.

Once I adapted to the old brick schoolhouse in Dozier, it became my second home for the next 12 years. During that time period, my father bought a sawmill. If he could work any harder than he did farming, he managed to do so at the mill. I learned so many positive things from my folks. Hard work and loyalty were certainly two that would sustain me throughout my career.

It's pretty safe to say that you can ask anyone who grew up in the same time frame as I did, and they'll tell you how families would gather around the radio and listen to the programs that I found just as entertaining as the ones that I would later view on television.

If I had to pick my two favorites, they would be *"The Shadow"* and *"The Lone Ranger."* The Shadow was a crime-busting vigilante who had psychic powers and, the best I can remember, he always got his man. The intro of the show went, "Who knows what evil lurks in the hearts of men? The Shadow knows."

I could also envision myself being the Lone Ranger; riding the white stallion, wearing the mask; and bringing in the bad guy. Yes, those were my two favorites.

What memories.

Dozier didn't have a theater either, but there was a company that would set up tents and a projector near the downtown area and show movies on one Saturday in the summer. I'd ride my bicycle there and meet up with some friends for what we deemed about as good a time as you could have.

They'd sell soft drinks for a nickel. If I was lucky I'd have a dime and could get a bar of candy, a bag of popcorn, or a bag of salted Planters' peanuts. You know the ones that had the little peanut man with the monocle as a logo.

Mainly, they'd show old westerns, and I loved the ones that featured Johnny Mack Brown, Hopalong Cassidy, and of course, the Lone Ranger. At that time I didn't have a clue that Johnny Mack Brown had been one of the early football heroes at the University of Alabama, but I knew he was one of heck of a cowboy.

We'd fill that tent up, too. There was never an empty spot. After their day in Dozier, the owners of the traveling movie shows would fold up the tents and move to another little town, where I'm sure they were embraced just as warmly.

Sometimes, I wonder if Andy Griffith didn't use Dozier as his model for Mayberry on his hit television show of the 1960s. Several times on the show the Mayberry bank gets robbed; and it happened in Dozier three times when I was living there. The most memorable for me happened when I was still in elementary school.

I don't remember exactly how old I was, but I had a bicycle and we'd moved from the farm into Dozier. It was summertime and when everyone at the bank had left for lunch it was robbed. The robbery was the buzz around the community. Two FBI agents came in to investigate and I trailed them around on my bicycle because I was so excited about seeing them and wondering if they'd catch the robbers.

I'll never forget one of them in a short sleeve shirt with a tie. He had two pistols, and I asked him if he was going to catch the crooks, and he said "Ya betcha." For a kid this was as exciting as it could be.

Years later, when I was an assistant coach at Alabama, the bank was robbed again. My first thought was "not again!" We used to get all the newspapers from across the state in the office, and Coach Bryant was reading the article in the Crenshaw newspaper about the robbery. I'll never forget him saying, "This could only happen in a small town in the South."

When the bank was robbed on this occasion, there was only one person in the bank. I guess you'd call him the security guard. He was blind in one eye and wore glasses so he could see out of the other. The robber just came in, grabbed the guard, yanked off his glasses, and locked him in a safe.

When the robbers were leaving the bank, the mayor, Bud Johnson, and one of the teachers in Dozier, Kenneth Cook, tried to stop them. Kenneth had a shotgun and took a shot at the car, and then hopped in a car with the mayor to give chase. In the article, it said Bud was gaining on them when he ran out of gas on Highway 29 near Andalusia.

Coach Bryant loved that story and told me to call Bud and find out what happened. So, I called Bud and said "Hell, Bud, I can read through the lines. You were gaining on them, didn't know what to do, so you just pulled off the road!" I laughed and asked him, "How does it feel to be like Barney Fife in Mayberry?"

For a town of 300, that was some kind of action.

While the radio, the movies and the bank robberies provided some real entertainment, I have to confess one of the most mesmerizing moments for me as a child was when we got our first washing machine.

After we got electricity, my dad brought home an old Coldspot refrigerator that was a Sears Roebuck product. It was unbelievable to us, but not nearly as much so as the first washing machine I ever saw.

Growing up, I'd watch my parents build a fire down by the springs near our house and boil water in these big old pots. Then my mother would wash our clothes in the hot water in those pots. Then one day, Dad brings home a washing machine for my mother and her first words were: "Now Dempsey, don't tell me that thing can clean clothes."

I always thought Norman Rockwell missed a great opportunity to illustrate southern Americana that day. We pushed the washing machine through the house into the kitchen area, and my father plugged it in and turned on the water.

Here we are --my parents, my sister Martha and me --gaping as our first washing machine started up. I got up on my toes and pulled myself up where I could peek into the machine and thought to myself, "This is the most amazing machine ever invented."

My mother still wasn't too convinced of its effectiveness, but it didn't take her long to appreciate the function of the machine over building fires, boiling water and doing it all by hand. As I was nearing double digits in age, my interests were shifting, too. I would soon learn about a couple of popular sports in the Moore household, bird hunting and football.

WEARING A FOOTBALL UNIFORM
FOR THE FIRST TIME

Being involved in sports also would become a lifetime passion for me; from the sandlots and playgrounds around Dozier on to the organized teams I would compete on from junior high until I graduated from Alabama. Both football and bird hunting would become my passions.

The love of hunting was passed down through the generations of my family. My great-grandfather, Ransom Moore, had moved south from Boston, Massachusetts to Milledgeville, Georgia where he opened a flour-mill not many years before the Civil War began.

One night, he got into a heated argument with some of the local town folks about the imminent war and made the mistake of telling them that the South had little chance because of all the factories and manufacturers in the North. It was a scene right out of *Gone With the Wind* except one of the men stabbed and fatally wounded my great-grandfather that night.

Eventually, my grandfather, Joseph Jones Moore, would move to Crenshaw County with his 10 children, including my dad, Dempsey. Hunting and fishing were pastimes in the Moore household as far back anyone can remember.

So was my family's affection for bird dogs. When I played at Alabama, my teammates nicknamed me "Bird Dog" because I always owned one, usually a pointer. One of the best ones I ever had was a lemon-and-white pointer named

Gal. She was one good dog, and we spent many a Saturday hunting quail, doves or ducks. Gal was also my daughter Heather's best buddy for years.

I tell you just how much I loved quail hunting. When I was in high school, I made a speech about quail conservation and protecting their natural habitat. It was such an easy subject for me that I won the Dozier contest for the best speech. I just stood behind the podium and made my spiel, talking from the heart.

After I won the speech contest, I was entered in the Crenshaw County regional contest, held in Luverne. I won first place again. I thought I must be this great orator; at least, until I went to the state finals in Montgomery. They didn't have a podium there, and I just froze up and couldn't say a word. After I got into coaching and administration, I have made many a speech, and I always feel better if I walk into a room and see a podium there!

My love affair with Alabama football began during those formative years as well. My dad owned a pickup truck, and we'd go out on Saturday mornings in the fall. He'd always have the Alabama football game on the truck radio so we could hear the Crimson Tide play in the afternoons.

The first teams I really remember were those in the early 1950s that featured Bobby Marlow, the great running back who would lead Alabama to the Orange Bowl against Syracuse during the 1952 season. I never dreamed I'd ever see a game in person. As I noted we didn't have a television, so the rare times Alabama was on TV, we didn't see those games either.

The next year, 1953, Alabama won the SEC Championship. That's the year the team went on to play Rice in the Cotton Bowl and Tommy Lewis became a nationally known figure when he came off the bench to tackle the Owls' Dicky Moegle. Bart Starr and Hootie Ingram were also on that team. I never dreamed that one day I would become friends with those guys.

It's probably hard for fans now to understand how addicting listening to the games on the radio was back then. Maury Farrell and John Forney were the broadcasting team, until Maury eventually left and John became the play-by-play man and was later joined by Doug Layton as his color analyst.

Even when I joined the Crimson Tide staff, my dad would rarely come to a game, but he would always listen to the broadcasts on his radio. When we'd win, he'd go to downtown Dozier and walk through Dink's Sports store, to the grocery store, and the hardware store, telling them, "Well, Mal and them won another one."

They'd all nod their heads. When we'd lose, my dad would say, "Well, Coach Bryant lost that one today."

It became part of Dozier's weekly football routine and everyone would already know what Dad was going to say before he ever got there. My father died in 1970, when my daughter Heather was only a year old, so I'm sorry that he didn't get to see her grow up and be around for our magical football run in the 1970s. I am grateful he was there to be a constant for me during my years growing up in Dozier and those early years at Alabama.

My dad was also always there to see my games, and my older brother Frank's games, during our seasons on the Dozier varsity. When I was in elementary school, Frank was the star of the high school football team, and I guess I wanted to emulate him.

There were only about 300 students from the first through the twelfth grades, and we were all housed in the same building. If you walked in the front door and went right, you'd be in the first through sixth grades; to the left were the seventh through the twelfth.

I'd get all excited when Frank would walk down the hall where the lower grades were, because he was a big sports star in Dozier, and all the kids knew it, too. Even though he was my idol, I was his proverbial punching bag on an occasion or two.

When Frank joined the United States Navy, he started boxing and he'd come home and give me a lesson on his pugilistic skills. I don't think my mother ever knew about it. I can only imagine what her reaction would have been. Frank would get down on his knees, and he'd still beat me up. Then he'd add another handicap by putting one arm behind his back. I think I finally got in a few punches then.

I was a tall, lanky kid for a sixth-grader, but I aspired to be on the Dozier football team one day, like Frank, and joined the team that year by becoming its manager. Never did I think I'd be dressing out with the varsity.

We were playing a Thursday night game in Evergreen, Alabama. When the bus was ready to pull out, one of the players, John Lewis Reeves, was not there, so the bus left without him. We only had 12 players, so the coach gave me John Lewis' uniform and told me to be prepared to go in if someone got hurt.

I was terrified. My mother and father, watching from the stands, told me later they were worried because they didn't see me on the sidelines. They didn't know I was dressed out for the first half. I was scared to death that I was going to have to play, but that was resolved at the half when John Lewis showed up. I changed back into my regular clothes while John Lewis put on his uniform.

When I had to give up the uniform, I had a big letdown, because I had enjoyed the feel of it and I was reluctant to turn it over to its rightful owner. I couldn't wait until the day I'd be able to play for Dozier. Two years later I was in the eighth grade and became the team's quarterback. I'd remain there as the starter for the next five seasons.

That's not to say that I didn't have some moments I'd rather forget. One that stands out is a game against Red Level when I was in the tenth grade. They had a great player – Dan Pitts, who signed with Alabama, and he'd become a good friend, too.

When I was growing up, I had crooked front teeth, and my folks struggled like heck to pay for me to have braces. I'd worn the braces for a year, and unfortunately the day I had them taken off was the day before we played Red Level.

I was the up-back on the punting team, and I'll never forget the play. Dan Pitts broke through the line and hit me in the face with his forearm. When I got up, I knew I didn't want to see a mirror after the game, much less show my parents my teeth. I spit out part of one of my front teeth, and another one had three cracks in it.

That was painful, but not nearly as painful as knowing how much my parents had sacrificed to get my teeth straightened, and now this. When I saw my mother after the game, I asked her if she noticed anything different about me, and she said, "No." Then I opened my mouth. She just gasped and said, "Oh, no!"

I told my parents not to worry about getting my teeth fixed until my football career was over. And I didn't until I was an assistant coach in the 1960s. Dan Pitts would play another major role in my life during a summer job I had at Alabama, but I'll tell that story later on.

Sports were fun and games to us, and by the time I was a junior, I made honorable mention all-state. Then in my senior year, I was chosen on the all-state's second team. Of course, we were in the lowest classification but it was a proud moment for me to earn such recognition. More importantly, I started getting some letters from Coach J.B. "Ears" Whitworth's coaching staff at Alabama.

During my senior year in 1957, I was invited to visit Tuscaloosa to watch

Alabama play Mississippi State. About the only excitement for most of the fans was the persistent rumor that there was about to be a coaching change which really didn't faze me that afternoon.

I was just overwhelmed to be in Tuscaloosa, watching a college football game. Jim Loftin, who would become a long-time friend, was the star in a losing effort for Alabama. Unfortunately, most games during that time frame were losses.

A few weeks later, I was invited to attend the Alabama-Auburn game at Legion Field in Birmingham. Mr. Steve Hicks, who owned Hicks' Tackle and Bait in Luverne, Alabama, drove me to the game along with his daughter Lilellen, and her boyfriend, John Wise. They would become close and lifelong friends.

We even went by the Bankhead Hotel in downtown Birmingham where the Alabama football team was staying; it was the first time I'd ever been in a real hotel. That might have been about the only highlight of the trip.

Most of the celebrating before, during, and after the game was by Auburn fans. The Tigers won 40-0, earning them a national title. Monday after the game Coach Whitworth was fired, and I was wondering who the next coach was going to be at Alabama.

The rumors started circulating that the coach at Texas A&M, Paul "Bear" Bryant was coming home to Alabama. I don't think I'd ever heard of him, but I thought with a nickname like that he must be one tough man. I was going to learn just how tough he was first-hand.

Bert Bank, who would become a longtime friend of just about anyone who had any affiliation with the Crimson Tide, liked to tell the story that in the early months of 1958, Coach Bryant asked him how many radio affiliates he had for the football team. Bert said, "Six." Coach Bryant said, "Six! Is that all?"

And, Bert responded, "Well, we are so bad, nobody's interested in Alabama football."

Coach Bryant told him, "That's getting ready to change, and change in a hurry."

Little did I realize that for 24 of the next 25 years, I would have a first-class seat on Coach Bryant's ride into history.

4

FROM THE TURKEY BOWL
TO TUSCALOOSA

W hen people ask me about all the bowls I've been to as a player, coach and administrator, I ask them to guess where the first post-season game I competed was. There are only a few who can answer that question.

Heck, I can barely answer that question myself. When I was playing high school football, we didn't have playoffs in the State of Alabama. Our Dozier team had a really good season, losing only once all year. We only had 18 seniors in my entire class, and most boys in the entire school played football. I'd been playing on the varsity since I was in the eighth grade, and because I had the strongest arm, I was the quarterback.

We had some pretty good players in 1957, including old friends Joe Kimbrough and Dan Merrill, and we went 9-1. Red Level High School was the best team in our area, and we lost to them. They had five players sign to play college football, which was unimaginable to us. One of them, Mickey Lee, signed with Alabama.

After the season, we were invited to play Lincoln High School in the Turkey Bowl, played in Reform, Alabama, just about a half-hour from Tuscaloosa.

Talk about thinking I'd hit the big time! I never dreamed I'd ever play in another bowl game much less coach in some of the most famous post-season contests of all time. Lincoln had a player, Richard O'Dell, who would become my teammate at Alabama.

(As a side item, Richard would forever etch his name in Crimson lore in 1960 when he kicked the game-winning field goal to beat Georgia Tech 16-15 at Grant Field in Atlanta in one of the most improbable comeback wins in Alabama history. It was actually the only field goal he ever attempted, too, because he had to sub for an injured Tommy Brooker in that particular game.)

You would think that the details of the Turkey Bowl would be hard to forget. Unfortunately, I can't even remember the score, but we lost to Lincoln. Regardless, I didn't think the game of football could be more fun. Within the next few months, I would learn the harsh reality that the fun and games of high school football differed radically from that of big-time college football.

Back in those days, we had an early signing period for the SEC, and those conference letters were binding to the league. I had dreamed about playing at Alabama. Although several other schools, including Georgia and Auburn, had shown some interest in me, the decision to become a member of the Crimson Tide was a no-brainer for me. Even though the team had suffered through four straight losing seasons, I was going to Alabama. We were always Alabama fans.

Quite frankly, I didn't even know who Coach Bryant was when I signed, other than he was set to be the new coach after his Texas A&M team completed its season in the Gator Bowl. I think that was true of the other 82 or so freshmen who reported that August.

Billy Neighbors, a freshman with me, was one of the few who had any inkling about what we were getting ready to experience. He always liked to tell the story of going to the library and reading up on this Coach Bryant. He told us before our first meeting, "This has to be the meanest man alive."

Billy's report was mesmerizing to some but it scared me to death!

The first coach I ever met from Coach Bryant's staff was Jerry Claiborne. He reported early to the University and started recruiting players, visiting those of us who had already signed the conference letter or had committed to Alabama.

I told him I was coming to Alabama and not to worry about me. Even though I had hardly been away from home in my entire life, I actually looked forward to getting to Tuscaloosa and trying to compete with the other freshmen for playing time.

You talk about a different time and place! One day during that summer of '58, my mother picked up the phone and called Coach Bryant-- out of the blue-- and started asking him questions. She found out when I was supposed to report. I had hardly met anyone at the University at that point, so I have to admit that the three-and-a-half hour drive from Dozier to Tuscaloosa seemed like a blur. I think I was already homesick by the time we pulled up in front of Friedman Hall where my folks dropped me off.

I had two suitcases with all my belongings in the world. I'll never forget my dad shaking my hand, and my mother hugging me tightly. My father told me he was worried about driving in the dark, so as soon as they said their good-byes, they headed back to Dozier.

How I survived the next month, I'll never know. Most of the 82 players who reported with me didn't make it. I can assure you it was the ultimate survival of the fittest. Coach Bryant told us in no uncertain terms in our first team meeting what he expected. I'll tell you how quickly players were leaving. During my freshmen year, I had six roommates.

Because there had been so many varsity members dismissed in the spring for showing up for meetings late, the freshman class of 1958 knew we'd better be on time.

That first meeting was the one when another freshman quarterback, Pat Trammell, from Scottsboro, stood in front of the rest of the players and told everyone that he was going to be the "damn quarterback." He pulled out a knife and hurled it into the top of the desk where he was sitting. People ask me if I remember that. I was too worried about what Coach Bryant was going to say when he got there than to worry about Pat or anyone else.

When Coach Bryant started speaking, there was no doubt who was in charge. He commanded respect by his words and demeanor. He told us that if those who remained for four years did what he asked of us, that we would win the National Championship in 1961. You have to remember that Alabama had won only four games in the previous three seasons combined and he's telling us we are going to be the best team in college football.

Had it been anyone else saying that, I would have said he was crazy, but somehow I believed him. There was something about Coach Bryant that made you believe. I was just learning how much.

The great George Blanda, who played quarterback for Coach Bryant at

Kentucky before going on to become an all-time NFL great, said the first time he saw Coach Bryant, "this must be what God looks like." All I can say is I'd never seen such a presence in a man.

After he had finished talking to us, he started to leave the room, then stopped. He told us to look around the room, because in four years, there would only be a handful of us left to play on that championship team. I believed that too, and was just hoping I'd be one of the survivors. Still I have to admit there wasn't a night until the season ended that I didn't think about quitting. Most of my freshmen teammates of 1958 would do exactly that -- leave the team. There were only a couple of handfuls of us around in 1961.

Football had always been fun for me growing up and I was one of the better players among a group of guys who hardly had the ability to play on the high school level much less on the next one. I learned on day one that football at Alabama wasn't just tough; it was harder than anything I can ever be able to describe.

When I hear of the tales of Coach Bryant and the Junction Boys of Texas A&M and how miserable it was, then all I can say is if it was more brutal than what I experienced in 1958, I would never want to experience it.

I thought we hit hard in high school until I took my first lick on the practice field at Alabama. Jim Blevins had been in the Navy for five years before coming to Alabama. He had a big old ship tattooed on his chest and had tattoos on his arm, too. I'd never seen a person with a tattoo before, so I just thought from the get-go this had to be one tough guy.

Man, was I right. He was the first player to hit me in practice, and when I managed to get off the ground, it took me another minute just to turn my helmet back in front of my face. I had no clue what football was really like until that day and that hit by Jim. It was shocking to me how hard he hit and just how tough college football really was.

Well, I was just an old country boy, being away from home for the first time. I was experiencing what football was truly all about for the first time, too. Witnessing how hard the coaches worked us and how much Coach Bryant demanded from not only the players but his staff as well was eye-opening.

Coach Bryant was building a team, but I didn't know that at the time. I would learn through the years that his magic worked more often times than not. Maybe the players from the bigger high schools had been in more competitive situations, but sometimes I wondered about that too.

At least they had had some competition, where at Dozier there were barely enough players to field a team. The coach just sent us out there with a few plays, and we had fun and hoped to win the game. If we didn't, it just wasn't that big a deal. At Alabama, I learned it was a really big deal.

Coach Bryant had inherited an absolute mess in Tuscaloosa. The other students made fun of the football program and they called the athletic dorm, the "ape dorm" because it was like a zoo with no manager. The players were just a wild bunch with no discipline and no respect. Well, I can assure you, Paul Bryant was one hell of a manager. I can assure you no one was calling it the "ape dorm" in the fall of 1958.

My teammates and I would sit around the dorm, talking about how unimaginable playing college football at Alabama was. Every day someone was packing up and leaving. The only thing that was keeping me there was my father's love of Alabama football, and I knew how crushed he'd be if I left. It was a source of great pride for him to tell his friends that I was in Tuscaloosa and part of the Alabama team, but one night I decided I couldn't endure any more of it.

I called my dad and told him I didn't think I could take it anymore and asked him to come get me. There was this long pause on the phone, and he told me to take it a day at a time and I would get used to it. He was right, too. Each week and each month seemed to make it easier, though the practices were just as mentally and physically draining as the previous ones.

Thankfully, I was a survivor, while the door of those leaving revolved continually. Coach Bryant was right. There weren't many of my freshman class around when we won the national title in 1961. I somehow managed to survive the daily war of attrition.

Freshmen wouldn't be eligible to play on the varsity until 1972, and even if we had been, there is no way I would have made the varsity. That being said, I'll never forget Coach Bryant's first game. It was played at Ladd Stadium in Mobile, and the opponent was eventual National Champion LSU led by its great player Billy Cannon.

I listened to the game on a radio in the dorm. Somehow, we were ahead 3-0 at the half on a field goal by Fred Sington, Jr., whose father had been one of the all-time greats at Alabama and on the committee that hired Coach Bryant.

That was the game in which part of the stadium caved in; however I think most Alabama fans remember the part about giving the Tide players and coaches a standing ovation as they left the field at half. Cannon would eventually make some game-changing plays on offense and defense and LSU would win 13-3, but I think that performance heralded a new day for Alabama football. No one was going to look forward to playing a Paul Bryant team.

One thing I would like to add about Billy Cannon is this story that occurred at the Heisman Trophy presentation in 2009. I was there for the event when Alabama's Mark Ingram would win the award, and it was the first time I ever had the opportunity to meet Dr. Cannon.

I told him that my good friend and old teammate Scooter Dyess told me that the only person who ever beat him in the 100-yard dash race was Billy Cannon. Not only was Cannon the SEC champ in the sprints but he also was the winner of the shot put as well. I told Billy I didn't think Scooter could beat you in the shot either!

Billy started laughing and told me to tell Scooter that he didn't remember what he looked like because every time he saw Scooter, he had cinders in his face "from trailing me on those old cinder tracks." I called Scooter that night from New York and we had a good time rehashing his old days in football and track.

I'll tell you one thing about Scooter. He had one of the biggest plays in Alabama history against Auburn in 1959. Our coaches had picked up on a certain defensive formation that Auburn ran and coached us on it all week. If the Tigers were aligned in that formation, Scooter was to look at Pat Trammell and communicate to him he had one-on-one coverage.

Sure enough, it happened. When Auburn lined up in that defense, Scooter signaled to Trammell. Pat just took the snap and tossed it to Scooter, who sped for a touchdown in a game we ultimately won 10-0, marking the first time since 1953 that Alabama had defeated Auburn. During that drought Auburn had outscored the Crimson Tide 142-15. Winning the state championship felt awfully good, too.

Although I had a pretty strong arm, I never had the running ability to execute the offense that we ran back in those days, and I spent most of those early years backing up Trammell and Bobby Skelton.

During my individual meeting with Coach Bryant after my freshman year in 1958, he told me that I probably could start for most teams, but he didn't think I could ever beat out Pat or Bobby. He told me that if I wanted to transfer, he'd help me get a scholarship at any school outside our conference I wanted.

I looked at Coach Bryant and told him that my heart was at Alabama and I didn't want to leave. We shook hands as I walked out, and even though I eventually left Tuscaloosa on two occasions, once after completing my eligibility and later when Coach Bryant retired, my heart would always be crimson and completely belong to the Crimson Tide.

The only game I ever started at Denny Stadium, was a freshman game in 1958 against Tulane. Sam Bailey was the freshman coach then, and the varsity had played in Knoxville that afternoon, losing 14-7 in a game that Coach Bryant obviously felt we should have won.

Coach Bailey was giving us a pep talk at halftime when the doors burst open. There in this big overcoat and hat was Coach Bryant. We knew he was mad about losing that afternoon, and he stood in front of us and told us that he'd seen enough bad football for one day, and he had better see some effort from us in the second half, or he was going to put all of us on the highway come Monday.

He was looking for competitors. He wanted players who would compete right down to the last whistle, and if football wasn't that important, then we could move on. We knew he meant it too.

At the time, I didn't know Coach Bryant probably staged this performance to get our attention and to help us develop an air of confidence in what we were doing. He really believed if you played to your maximum talent, you could be a champion.

I think all of us who stayed started buying into his philosophy that night. We didn't have a lot of great players in our group. Billy Neighbors was big time and made All-American. As I said, Pat Trammell was a great leader and was mean on the football field, too. He just hated to lose and would fight to the last second to win a game. Mostly, we were just a band of young men who believed in Alabama and Coach Bryant. And the wins started coming, too. I also learned that there were other bowls besides the Turkey Bowl.

5

GIVE ME LIBERTY

When I enrolled at Alabama in the fall of 1958, there was no such thing as a weight room and to the best of my memory, the school didn't have one barbell, dumbbell or any other type of weight training equipment, at least in the athletic department. Our off-season conditioning was all about speed, quickness, stamina and coordination.

There was no such thing as Coleman Coliseum or Bryant Hall either. We worked out in the upper gym at old Moore Hall, where Coach Bryant's office was located. Those drills were brutal, too. We started working out as soon as the 1958 season ended --agility drills, wrestling, anything to improve our quickness and speed.

We only worked out 45 minutes, but those were the toughest minutes I'd ever endured. You know, we were assigned to small groups. If one player loafed, it meant everyone had to repeat the drills. Coach Bryant didn't tell us, but he knew it was building team camaraderie and leadership. All I knew was that I didn't want to be the one loafing. Usually, if a player did lollygag, he wasn't going to be around too long.

Having everyone perform at his highest level and being mentally tougher than the opponent was the mantra instilled in us. Coach Bryant would get in front of the team and use percentages to describe opposing teams.

He'd tell us stuff like this: Georgia Tech has an 85% level of talent, and we have 75%. But if they play at 85%, which they probably will, and if we play to 100% of our ability, we will win. Getting that maximum effort is what separated Coach Bryant from other coaches.

School didn't get out until late May or early June back in my college days, and we had spring practice in the hottest part of the spring to help get us ready for the fall. I doubt, in the history of football, if there have ever been better conditioned teams than those Bryant-coached ones in that era.

It was ingrained into our psyches that we would play 60 minutes. We would not be tired, ever, especially in the fourth quarter when the other team would start feeling the effects of fatigue from all the hitting and running in the preceding three quarters.

I don't know exactly when we started raising four fingers to signal the fourth quarter was ours, but Alabama was the first school to do it, and that tradition has endured through the years.

Friedman Hall housed the football players, and every Wednesday night, Coach Bryant would meet with the team there. We felt privileged because Coach Bryant had made certain that some supporters of the school came up with the money to air-condition our dorm. I think it was the only one on campus afforded such a luxury.

Some of the other students may have resented it, but I don't think they had a clue what we were going through, playing football. There is no way imaginable to describe the mental and physical conditioning we were enduring. Years after Coach Bryant was gone, someone asked me what made him so great.

I said, "He brainwashed us into believing we could achieve anything if we dedicated ourselves to achieving our goals. He made us believe in ourselves when maybe no one else did. It's a trait I don't think I've ever seen in any other person I've ever known."

Another thing I learned early was that Coach Bryant's quarterbacks were an extension of the Coach himself. He put immense pressure on his quarterbacks to be mentally focused and prepared to compete, no matter what the situation in any given game. Expect the unexpected. When we ran on to the field, he wanted his whole team to have an air of confidence, but especially his quarterbacks.

When I played, Coach Bryant would eat lunch with all the quarterbacks once or twice a week and we'd talk about everything from situations in games to situations in life. I cherish those moments, too. He was a teacher, giving us a test of life lessons. Years later, when I became the quarterbacks coach, we would have our Monday morning meetings to discuss personnel.

All the assistants would give their grades on their players, talk about the positions, and how the players were developing. Coach Bryant always wanted to know who the winners were, but he never asked me to talk about the quarterbacks in front of the other coaches. As soon as the meeting was over, I'd go into Coach Bryant's office where we would evaluate the quarterbacks. He didn't even want me to comment on the quarterback's performances to the press. He handled that.

Game day was fun when I played, and when I coached, too. Practices were anything but that. Players would try to become friendly with the head manager because he always had the practice schedule. Finding out what was on that sheet of paper was a daily mission.

Coach Bryant would write it out: first period – 20 minutes. Second period – 15 minutes. Third period-- "N/T." Well, when we'd be tipped off about the N/T or "no-time," we knew it was going to be a long day.

They could vary in length, and I've been there when they've dragged on for well over an hour, or until we got it right. I tell you when Coach Bryant had two or three of those N/Ts written down for one practice, then we knew it was going to be one long day on the practice field.

Of course, everyone knows now about the legend of Coach Bryant's tower that still stands tall on the Thomas-Drew practice field. When I played, it was an old wooden tower. Coach had an eagle eye, too. I don't think he ever missed anything. And, I learned early on -- and never forgot it either -- you didn't want him coming down from his tower. I can assure you when he did, it wasn't good news.

When we won five games that first year, it was like a miracle. There was no doubt he had us believing that we would, indeed, be National Champions before we left Alabama. We knew we were going to get better and better and better. For those of us who survived, it was magical. We didn't have many great players, either, but every new player learned from the older ones that playing here meant something special, and that bowls and championships were coming.

That first staff was special, too. Jerry Claiborne was the defensive coach, although there were no titles, and Phil Cutchin was the offensive coach and my first quarterback coach. It was a young staff comprised of excellent teachers and men who were mentally tough like Coach Bryant. They believed in his plan and they made us believe.

I tell you what, his commitment to excellence didn't start and finish with his coaches and players either. When he first got to Tuscaloosa, he asked his secretary Mrs. Marie Penton, to set up a meeting with all the managers at 1:00 p.m.

When some of them showed up late, he looked up and told them, "Today would be a good day for you to go call your father and let him know that from now on that he's paying your way to school."

The message was clear who was in control. He also made it clear to the players that he didn't care who their daddies were. He also made it abundantly clear to the alumni and supporters that he was in charge, not them. As the old saying goes, there was a new sheriff in town and that sheriff was Paul Bryant.

You know, people ask me when I thought the players really started believing. Well I think you have to have a victory against a great opponent to turn the proverbial tide, and I think Alabama's came in 1958 when the team beat Georgia, 12-0. That Georgia team had the great Fran Tarkenton as well as the Dye Brothers, Pat and Nat.

When we went into the 1959 season, I think we felt we were close to being a championship-caliber team, and by the time we beat Auburn, we had secured a spot in the first-ever Liberty Bowl.

I had one of my career highlights late in the season when I came off the bench to throw a 15-yard touchdown pass to Bill Rice in a 14-7 win over Memphis State and help put us in the bowl talks and get a bid.

Bud Dudley, who was a friend of Coach Bryant's, founded the bowl in Philadelphia and set up that initial meeting between Penn State and Alabama. Since Penn State had an integrated team, there was some question whether the governor's office would interfere and even allow us to travel to Philadelphia to play.

Coach Bryant worked it out with Alabama Governor John Patterson, and we boarded a train in Tuscaloosa and traveled north to Philadelphia. I don't think many of us were prepared for the cold weather that would greet us, though. It was about 25 degrees and the wind was gusting as much as 40 miles an hour, hardly ideal conditions for a football game. Penn State – coached by Rip Engle, along with a young assistant named Joe Paterno – might have been better adapted to the inclement weather than we were. I just know it was miserably cold that day for my teammates and me.

I'll never forget us practicing in the hotel meeting room the day before the game. One of the Philadelphia newspapers even snapped a picture of it. The coaches had set up chairs in the room, which we used to make sure players were lined up properly.

The game was played in what is now John F. Kennedy Stadium but it was known as Philadelphia Municipal back then, and we lost 7-0, thanks to a fake field goal. Galen Hall, who would go on to become a long time assistant at Oklahoma and then the head coach at Florida, was the holder and he threw a touchdown pass right before the halftime break.

It was probably the only time Pat Trammell had a mental lapse. He didn't cover the receiver, who broke wide open; and Galen hit him for the only score of the day.

What I remember most about the bowl trip was Coach Bryant taking us to New York City after the game. What a treat. Mel Allen, the fabled voice of the New York Yankees and alumnus of Alabama, set up a dinner for us at Mama Leone's, the famous Italian restaurant of that era.

Joe DiMaggio was there and had his picture taken with Coach Bryant. Of course, a few years earlier DiMaggio had been married to Marilyn Monroe, and the two of them were about as big time as celebrities could be. I'm sure most of the players would have preferred to see Marilyn, but seeing the great DiMaggio was pretty special.

Our gift item from the bowl was a transistor radio, something I guess we all wanted back in 1959, which is quite a difference from the high definition television that one of the bowls gave away in 2012.

Going to the Liberty Bowl in Philadelphia and subsequently being able to tell folks back home that I'd been in the Big Apple at Christmas time made playing in the Turkey Bowl two years earlier seem pretty ordinary. Little did I know my bowl experiences were just beginning.

6

NEAR DEATH EXPERIENCE

W hen I was playing at Alabama and during my years on Coach Bryant's staff, the student-athletes would work in the summers to earn some extra cash. It's not like that anymore. When I came back to college football in 1990, the players were pretty much in Tuscaloosa year-round, working out and preparing for the next season.

Let me assure you the summer jobs we had were anything but cushy positions. It was hard labor and almost as tough as the spring and August practices that we endured. We had to run the mile under a certain time, so the summer jobs were in essence endurance tests, too. Most of us came back in running condition, able to endure those hot summer practices.

Before my sophomore year at Alabama, the summer of 1959, Coach Bryant got me a job working for Holt Rast, who had been a great football player at Alabama in the early 1940s. Mr. Rast owned a company that had a project in Andalusia installing a new sewer system throughout the town. Andalusia is only nineteen miles from Dozier, so I could live at home and pocket my paychecks without having to worry too much about paying many bills.

There were two other teammates working on the same project, Dan Pitts and Ashton Wells. We had three different crews, and the one I was on was laying pipelines and this pipe had to stay on grade. It was a difficult task because the area we were working was really low and then you came to a hill. It made the ditches much deeper at this particular part and made it extremely hard to keep the pipe level.

Because of heavy rainstorms in the area, the dirt was very saturated, almost marsh-like, making it challenging to keep good footing where we were stationed. Our assignment was to lay 20-foot long pipes in the ditches. On this particular July day, one of our co-workers called in sick, which complicated the entire process.

The foreman told me that I would be working in the ditch that day along with a gentleman from Louisiana, named Leroy Jackson. He was an affable man, who really knew what he was doing. He was certainly no novice in this business, like I certainly was. Everyone called him "Jelly Leroy." He liked to tell us he got his nickname because he always loved to put jelly on his biscuits. I don't know if that was true, because he always laughed when he said it, but I know he was a good man.

After our lunch break, we returned around 1:30 to finish laying this pipe. Because of the heat that day, Jelly Leroy had pulled off his shirt. He was wearing one of those old V-shaped undershirts, and he wrapped a bandana around his head. My job was to help when the pipe was swung in by the big crane to guide it into the "bell hole," put the bolts in, and then tighten it.

Our task had become more treacherous because our feet sank into the mud in the ditch, almost coming up above our ankles. Finally, we got the pipe properly laid but we still hadn't finished bolting it in. I got out of the mud and was standing on the pipe, kicking the mud off my work boots. I looked up to see Jelly Leroy doing the same on the other end of the pipe.

I started walking down toward Jelly when I heard this screaming from above the ditch. I looked up to my left and I saw the entire side of the hill caving in on us. We were down about 14 feet, so you can imagine how terrified I was when I saw this mud slide, knowing that we could be buried alive.

The entire hill started sliding down, knocking down trees in this landslide. Instinctively, I started climbing the wall away from the landslide of mud. I jumped as high as I could, grabbed the mud wall, and climbed to the cusp of the ditch. Jelly was running down the pipe, slipped and I heard him screaming.

We locked eyes for an instant and then I saw the entire side of the hill cave in on him, muffling his screams. The weight of the landslide killed him instantly.

I kept sliding down, but I got my hands to the top of the ditch. With all the effort I could muster, I managed to keep my head above the ditch, but I had it at a slant, tilted skyward. The rest of my body was covered in mud. Only my hands and my face, from the chin up, remained above the ground and not buried in mud.

The foreman rushed over, digging dirt off my face to keep me from being buried alive. He sent Ashton Wells to get help from the local fire department, the sheriff's office and Rural Electric crews. By the end of the day, hundreds of people worked urgently for the rest of the day trying to rescue me from the mudslide.

I was losing feeling in my legs and Dan Pitts came over, frantically trying to help me. Dan had experienced all kind of problems with heat-related ailments while playing football which ultimately ended his career. That didn't stop him from doing everything he could to rescue me that afternoon.

Dan was doing everything possible to dig dirt away from my face and keep my head from sinking under the mud. While he was keeping me alive, I heard some of the workers say they couldn't use big machinery to dig me out because they thought the weight would buckle the ground even more and bury everyone there. Meanwhile, I was praying and pleading with Dan not to let me die.

The Rural Electric crew, which is now Alabama Power, attempted to get me out by putting leather straps under my arms. They tried to pull me up, but it just didn't work. When you get in wet dirt like that, and the water drains down, a suction forms around your body, and it's just like having a cast all around you. You can't move and it becomes hard to even breathe.

I could literally feel my joints pulling apart as their efforts to get me out were unsuccessful. That made me even more scared, if that was humanly possible. Then they got plywood boards and tried to form a wall around me and the mud. But when they would dig it out on one side, the weight of the upper side of the hill would push the plywood in on me, almost crushing me.

I'd been there for several hours, and I think everyone knew the situation was grave and time was becoming an issue to save me. One of the firemen suggested he might be able to buoy me out by pouring water into the mud.

It seemed like a desperate plan, but this was a desperate situation. The firemen got one of their hoses and pulled it down to where I was. They hooked a harness around me to keep me from drowning in mud.

One of the firemen put the hose as far down in the mud as he could, and they turned on the water pressure as high as they possibly could. The other firemen pulled hard on the harness that they had wrapped around my shoulders.

As the water pumped under me, I could feel the dirt loosening. With the help of those pulling me, I just floated up out of the mud and onto the safety of the ground. When I was out of the ditch, I went into shock and was rushed to the Andalusia hospital, where I would spend the next three days recovering.

At first, I didn't think the doctors were going to be able to save my legs, because I had no sensation in them. That was a terrifying feeling. Finally, I started getting twitches in both legs and I couldn't keep them still. I didn't know whether that was good or bad, but I knew it was better than not having any feeling in them.

When the doctors told me that I was going to be all right physically, and although it was a great relief, I couldn't stop thinking about Jelly Leroy. He was about 40-years-old, and he was the most adept worker we had laying pipe. After they got me to the hospital, they finally excavated Jelly out of the mudslide that had claimed his life and had almost taken mine.

Today, we have grief counseling in these cases to help individuals overcome the emotional scars, but back then it was almost taboo to even talk about it. I know when I thought about the cave-in, I'd be overwhelmed with a rush of sadness for Jelly, and yet relief that I had somehow survived.

Maybe everyone has a near-death experience. I know I had one on that summer job. I doubt if I've had many days that I have not thought about that summer and about Jelly. Every time I've heard about a mining accident or a cave-in of any type, I just pray for the victims and their families.

It certainly gave me a different perspective of the sanctity of life and to appreciate our blessings.

7

COACH BRYANT'S PROMISE COMES TRUE

I guess you could say I was a double survivor when I entered my junior year in 1960. Not only had I endured the rigors of playing two years for Coach Bryant, but I had certainly survived the horror of having been virtually buried alive in the cave-in that summer in Andalusia before my sophomore season of 1959.

In August, 1960, Coach Bryant told me that he had decided to redshirt me. I wasn't disappointed, though, because Pat Trammell and Bobby Skelton were a formidable one-two punch at quarterback and there were high expectations for a team coming off its first bowl appearance since the 1954 Cotton Bowl.

I would like to interject that there was only a handful of bowl games back then, and just to earn a spot in a post-season contest really meant that you had a pretty good football team. Having most of our players back for 1960 made us a legitimate contender for conference and national recognition.

Our team really didn't live up to expectations in a road loss at Tennessee, when we fumbled the ball away five times. Plus, we inexplicably tied an average Tulane team in New Orleans. Certainly, it looked like our road miseries had continued when we fell behind Georgia Tech 15-0 in Atlanta. Thankfully, Bobby Skelton came off the bench to replace an injured Trammell and rallied Alabama for a 16-15 victory. My old friend Richard O'Dell kicked the game-winning field goal as the clock reached zero.

If there was ever a confidence-booster, it was that win. It would live in Alabama folklore for an awfully long time.

For the second consecutive year, we ended the season with a dramatic win over Auburn at Legion Field. Auburn had its typically solid football team under Shug Jordan, a squad that was ranked No. 8 in the country entering the game. We were fortunate to escape with a 3-0 victory, thanks to a second quarter field goal by Tommy Brooker.

Auburn crossed the 50-yard line only twice during the entire game. Defensively, it was a vintage Coach Bryant team. After the season, we were invited to play Texas in the inaugural Bluebonnet Bowl in Houston. The game ended in a 3-3 tie, even though we all thought Skelton scored the game-winning touchdown when he crossed the goal line in the fourth quarter. Unfortunately, the official ruled him down inches from the goal.

Regardless, we entered the 1961 season primed to compete for it all, and we did. Winning the SEC was almost as difficult as winning the national championship. When the season ended, three SEC teams were ranked in the top-five, with Alabama being National Champions and LSU finishing third and Ole Miss fifth.

We opened that year with a 32-6 win against Georgia in Athens. It was a noteworthy game for me because I came in to throw a touchdown pass to Red Wilkins. Most of the time when I got to play it was on the defensive side at safety, but candidly I was more of a sideline spectator than a performer. I don't want to give any false impressions that any game depended on me having to throw a winning pass or deflect one on defense.

Throughout the season, we only trailed one time the entire year and that was against a good North Carolina State team that featured future NFL star quarterback Roman Gabriel. Ultimately, we would win that game 26-7. No other team would score a touchdown on us the rest of the season.

The next week we played Tennessee in Birmingham, and that was one of those monumental games for the Alabama program. In a series marked by incomprehensible winning streaks that seemed to be never-ending, the Volunteers were the ones holding the upper hand, having not lost to us since 1954.

In a game we should have won in 1959, the final score was 7-7. Sometimes, the end results of games like these lead you to wonder what it takes to win against that rival. It becomes a mental nightmare to get over that proverbial hump.

Entering the 1961 game, there was no doubt that we were a much better team, but we had felt that way the previous two seasons as well. Yet, we had nothing to show for it. You could always sense how important the Tennessee game was to Coach Bryant. Let me tell you something, there was an extra hop in his step the third week in October, the traditional time that Alabama had been playing the Big Orange for years.

When Coach Bryant had played, Alabama didn't have Auburn on the schedule, so it was well known just how important the Tennessee rivalry was. There were always the ghosts of the past lingering, too.

Tennessee's fabled coach, General Robert Neyland, had once remarked, "You don't know how good a team is until they play Alabama." High praise indeed. Former Crimson Tide back Gordon Pettus once told me about the time he was a freshman when Coach Frank Thomas walked into the team room, grabbed a piece of chalk and wrote on the blackboard, "T-E-N-N-E-S-S-E-E."

And when Coach Thomas abruptly left the room, Pettus asked his old high school teammate Harry Gilmer what that meant. Harry said, "That means we better beat Tennessee."

Yeah, we had endured a long drought against Tennessee, whether the game was played in Birmingham or in Knoxville. In 1961, before a sellout crowd of 48,000 and the only television audience of the regular season, we didn't exactly get off to a banner start either.

George Shuford kicked a then-record 53-yard field goal, which turned out to be about the only thing Tennessee fans could cheer about that day. Our defense held them to 61 total yards and by halftime we were up 20-3. I remember Billy Neighbors and Lee Roy Jordan just dominating them all day, but frankly those two pretty much overwhelmed everybody we played. Those two were just about as big-time players as you could ever imagine.

Pat Trammell, Butch Wilson, Mike Fracchia and Billy Richardson scored touchdowns and the Crimson Tide prevailed 34-3. If there were any doubts about how good we were, I think we answered all questions that afternoon.

It was also the beginning of the cigar tradition, one that still lives on for the winner of this rivalry. Jim Goostree, our trainer and a Tennessee alumnus, brought the cigars in a big chest, and Coach Bryant handed them out to the team. What's funny is Coach Bryant really didn't like anything about cigars. On this day, though, he sure didn't have any problem with the billowing smoke in the winning locker room.

When I was coaching at Alabama, some of the happiest memories I ever experienced were smoking the traditional victory cigar, but it was even more fun during those years when defensive coach Ken Donahue, also a Tennessee graduate, and Coach Goostree would dance in the dressing room. Man, what memories I have of those days

A few weeks later, LSU beat Ole Miss 10-7, elevating us to the No. 3 position in the country, behind Ohio State and Texas. In the ensuing weeks, TCU would virtually hand us the national title, first by tying Ohio State and then beating Texas on the same day we beat Georgia Tech.

All of a sudden we were top-ranked, but back then there wasn't a lot of hoopla about it. Among the players, though, there was that lingering thought: Coach Bryant had told us this was going to happen.

We closed the deal with a 34-0 win over Auburn, marking our fifth straight shutout and clinching the national championship. Those were the years before the voters were polled after the bowl games. In December, Coach Bryant and Pat Trammell went to New York for the National Football Foundation dinner to receive the McArthur National Championship trophy from President John F. Kennedy.

There was some controversy about the bowl game that year, one that almost enabled us to return to Pasadena to play in the Rose Bowl. Ohio State's faculty senate voted not to allow the Buckeyes to compete in the game against UCLA. There was a push from the West Coast to find a loophole in the contract between the Big 10 and Pac-8, to allow us to play there.

Unfortunately, for us at least, the prevalent image of the Deep South and some caustic editorials from some well-known national columnists derailed us from having that opportunity.

As players, we were pretty much oblivious to such back room politics; so earning a spot in the Sugar Bowl to play Arkansas in New Orleans seemed rewarding enough. We practiced in Biloxi and went over to New Orleans a few days before the game. I'll never forget staying in the Roosevelt for the first time, and what a thrill it was for me to be in one of the most renowned hotels in the city.

The game was big enough anyway, but there was little doubt that Coach Bryant wanted this one for a number of reasons. Foremost was for us to become the first undefeated Alabama team since 1945, but also to become the first one ever to win the Sugar Bowl.

Coach Bryant, of course, had been born and raised in Arkansas, and had even accepted the job to become the Razorback head coach on December 7, 1941. The Japanese bombing of Pearl Harbor changed everything that day. At the same time my brother Douglas was enlisting in the Navy, so was Coach Bryant. That fateful day in American history also had a far-reaching impact on college football and Alabama.

Although many of our players had traveled to New Orleans the year before to play Tulane, it was my initial trip to the Big Easy. For an old country boy from Dozier, experiencing the culture and walking down Bourbon Street for the first time were eye-opening events. So was walking into old Tulane Stadium on New Year's Day and seeing that legendary facility with 82,000 people. I couldn't imagine that many people being in one venue.

We won the game 10-3, with Mike Fracchia earning MVP honors. There were some dramatics late in the game when Arkansas superstar Lance Alworth got behind our secondary, but a potential touchdown pass was thrown just inches too long and we had etched our mark in Crimson Tide history.

Back in the years that Alabama had played in the Rose Bowl and won national titles, the team had returned to massive crowds at the Tuscaloosa train depot. Back then, the crowds waiting and cheering the Crimson Tide as the train passed through all the small Southern towns en route to Tuscaloosa had become legendary. There had been even bigger celebrations in Tuscaloosa, not only at the station but also on the quad, where tens of thousands welcomed home the conquering heroes.

I don't remember much about our flight back to Tuscaloosa, but I do remember the victory parade that began at the old courthouse, turned up University Boulevard and wound through campus. I think it was during that parade that I realized for the first time just what a big deal the National Championship really was.

After winning it all in 1961, I think the prevailing feeling was we were going to be even better in 1962. We had a strong senior leadership with players like Lee Roy Jordan, Richard Williamson, Bill Battle, and Butch Wilson. I don't think there was any doubt that Mike Fracchia was the best running back in the country.

I've always loved to tell the story that I was the No. 1 quarterback when we started spring practice for the 1962 season. I took one snap and then Joe Namath stepped under center and took his first snap. All of a sudden the coaches thought he should be first team! Actually, I was first team a whole day before they moved Joe up to the starting spot, and rightfully so. He was something special.

While we would have a remarkable year by most accounts, it was one filled with trying moments. One of our linemen, Tom Bible, got killed in an accident that June. Fracchia tore up his knee, which basically ended a brilliant career.

Late in the season we were undefeated and ranked No 1, when we traveled to Grant Field to play Georgia Tech. It was one of those games that haunt you. We should have won easily but lost 7-6. Despite the devastation of that one, we did come back to shutout Auburn for the fourth straight year and set up an Orange Bowl match with Oklahoma, coached by the legendary Bud Wilkinson.

There were several plot lines to that game. President John Kennedy attended the game, dropped by the Sooner dressing room before the game and sat on their side during the game. Coach Bryant used that to serve as a motivation for us. It was also the game in which the nation saw first-hand just how great Joe Namath really was.

Joe threw a long touchdown pass to Richard Williamson, and Cotton Clark scored a touchdown in a 17-0 victory. Our defense, just like it had done most of the year, completely stifled the Sooner offense. It was a game most remembered for Lee Roy making 31 tackles, and it should be, but our coaches had noticed on their film studies that an Oklahoma player tipped off which side the ball was going.

Two of our defensive linemen, Charley Pell and Richard O'Dell, also had memorable days. After the game, some reporter asked Coach Bryant about his quarterback, and that's when he said, "His name is Namath and you better learn to spell it: N-A-M-A-T-H."

We stayed at the Seaview Hotel in Miami, and back then the Orange Bowl had this gigantic party the night after the game. It was held at the Indian Creek Country Club. Man, what a place. It was on an island right there at Miami Beach, and there were like 28 mansions on it, including one owned by J.C. Penney. It was a memorable way to close out my playing career.

I would have never dreamed when I arrived on campus in 1958 that in four years, I would be part of teams that won a National Championship and traveled to Philadelphia, New York, New Orleans and Miami as part of bowl experiences. And thinking back on it, I thought that the bus ride from Dozier to Reform to play in the high school Turkey Bowl was a really big deal.

8

BIG SKY MEMORIES

A‌t some point during my junior year at Alabama, during our drive to Coach Bryant's first national championship, I started thinking about my future away from football and what I was going to do when I finished my degree requirements at the Capstone.

As I've said before, I wasn't a very good player, but I enjoyed the strategies involved in football, and I had learned some harsh realities of what it took to build a champion during my seasons under Coach Bryant as a player. Although I don't recall ever having many conversations with my teammates about our futures in the game, I knew I wanted to coach.

You have to remember our teams during that time period were filled with players who were not only going on to coach, but become quite successful in the profession. We had some unbelievable teachers, too, and not only Coach Bryant.

Two of the staff members, Howard Schnellenberger and Gene Stallings, would go on to win national championships and earn entry into the College Football Hall of Fame. One of the best coaches I've ever been around was Jerry Claiborne, and he would have his own Hall of Fame career as head coach at Virginia Tech, Maryland and Kentucky. Maybe the best coach on that entire staff was Pat James, who helped develop championship teams at Alabama and Oklahoma.

During the 1961 and 1962 seasons, our roster included future major college head coaches Bill Battle, Charley Pell, Jimmy Sharpe and Richard Williamson, and I was lucky enough to be an assistant alongside teammates Brother Oliver and Jack Rutledge.

And, then there was Mickey Andrews, who would have a remarkable career at Florida State. I'm sure I'm missing somebody, quite unintentionally, because I have had nothing but the utmost respect for all the men who spent their lives serving as mentors and teachers of young men who found a common outlet in the game of football.

After we defeated Oklahoma in the Orange Bowl, I graduated and enrolled in graduate school, figuring it would help pave the way for me getting a good high school job as a coach and a teacher in Alabama.

Since I had graduated, I was going off scholarship, so I was looking around campus for a job to allow me to stay and complete my master's degree. One day I dropped by and saw Coach Bryant and told him that I was looking for some work to help me pay my way through school. He just kind of nodded and didn't say much.

I should have known him well enough to know that the proverbial wheels were turning in his head. A few weeks later I was over at the old Union Building that is now Reese Phifer Hall. It had the Supe Store, the post office and a cafeteria.

It was the hangout for students, and I was leaving there when I ran into Coach Sam Bailey, who was Coach Bryant's right hand man for so many years. Coach Bailey told me Coach Bryant wanted to see me, so I guess I should have thought it was my lucky day, but when Coach Bryant summoned you to his office, well, it made everyone a little nervous.

When I got over to his office, one of the secretaries, Mrs. Penton, told me Coach Bryant was expecting me. I had no idea what this was about. I was concerned, and probably showed it, too. When I went into his office, he was shuffling through some papers, and it seemed like forever before he looked at me. Coach said, "Mal I have just returned from speaking at a high school football clinic in Bozeman, Montana at Montana State University.

"They've just hired a new coach. His name is Jim Sweeney, and he told me he wanted one of my players to come out there and coach for him. I recommended you to him."

Coach Bryant handed me his telephone number and told me to call him, and he cautioned me, "Don't act like you know you have the job, but I've worked it out, and you've got it." Although he didn't say it, I think his message was clear: "Don't screw this up, Mal!"

So, I took the number from Coach Bryant and I went back to my apartment to get an atlas, so I could figure out where exactly Montana was, and particularly where Bozeman was located in the state. All I knew was that it was up in the Northwest. Two hours earlier I was walking through the student union, wondering what I was going to do. Now, I was preparing to move to the Big Sky Country!

I couldn't believe how quickly my life was changing, and I started looking at routes to drive there and determining what sites I would see as I drove from Alabama to Montana. Of course, I was doing all this before I called Coach Sweeney, but when Coach Bryant told you something you knew it was a done deal.

Back in those days, you had to go through an operator to make a long-distance call, and the one who answered my call had this distinct Southern drawl. We chatted a second, and she told me that she was from Tuscaloosa, and I guess I thought this was fortuitous.

She got Coach Sweeney on the line, and she said, "Jim Sweeney, will you accept a collect call from Mal Moore?"

After a long pause, the first words I ever heard him say were, "My, I can just smell the magnolias."

I knew right then I would like him and enjoy working for him. He told me that he had a job opening coaching the defensive backs and I'd be a graduate assistant finishing up my master's degree. Back then, graduate student coaches were part of the staff, and you had the responsibilities of a full-time coach, but without the salary.

I'd be remiss in not mentioning my conversation with Coach Bryant when I told him I wanted to go into coaching. I'm sure he gave me the same lecture that he did every other player who went to see him with the dreams of coaching.

Anyway, he said, "Mal, if you go into coaching, you'll never make much money, and you'll be married to your job. When you get married, you better have a wife who understands you'll be working year-round. There will be many a night you'll either be in your office or on the road recruiting. There is nothing easy about it."

And he was right, too.

After Coach Sweeney told me when to report to Bozeman, I called my Dad to let him know of my first coaching job. He had given me a Chevrolet Corvair with four gears, a motor in the back and the trunk up front. I really didn't think life could get much better.

On the way there, I zigzagged my way through as many states as I could, and it was quite an experience crossing the Continental Divide right above Jackson Hole, Wyoming. I didn't even know what the Continental Divide was before I started my trip, but I had educated myself and learned it extended all the way from the top of Canada to the bottom of South America.

When I was driving into Bozeman, I didn't think there could be a more beautiful setting in the world. The Bridger Mountains were on the right and the Spanish Peaks on the left. Bozeman is in the southwest corner of the state and at the time had a population of about 8,000 people.

Coach Sweeney had gotten me a room at the Bozeman Motel. I went into the lobby where there was a pay phone and I called him, and he told me to come out to his house. When I got there, I met Coach Sweeney for the first time, along with his wife, Cille, and their nine children. He was an affable Irishman, and his wife and children were just as nice he was.

I'll never forget him saying, "Come on, Mal, I have to go get some milk. We go through a lot of milk at our house."

I told him I could relate, having grown up in a houseful of children, too. We drove through town and passed the stores there, and I said, "Where are you going to get milk?"

And, he said, "Mal, I have to go to the dairy to get milk."

He bought eight gallons of milk. When we got back to his house, he showed me they had two refrigerators, something I'd never seen before. One held all their dairy products; and the other one was for everything else. The family wouldn't let me stay at the hotel. I just moved in with them for the next couple of weeks while waiting for the apartment I had rented to come open.

It was quite an operation there with Cille managing the household. She was also a great cook. They became like a second family to me, and years later I would help recruit their son Jim, Jr., to Alabama. He ended up getting injured and never played for us, but that didn't lessen the love the Sweeney family had for Coach Bryant and Alabama.

I should have known then the impact Coach Bryant had on people and college football. Coach Sweeney absolutely loved Coach Bryant. Sweeney had grown up in Butte, Montana, played college football at Portland, and begun his coaching career at the high school level in Kalispell, Montana. He had become one of Coach Bryant's most ardent admirers and studied everything about him.

When he was a high school coach, Sweeney drove several hours to hear Coach Bryant speak at a clinic, and through the years, he would come to Tuscaloosa just to watch our team practice. When he was coaching Fresno State, the school was honoring him and he called Coach Bryant to ask if he would come and make a talk. Coach Bryant agreed, even though he was at a point where he wasn't making many speeches. He did it for Coach Sweeney.

I learned just how important coaching clinics were and the tremendous impact they had. In fact, one clinic in particular would ultimately be a key factor in Coach Saban's decision to come to Alabama. More on that later.

Let me say this about Coach Sweeney: he was an innovator who had a unique eye for talent and a knack of knowing who could coach. He convinced a skier by the name of Jan Stenerud to come out for the Montana State football team as a kicker, and Stenerud would become the first full-time place kicker elected to the NFL Hall of Fame.

And he had a quarterback named Dennis Erickson who would go on to coach a couple of National Championship teams at Miami, and losing a chance for a third when Alabama beat them in the 1993 Sugar Bowl.

Among our players on that 1963 Montana State team was Joe Tiller, another player who would go on to have a successful coaching career. He was one of our tackles and quite a player at that. We went 7-3 that year, with one of the losses to a really good Tulsa team that featured three big-time players in quarterback Jerry Rhome, his favorite receiver Howard Twilley, and defensive lineman Willie Townes, so we had a good team.

The highlight of our 1963 year was a season-ending win over our archrival Montana. We beat them in Bozeman, 18-3, and that made Coach Sweeney's first year a rousing success as far as all of us were concerned.

Just as a side note, when I left Montana State, Coach Sweeney hired Joe Tiller to replace me, and he would go on to have quite a career, including being a top-notch head coach at Wyoming and Purdue. Joe and I stayed in touch through the years, and I always tried to visit with him in person during the annual National Football Foundation and Hall of Fame weekend in New York.

I really enjoyed my year in Montana and the time I spent with the Sweeneys. He knew I wasn't making any money, so one night a week, he told me to go the local country club and sign my name on his tab. They had this great piano player who entertained there. Every time I walked into the club, he'd quit playing, look up, nod at me, and start playing "*Stars Fell on Alabama.*"

Another thing that I remember about Montana was that no one had a paper dollar bill. Everyone paid in silver dollars. That was "the thing" then. Of course, the government started taking up silver dollars a year later and they disappeared for the most part as a result of a Congressional Act.

It had been an eventful year for me in Bozeman, but I would soon get a call that would bring me back home to Alabama.

9

RETURNING HOME - 1964

While I had thoroughly enjoyed my year at Montana State and was close to finishing my master's requirements, I really wanted to earn the degree from the University of Alabama. Coach Bryant routinely checked on his former players. I got a note from him, making sure I was doing okay in school and learning as much as I could from Coach Sweeney.

On an impulse, I called Coach Bryant and told him that I would really like to complete my degree in Tuscaloosa. He told me if he had a graduate job come open, then he'd bring me back. That's exactly how it worked out for me.

It was a time of turmoil in the United States with the assassination of President John Kennedy, the impending escalation of the war in Vietnam, and of course the Civil Rights movement in the South. About the only constant to me seemed to be Alabama football and Coach Bryant.

Football was changing too, with the new substitution rule. Basically, everyone had played both offensively and defensively, but the more liberal substitution rule introduced two platoon football back into the colleges. When I came back home to Tuscaloosa, Coach Bryant told me that I would be working with Coach Gene Stallings and to learn everything I possibly could from him.

It never occurred to me that Coach Bryant was probably testing me to see if I would be an adequate replacement if Coach Stallings received an opportunity to head up his own program. In retrospect, it was pretty obvious that Gene was on course to soon become a head coach at the highest level of college football.

We also thought early in the spring that we were on course to win the national championship. Joe Namath was back for his senior season, and my old friend had matured dramatically since I had left. There was little doubt to anyone who had the pleasure of watching him play, that Joe was truly one of the most gifted quarterbacks ever.

Talk about an incredible player and athlete. When he came out of high school, Joe had been offered a substantial baseball contract by the Chicago Cubs. The rumor around the football team was he had turned down as much as a $75,000 signing bonus to play college football, and none of us thought we'd ever see that much money in a lifetime. That was before they had a baseball draft, but there is little doubt he would have been the first player picked if there had been one.

Our longtime trainer, Jim Goostree, liked to tell the story about walking through Foster Auditorium in 1961 and seeing a player dunking the ball. Goose said he told the basketball coach and football assistant Hayden Riley, "Hey, Coach I see you finally got a real player."

To which Hayden responded, "Basketball player? That's Joe Namath. Coach Bryant will never let him play basketball!"

I don't think there was a sport in which Joe wasn't an A-plus performer. When you hear old NFL coaches say that they could literally hear the ball whistle when he threw -- well that's absolutely true.

Joe would have been our best defensive back, too, and he was brilliant on the option as well. We were undefeated in October when he suffered a severe knee injury against North Carolina State. He wasn't even touched on the play.

If Joe hadn't gotten hurt, I doubt if we would have been challenged that year but he did. I learned an important lesson as a young coach, too. Coach Bryant didn't bemoan the fact that we had lost the best talent in football. He just expected the backup, Steve Sloan, to step in, and he did, in leading us to a 21-0 victory over the Wolfpack.

Sloan played a major role in three of our most magical wins that season, including rallying to beat Florida, led by quarterback Steve Spurrier, 17-14. When we played LSU at Legion Field, both teams were undefeated; and we led 10-9 in the fourth quarter when the Tigers were driving for what would have been a go-ahead score.

One of our unyielding beliefs was that someone had to make a play to win the game. On that November afternoon, one of our defensive backs made the big play. Hudson Harris intercepted a pass and returned it for a touchdown, and we escaped with a 17-9 victory.

The Auburn game was for the SEC title and it was a talented Tiger team, with quarterback Jimmy Sidle and halfback Tucker Frederickson, who was one of the last great two-way players. Joe came off the bench to throw a touchdown pass to Ray Perkins and Ray Ogden ran the second half kickoff back 108 yards.

Ogden always said he was running for his life because he knew Coach Bryant would have killed him for returning a kick that far back in the end zone. Ray was right, too. We won it 21-14, setting up the Orange Bowl showdown with Texas.

That was the game when Joe Namath came off the bench in the second quarter and rallied us to what we thought was a winning touchdown on his sneak in the final minute. One official ruled he didn't score. It was frustrating as heck but Coach Bryant told us never leave it in the officials' hands; and it shouldn't have come down to that one play anyway.

Nevertheless, we were consensus National Champions because in those days both the Associated Press and United Press voted before the bowls and awarded their respective championships.

On a more positive ending for me in 1964, I completed my degree but I never had the opportunity to start looking for full-time employment. One day I went by the post office and in the box was a draft notice to report for military duty.

ROTC was mandatory at the University in those days and like I mentioned earlier, the situation in Vietnam became more and more ominous each day. Regardless, I wanted to fulfill my military duties, and I told Coach Bryant I had been drafted.

He offered me some advice, telling me that if I wanted to coach and went on active duty for three or four years, I probably would have a difficult time ever advancing in the profession. My other option was to join the Air National Guard, so that's what I did, driving to Birmingham and enlisting in January of 1965.

Almost immediately, I was sent to basic training at Lackland Air Force Base in San Antonio and then to the Amarillo Air Force Base in Amarillo, Texas. I was going to be discharged in July, and I didn't have a job, so I called Coach Bryant and asked for his advice. He told me that he would help me find a coaching job somewhere.

Quite frankly, I really wanted to work for him and was admittedly disappointed, but I felt strongly that everything would work out for the best. When I got a call from Jerry Claiborne, I really thought my next stop would be at Virginia Tech.

Jerry offered me a job coaching tight ends, telling me that I could live in the dorm since I was single, and that would help me save some money. Before we hung up, Coach Claiborne told me that he would have to clear everything with the University president and that he would call me as soon as he had official permission to offer me the job.

Well, I flew back into Birmingham and I remember it being a typical hot, muggy July night. My sister, Martha, was living in Birmingham then, so I called her and asked if she would pick me up. I didn't mention to her that I had unofficially accepted a job at Virginia Tech.

When I got off the plane, I saw Martha just beaming, and she congratulated me on my new job and I wondered how she found out about the Tech offer. I asked her what she was talking about and she said, "It's in *The Birmingham News.* Coach Bryant has hired you as the defensive back coach."

I was shocked because Coach Bryant had never hinted to me that he was going to hire me. That night I got a call from Coach Claiborne, but I didn't want to take it, because I still hadn't talked to Coach Bryant. I didn't want to do anything until I knew for sure he was offering me a job. Talk about a long night. I felt awful about not talking to Coach Claiborne, but I didn't want to promise him something and have to back out.

I didn't sleep but a couple of hours that night and probably should have gotten a speeding ticket, getting to Tuscaloosa to see Coach Bryant. When I got to the football offices, much to my disappointment, I learned Coach Bryant was out of town and wouldn't to be back until the next week.

Well, I really didn't know what to do at that point, but I ran into Coach Sam Bailey and told him my dilemma. Sam and Jerry were not only close friends, but at that time Sam's son Darryl was playing for Jerry at Virginia Tech, and Sam wanted to make darn sure there was no hard feelings with Coach Claiborne.

Sam told me, "Coach Bryant has hired you, so call Jerry and let him know." And that's exactly what I did. I became a full-time assistant coach at Alabama without ever officially being offered the job!

I was assigned the secondary, taking over for Coach Stallings, who had become the head coach and athletic director at Texas A&M at the age of 29. Ken Donahue, who had come to Alabama from Mississippi State the year before, was in essence the defensive coordinator, though I don't think Coach Bryant ever gave out titles like that back then. Dude Hennessey was the other holdover on the defensive staff, and the other new member was the linebacker coach Pat Dye.

Together, we would work to produce two memorable defensive units during the 1965 and 1966 seasons.

10

THERE IS TISSUE
ON THE TURF

For years it was legal to scout opponents in person, and I always enjoyed that aspect of coaching. I always felt you could really get a feel for a team, its personnel, how they were coached and how hard they played by watching them in person as opposed to just rewinding tapes and watching it on a projector.

I'll never forget my first scouting experience. We were in the staff room before the 1965 season opened. Dude Hennessey was assigned to report on Tulane, our second opponent that year. Coach Bryant looked around the room in his unique style of sizing up everything and said, "Dude don't you bring back a blankety-blank report like you did last year."

Then he looked at me and said, "Mal, you go with him, and you heard what I said."

Tulane was opening against Texas in Austin and Coach Bryant told us that Darrell Royal would get in touch with us when we got there, which he did. We went to the Texas football office and three of his assistants -- Mike Campbell, Charley Shira and Jim Pittman -- took care of us, telling us what they thought of Tulane. Then Mike invited us to a get together on Friday night.

Lord bless Dude, because there was only one like him. He just had that knack of making people like him, and he regaled everyone at the get-together. They all wanted us to come back Saturday night for an even bigger party. Dude had taken on the persona of Tonto from the Lone Ranger television series and would mimic the Ranger's faithful companion. He had the Texas coaches and support staff rolling that night. Naturally, we accepted the invitation to come back on Saturday.

Back in those days, and up until 1984 when the Supreme Court ruled that NCAA couldn't control television rights, you could only be on television a couple of times a year. Texas and Tulane were playing Saturday night, and we were playing Georgia in Athens on television, so Dude and I settled in our room to watch the game.

It was memorable in a bad way for us, because Georgia scored late in the game on a flea flicker from Kirby Moore to Pat Hodgson to Bob Taylor. The play went for more than 70 yards for a score.

I don't think there was any doubt that both of Hodgson's knees were on the ground when he caught the pass. Under today's rule with replays, the play would have been ruled dead at the point of the reception, and we would have won the game.

In retrospect, if there had been replays back then, we more than likely would not have lost a game during the 1964-66 seasons. We only lost two, and both controversial games, to Georgia and to Texas in the Orange Bowl.

Dude and I were stunned, and we could just imagine how tough it was going to be in Tuscaloosa when we got back. I asked Dude if we were still going to the party after the Texas game and in his best Tonto voice, he said, "Me not want to get scalped by Coach Bryant. Me gonna give good scouting report tomorrow."

And he did.

I always liked scouting at LSU because they played their games at night, and we would fly down after we played in the afternoon, watch three quarters and leave to get back.

My, how things have changed over the years! We would bring all of our films down with us and exchange them with the LSU managers, who would bring their game films up to the press box before kickoff.

Although we won most of the time against LSU while Coach Bryant was the coach, the games were never easy. It was usually our most physical game of the season, probably because the LSU coach, Charlie McClendon, had played for Coach Bryant and with Dude Hennessey at Kentucky.

On my first trip to LSU, I was taking notes in the press box when I heard the interior PA announcer in his distinctive South Louisiana accent say, "There is tissue on the turf."

I didn't have a clue what he was talking about, and I was looking on the field when Dude tapped me and said, "Rookie, it means there was a penalty called." In all the years I went back to Baton Rouge as a coach, every time I saw an official throw a flag, those words "tissue on the turf" would ring in my ears.

By far, my most memorable scouting trip occurred in 1967 when Coach Bryant shipped Dude and me to Los Angeles to scout Tennessee, who was opening the season against UCLA. We flew out on Thursday and had barely checked into our room when there was a knock on the door and one of the bellhops was there with a dozen roses for me.

I knew I'd been set up, probably by Dude or the assistant coaches back in Tuscaloosa, so I waited until the bellhop left before I looked at the tag to see who sent them. Of course, Dude was right there, looking and said, "They are from Barbara Parkins."

He was really giving me a tough time.

The problem was I didn't have a clue who Barbara Parkins was. Of course, Dude did and he told me she was the star of the movie, *Valley of the Dolls*, and the TV show *Peyton Place*.

Not long after that the telephone in the room rang. I knew it had to be someone else trying to pull a quick one on me, and I thought so when the person on the other end of the line said it was Jim Nabors, and he was sending a limousine to pick Dude and me up to take us to the studio where we could watch him tape the *Gomer Pyle Show* and then we would all go to the airing of the *Carol Burnett Show*.

I just laughed and told Dude I was tired of his tricks, but he got all excited and said he didn't know anything about it. Sure enough, a driver pulled up in a limo and took us to the CBS studios where we had the opportunity to meet another of that era's top TV stars.

Carol Burnett and Tim Conway spent a lot of time with us and introduced us during the taping of the show as Alabama coaches who were in Hollywood scouting. Carol even invited us to a party that night and we accepted. It turned out to be quite an evening.

I promise you Dude Hennessey was the star of the night. He had all the top comedians in Hollywood laughing so hard that you would have thought he was the television star. Of course, no one really had a clue who we were, or why we were even there. When we left the party, there were a lot of autograph seekers wanting celebrity autographs.

They ran up to Dude and asked him who I was. He whispered, "That's the actor Aldo Ray." I bet I signed a hundred autographs that night as Aldo Ray. The next night Tennessee and UCLA played an intense, great game, especially for a season opener, and the Bruins scored late to win it.

When we were flying back the next morning, I got to my seat and there was a distinguished gray-haired gentleman sitting next to me. Dude was seated about three rows behind us. I introduced myself, and the gentleman said he was Tom Siler. I didn't know he was the sports editor of the *Knoxville News-Sentinel*. Naturally, Dude knew him personally and he was back there, trying to get my attention, but he couldn't.

Mr. Siler asked me what I thought of the game. I made the mistake of telling him that I thought Tennessee had some deficiencies and pointed out what they were. About that time, the plane had taken off and Dude had made his way up to where we were, and telling me that Tom Siler was the sports editor of the *Knoxville News-Sentinel*.

Here I am, a 27-year-old coach and I'm sinking in my seat, thinking if he writes what I just said, Coach Bryant is going to fire me when I get back home. I was miserable.

We used to subscribe to all the major newspapers from the areas where we had opponents, so we would get the Sunday editions usually on Tuesday or Wednesday. Coach Bryant always read those papers.

I made a mad scramble to get the Knoxville paper on Tuesday before it got to Coach Bryant and the paper wasn't there yet. Same thing on Wednesday morning. Dude came down to my office and whispered, "Coach Bryant already got it and he wants to see you immediately."

I was petrified as I made that walk down to his office and knocked on his door. When I knocked on the door that was half open, Coach Bryant looked up and asked what I needed. I said, "I heard you wanted to see me."

He mumbled, "Hell, if I wanted to see you, you'd know about it."

When I got back to my office, my good friend Dude was there just laughing and I was relieved when he told me that there wasn't anything in the Knoxville paper, that he and some of the other coaches had grabbed it earlier to make sure. More importantly Dude had told Tom Siler when we went our separate ways in the Atlanta airport to please not write anything I had said because Coach Bryant would kill me.

Mr. Siler and Coach Bryant were friends, and he assured Dude that he wouldn't write a thing. I wish I'd known that on Sunday because those next three or four days were mighty tough. Despite it all, I wouldn't trade those days for anything, being a young coach and surrounded by the best people you'd ever want to meet.

11

WHAT HAPPENED TO
THE CLASS OF 1965

W hen I reflect on my coaching career, being part of two championship stretches that have rarely been matched doesn't amaze me. It sure makes me proud that I played a small role being on a staff that came within several votes of winning three straight National Championships.

After I came back to Alabama in 1964, it had become almost expected among our players and fans, as well as our staff, that we were going to win every time we stepped on the field. I feel that what we accomplished in the 1960s was remarkable because we weren't loaded with a team filled with stars. Sure, there were extraordinary talents like Joe Namath and Kenny Stabler, but for the most part, we were a team of ultimate overachievers.

Jerry Duncan, who was a 190-pound all-star tackle for us and an improbable offensive weapon on the tackle eligible pass, probably summed it up best, "When you looked over there on the sideline and saw Coach Bryant, you had no doubt we were going to win. He instilled an iron resolution in each of us to overcome all obstacles."

And, we usually did. During my first three years on the staff, we went 30-2-1, and the only two losses were controversial ones to Texas in the 1965 Orange Bowl and to Georgia in the '65 season opener. Coach Bryant never blamed the calls, always emphasizing the games should have never hinged on those plays anyway.

I learned as a player and had it reinforced as a coach, that coaches and players who dwelled on one unexpected bad call or bad play usually got whipped. And, during those early days, we didn't get whipped much.

When I hear fans or writers remark about how great the SEC is now, they forget how good it was back then, too. It was great when I was a player and it was dominant in those mid-1960s.

Looking back on the 1965 season, the final polls had seven SEC schools in the top-17 in the nation, and some of the non-league victories were impressive to say the least. Entering the final game of the year against Auburn, we were tied for the conference lead, and the loser would drop to seventh or eighth in the league.

That's how bunched up the teams were in the standings. It took a lot of outside luck and a miracle or two for us to even get back into the SEC race, much less the national title chase. Tennessee was unbeaten with two ties, including one against us, late in the season, but Ole Miss beat them, and a week or two later the Vols upset UCLA, which really changed the entire season for us.

If the Bruins had beaten Tennessee, UCLA would have had a legitimate chance of winning the national title if they could knock off Michigan State in the Rose Bowl. Arkansas sat at No. 2 in the ratings and was riding a long winning streak when it clinched the Cotton Bowl bid that automatically went to the champion of the old Southwest Conference.

LSU, a team that had lost three SEC games, including a 31-7 contest to us in Baton Rouge, accepted a bid to play the Razorbacks in Dallas. No one really thought they had a chance, except Coach Bryant.

Nebraska also had a perfect record, was rated No. 3 and the Cornhuskers were set for an Orange Bowl berth. Coach Bryant had worked his magic and had managed for us to get a bid against them, regardless of our outcome against Auburn.

By the time we got to the Auburn game, we were playing with a high level of poise. We only had nine seniors, but we had great leadership among that group and I don't believe I was ever around a team more confident than this team was when we walked onto Legion Field.

Steve Sloan, I believe, had three touchdown passes, and Steve Bowman ran all over Auburn that day. We won 30-3 and we were elevated to No. 4 in the polls. For the first time ever, the Associated Press decided to wait until after the bowls to cast its vote for the national champions. So did the Football Writers, so we knew with a whole lot of luck, we had a chance of claiming back-to-back titles.

One day Coach Bryant came into a team meeting and told all of us that LSU was going to beat Arkansas; UCLA was going to upset Michigan State; and we were going to play Nebraska for the National Championship. I'd learned a long time ago not to question Coach Bryant, but I just didn't see how it could play out that way.

When we were down in Miami, preparing for Nebraska, Coach Bryant told us a few days before the game that he was really concerned about our offensive game plan and wasn't sure we could win with that plan.

Nebraska was much bigger than us. I think at some point, someone said they outweighed us about 70 pounds a man on the line, and that was probably right on target. I was coaching the secondary then, and we knew Nebraska had not only a power running game, but they were also efficient throwing it.

Coach Bryant knew we had to score -- and score a lot -- to win. He told Kenny Meyer, our play-caller on offense, that he wanted us to play the entire game like we were two touchdowns behind. Years later when I was the offensive coordinator, I had a similar meeting with Coach Bryant before the 1981 Penn State game.

I think he thought it would take pressure off Kenny that night. Coach Bryant always said to "Expect the unexpected." He probably fooled Kenny and the offensive staff as much as he did Nebraska that night. Candidly, it was a brilliant ploy.

When we were out on the field for warm-ups, there was a light mist falling and we were putting our defensive backs through their drills when the PA announcer said, "Final score from the Rose Bowl, UCLA 14 and Michigan State 12." We already knew LSU had indeed pulled off the upset in Dallas. Talk about a "buzz" that went through the crowd. Our players already had an extra bounce in their step, but when that score was announced, they were really intense and fired-up.

And that's exactly how we played that night, with a sense of urgency like we were two touchdowns behind. Steve Sloan set all kinds of bowl passing records and so did Ray Perkins in receiving. On our first offensive play, we ran the tackle-eligible pass and Jerry Duncan broke it for about 20 yards. We were off and running, and never looked back.

You think back on coaching decisions, some that work and some that don't.

That night Coach Bryant kicked an on-side kick right before halftime. We had just gone up 21-7 and Vernon Newbill recovered the kick and a few seconds later, David Ray hit a field goal to give us a 17-point lead at half.

I don't think I've ever been in a dressing room where the players were that excited. Let me tell you this, you never knew how Coach Bryant was going to react at half. I've seen him angry and I've seen him when we were behind, come in singing, "Oh, What a Friend We Have in Jesus."

That night he did an unbelievable job of settling everyone down and preparing for a second half that he knew would be much tougher. He told Coach Meyer to keep attacking and we did.

The final score was 39-28, but it was really never that close. I'll never forget the next day going to the office, worried about the final vote and there was a note on the bulletin board from Coach Bryant, saying "Congratulations National Champions."

Because we won two of the four polls that were recognized, we were the consensus National Champions for 1965, and the new goal was to make it three straight.

It's no sense rehashing what happened in 1966, other than to say that I don't think anyone could have beaten us. That team had as much leadership as any I've ever been around. They just refused to lose and they didn't either.

I guess the game that always stands out, other than the 34-7 victory over Nebraska in the Sugar Bowl, was the 11-10 victory in Knoxville. It was a typical "Third Saturday in October" game, but this one was marred by a downpour that really hampered our offense.

Snake Stabler was our quarterback, and we had two great receivers in Perkins and Dennis Homan, but it was almost impossible to pass. We fumbled around and basically gave up short drives for 10 points. I really didn't know if we could score, not only because of the conditions but because Tennessee had a great defense.

Snake rallied us though, scoring a TD, hitting Wayne Cook on a two-point conversion, and then driving us for the winning field goal. There is one play that will never get much mention, the field goal by Steve Davis. Kenny wasn't our regular holder but he stayed on the field that day because he had such great hands. He needed them, too.

There was a low snap that he had to dig the football out of the mud and then perfectly spot for us to make the field goal. The kick went through with 3:23 left on the clock. I don't think anyone really thought much about those numbers that day, but they sure would become historic for Coach Bryant when he finished his career with 323 wins.

I was lucky to be part of that defensive staff. We only allowed 37 points the entire season and I don't think we ever gave up a drive of more than 70 yards. I was up in the coaches' box in the press box that day.

Our two defensive coaches on the sideline, Ken Donahue and Dude Hennessey, got a triumphant ride on the shoulders of our players. I don't think I ever saw that before or since, but there were never two coaches more deserving of such an honor being bestowed on them by their troops than those two.

We ended up finishing third in the polls that year behind Notre Dame and Michigan State, who had played to that memorable 10-10 tie late in the season. The Irish didn't go to bowl games back then, and the Big 10 rule of repeat appearances in the Rose Bowl eliminated the Spartans from the bowl picture.

Unlike the year before, the Associated Press decided not to vote after the bowls, making our 1966 team forever known as the "Uncrowned Champions."

We just dominated Nebraska in the Sugar Bowl, winning 34-7, and it probably could have been a whole lot worse. Snake was brilliant and won the MVP award, but one of my defensive backs, Bobby Johns, intercepted three passes and should have received some kind of award as well.

Coach Bryant only gave out rings to teams that won the National Championship, so our players didn't receive much recognition for winning the SEC and the Sugar Bowl. Years later, after I had become athletic director, Mike Hall, who was a star linebacker on that team, came to see me, wanting me to authorize members of that team to be able to produce and purchase a ring that symbolized winning the league and the Sugar Bowl.

So, nearly 40 years after one of the most remarkable seasons Alabama ever experienced, the 1966 team finally wore a ring commemorating their undefeated season, but even that memento will never erase that thought of what might have been for the Crimson Tide.

12

THE ONE THAT GOT AWAY. DID IT CHANGE THE HISTORY OF ALABAMA FOOTBALL?

One morning during the spring of 1969 in a staff meeting, Coach Bryant came into the room and started writing the names of our personnel on the chalk board. When he finished, he looked around the room at our staff and said, "If Dr. (Frank) Rose knew how badly we've recruited and what condition our program is in, he'd fire me and all of you on the spot."

I think there was probably some denial among us that we were that short on talent, but reality didn't take long to set in during the season. Actually, there were plenty of warning signals the previous two seasons when we had struggled through disappointing 8-2-1 and 8-3 seasons. There had been a few highlights, especially Kenny Stabler's run in the mud to beat Auburn 7-3 in 1967, and Mike Hall's remarkable performance against the Tigers the next year.

That was the game Mike had 16 tackles and intercepted two passes on defense and we used him at tight end, too. I know he caught a TD pass from Scott Hunter to pretty much seal the victory.

After that game, my teammate Pat Trammell came into the locker room and Coach Bryant gave him the game ball. Pat was dying of cancer and a week later, he was gone. I'm not making excuses for our poor performance in the bowl, but Pat's death took a lot out of all us, especially Coach Bryant.

About the only highlight in 1969 came when we beat Ole Miss on national television 33-32 on a last minute pass from Scott Hunter to George Ranager. It was a classic offensive game, and long-time ABC announcer Chris Schenkel labeled it the most exciting game he ever called.

From a coaching standpoint, it only proved how prophetic Coach Bryant's words about our personnel were. Ole Miss, with Archie Manning, would go on to win the Sugar Bowl that year while we struggled the rest of the way, starting the next week when we lost to Vanderbilt in Nashville, the only time we ever lost to them during Coach's 25 years.

One thing Coach Bryant told us we were going to do -- and he meant it, too -- was get out and recruit some SEC-quality players. I think it is important to note from a historical perspective that we started recruiting black athletes prior to the much ballyhooed game against Southern California in 1970, a game that has become legendary over the passing years.

Back in those days, you had two signing periods, the first being the SEC "Letter of Intent" in December, which was binding against other conference schools, but the student-athlete could still sign a national letter with another team.

We were in the midst of not only actively recruiting two of the best black players in the state for the first time (Wilbur Jackson of Ozark and Bo Matthews of Huntsville) but we were also locked into a national recruiting battle for the two best quarterback prospects in the nation: David Jaynes of Bonner Springs, Kansas, and David Humm of Las Vegas, Nevada.

I think every coach on the staff wanted the opportunity of being assigned to recruit David Humm because of the natural allure of being able to go to Las Vegas. Not only was David from Las Vegas, but his dad was the credit manager at Caesar's Palace, and whoever got the job of trying to sign Humm would stay there.

Even though I was the defensive backfield coach at the time, Coach Bryant looked across the room in the staff meeting and said, "Mal, you're recruiting David Jaynes, and Dude you're recruiting David Humm."

Dude was a personality, and everyone just liked him. I think it was the late Benny Marshall of The *Birmingham News* who called him the clown prince of the staff. Every staff needs a Dude because he could lighten up a room in its darkest moments, and believe me he made the most of this opportunity.

We were suffering through that miserable 1969 season, and we'd come off the practice field into the dressing room that afternoon after Coach Bryant had assigned me to Jaynes and Dude to Humm.

Dude waited, of course, until Coach Bryant had left, and he'd start acting like he was rolling the dice, getting ready for his next few weeks in Las Vegas. Every day, he'd do a different routine, acting like he was throwing the dice behind his back or blowing on them and spinning them down the table. He'd never say a word but he'd get us all laughing and we couldn't wait until the next day to see what his routine would be.

As the December signing date approached, Coach Bryant told Dude and me to get to Las Vegas and Bonner Springs respectively and not come home without getting at least one of them. Let me emphasize both of the Davids were your traditional pro style type quarterbacks, so any thought of the eventual move to the wishbone never entered our minds in December, 1969.

Bonner Springs is a 20-minute drive from Kansas City, and I spent the first couple of weeks of December there trying to get a commitment from David. He was regarded by most as being the best drop-back passing quarterback in the nation and everyone was recruiting him, especially the University of Kansas, coached then by Pepper Rodgers. The Jayhawks had been to the Orange Bowl the previous year, and Pepper had them competing at the highest level.

His top assistant, Terry Donahue, was assigned to recruit him, and it seemed like I would visit David and then Terry would go in and see him. And, the next day, Terry would go in, and I would be next. We had a really good "in" with David, because his idol was my old teammate and then the toast of pro football, Joe Willie Namath. Joe had led the New York Jets to the Super Bowl title in January of 1969, and seemingly every top quarterback in the nation wanted to emulate Joe.

David Jaynes did a pretty good job of it. He looked like Joe on the field, with his mannerisms and his ability to really throw the football. I spent so much time with the Jaynes family that I even helped them decorate their Christmas tree, and one time when no one was at home, I even raked the leaves in their yard.

Back then, it was still legal to have former players call a prospect, and David really wanted me to get Joe to call him and talk to him about coming to the University. Since the Jets were still in the stretch drive of a season that ended with a division title, I didn't feel it was appropriate for me to bother him at such a crucial time of his season. Ultimately, I probably made a mistake in not getting Joe to do the University this favor.

I also found out early on that David's parents had been supporters of George Wallace for his independent run for the Presidency in 1968. One day when I was in Tuscaloosa, I called Governor Wallace and asked him if he would write or call David's parents, because I thought it might help persuade them to encourage their son to play for the Crimson Tide.

Governor Wallace's first question was, "Is Auburn recruiting him, Mal?" The implication was clear; if Auburn was indeed recruiting him, then the governor wasn't going to get involved. I assured him that Auburn was not involved in the recruitment of David. I'm not positive if Governor Wallace ever contacted the family or not.

It didn't matter, at least for a few weeks. David committed to play for the Crimson Tide but he wanted to make sure Coach Bryant was there for the signing. I called back to Tuscaloosa with the good news. There certainly weren't any of the football recruiting gurus back then or all the attention on recruiting, but this was a coup for Alabama.

Coach Bryant made arrangements to fly in to Kansas City where I would pick him up and get him to David's house for the official signing of the SEC letter of intent.

I was so nervous about wanting everything to go smoothly, that I actually drove the route from the airport to the Jaynes' house several times to make sure we had the timing down, because I didn't want anything to mess up the signing of the nation's top quarterback. Frankly, I was getting really concerned at the airport because there was no sign of an airplane arriving from Tuscaloosa with Coach Bryant.

Everything was racing through my mind about what could have happened to the plane. I was pacing back and forth. I'm sure everyone there thought I was nervous. I was more like frantic. When the plane finally landed in the private part of the Kansas City airport, I shook Coach Bryant's hand and tried to get him to the car as quickly as possible.

Well, Coach Bryant wanted to read the local newspaper, and we had to find him one for that 20-mile trip to David's house. By now we were really running late and I was scared if we weren't there, David wouldn't sign with us, so I tried to make up time by speeding back to Bonner Springs.

That was a big mistake. I saw the lights of a state trooper beaming into our car, so I pulled over and got out. I told Coach Bryant, "Well, I guess we are getting a ticket." He just looked over his reading glasses, and asked, "Who's getting a ticket?"

The trooper told me he could put me under the jail for going as fast as I was traveling, and I tried to explain that I was a coach at the University of Alabama and I had Coach Paul "Bear" Bryant in the car.

I could see the trooper leaning his head and peeping into the back window of the car to try to see if it was really Coach Bryant. I was hoping Coach would get out of the vehicle but he just stayed in there, reading the newspaper. I can still see him there with his bifocals, reading the paper while I was giving my spiel on how we had to get to David Jaynes' house for the signing party.

It seemed like an eternity but Coach Bryant never turned around. He finally put on his hat, and after that the trooper told me that he would give me a warning, but to slow it down. When I got back in the car, Coach was still reading the paper. Then, he slowly folded it and asked if I had gotten a ticket or had I talked my way out of it. I told him I had talked him out of it. He just had that wry grin appear and not another word was spoken on the trip to the house.

Well, we finally got to David's house and they had his signing party. There were five or six television stations there, and in a time and place when there wasn't much attention paid to a recruit signing with a school, this was a major media event. One thing David asked was that now that he was committed to Alabama, would we stop recruiting David Humm. I told him we couldn't because we had an offer to him and we couldn't go back on our word.

Anyway, a few days later, Dude was still in Las Vegas trying to get David Humm to sign with us. Lo and behold, who shows up at Caesar's Palace but Joe Namath. The Jets had lost their playoff game, ending their season. Of course, Joe and Dude had been close when he played for us, and Dude told him he was there trying to recruit David Humm to come to Alabama. Dude introduced Joe to David Humm and someone snapped a picture of the two of them.

It was just a happenstance, accidental meeting but every coach who was after David Jaynes let him know about Humm meeting Joe, and showed David the pictures that were in the Las Vegas newspapers of Joe and David Humm. They all told David Jaynes that Alabama really wanted David Humm. Eventually, we would not sign either one of them on national signing day.

David Jaynes ultimately signed with Kansas, while David Humm went on to play for Nebraska. If you could spin back the clock of time, it would be interesting to see if we had signed either one of them what it might have meant as far as the wishbone era was concerned. David Jaynes went on to be a consensus All-American at Kansas, though Pepper Rodgers left for UCLA after the 1970 season. Don Kimbrough was David's coach during his Jayhawk career. Likewise, David Humm had an outstanding career for the Cornhuskers.

As a footnote to this story, I remained friends through the years with Pepper and Terry Donahue. Whenever I saw them, I would ask about David Jaynes and we would reminisce about his recruitment. I would always remind Pepper that one time when I was in Bonner Springs I ran into him, and Pepper told me, "Mal, you know I can arrange to have your legs broken here in Kansas!"

As the years passed, David enjoyed a lot of success. He had a short NFL career with the Chiefs before moving to Los Angeles where he became quite successful in the real estate business and married Cary Grant's widow, Barbara Harris.

When we went out to Pasadena to play Texas for the National Championship in January 2010, I called David and asked him to meet me at the hotel where we were staying. I hadn't seen him since we recruited him in 1969, so I didn't know what to expect, or even if I would recognize him. When he walked into the hotel lobby, he looked the same. He walked up to me and said, "Coach, I don't remember you being as tall as you are."

We had a great visit, and he and Barbara attended our victory over Texas. Later that spring, David came to Tuscaloosa to play in our annual *Joe Namath Celebrity Golf Tournament* that raises money to endow athletic scholarships at the University. After 41 years, I finally got him together with Joe Namath.

Even though we signed David Jaynes in that class and didn't get him, it was particularly significant because we did attract a top-quality group of players. It was also the class that officially began the integration of the program. It should be duly noted that we had several walk-on black players prior to then, but none had been able to make the team during the difficult transition of that time period.

In December of 1969, the first two black football players committed to play for the Crimson Tide. Pat Dye signed a great receiver prospect in Wilbur Jackson. We would eventually move him to running back at Alabama, but he kept his No. 80 and became one of the greatest runners of the wishbone era.

His move to running back is a great story, too. Wilbur was one of the fastest players we had, but he really struggled catching the football. Our receiver coach,

Bobby Marks, was having a terrible time. Wilbur would be yards behind the secondary, but he seemed to drop every pass.

Finally, Coach Bryant had enough. He came down from the tower and said, "Why don't we just hand him the football." And, we did it a lot during those early wishbone days. Wilbur had a great NFL career, too.

We also went to Huntsville and signed the top running back prospect there, Bo Matthews. Eventually, Bo would sign a national letter with Colorado and play an important role on the outstanding teams the Buffaloes fielded during the early 1970s.

I think if we had signed either David Jaynes or David Humm, Coach Bryant would never have switched to the wishbone. Our failures there no doubt changed the history of Alabama football. Regardless of losing David and Bo Matthews, the December signing class of 1969 would help begin our climb back to national prominence.

13

SINK OR SWIM

Coach Bryant always brought in nationally recognized speakers to our annual coaches' clinic, which back in my coaching days with him fell during the last week of July, just before we began our August drills.

I was in my first year as quarterback coach, having moved over from defense, and we had drilled exclusively in the spring in our traditional pro-set offense. One thing we knew for sure that July morning was that we had a daunting task facing us in 1971. We were facing one of the toughest schedules any team had ever played.

Not only did we have pre-season top-20 SEC foes Florida, Tennessee, LSU and Ole Miss to play but we also played non-conference games with top-20 teams Southern California and Houston. After enduring 6-5 and 6-5-1 seasons, I think as a staff we were hopeful, but not overly optimistic, that the results would be much better this year. Quarterback Scott Hunter had moved on to the Green Bay Packers and our beleaguered defense was basically going to be the same cast of players.

One thing no one ever underestimated on our staff was the powerful presence of Coach Bryant, his steel-like resolve to reassert himself, and return the Crimson Tide to the national prominence. I know it had really stung him when Tennessee linebacker Steve Kiner made the statement "Alabama no longer has any pride left in those crimson jerseys."

I don't think Coach Bryant needed any inspiration to resurrect the program, but if he did, that one remark certainly left an impression. Regardless of all of our determination to right the so-called ship, the spring hardly uplifted the feeling that we were going to challenge for anything other than fighting to escape bottom half of the SEC.

Before that fateful day that Coach Bryant redefined Alabama football, we were discussing our personnel for the upcoming season. Offensively, we really only had two big-time players: guard John Hannah and running back Johnny Musso.

Let me say this about John Hannah. He was one of those rare talents that come around once in your coaching career, and I think John would tell you to this day that we didn't do a great job of coaching him. Frankly, we had never had a lineman with his size and ability. Our focus back then was keeping our linemen as sleek and as quick as possible.

I shudder to think how good he'd been if we had let him play at what his normal football weight should have been. He dominated anyway. During our Centennial celebration back in 1992, they picked an all-time team and he was easily picked as one of the linemen. *Sports Illustrated* called him the greatest lineman ever when he was a member of the Patriots and knocking NFL defenders around. He was just a magnificent football player.

During the Centennial celebration, they were showing me some video of John that the Bryant Museum had compiled years after he had played. There was one pass play in an LSU game that he literally knocked a defensive tackle about five yards backwards and then he peeled back and waylaid a blitzing corner. In all my years in football, I don't think I'd ever seen anything like it.

In another clip, he is leading Wilbur Jackson down the field, running step-for-step with him and knocking defenders over like a bowling ball. John was also an all-star in track and field, easily winning SEC Championships in the shot put and discus. He did the same in wrestling, winning heavyweight titles. Let me add, he did these things in track and wrestling without ever practicing.

Coach Bryant would let him compete in the meets, but the rest of the time, he was concentrating on football. I think if he had turned his attention to track or wrestling, he would have been an Olympian and probably a gold medalist to boot.

If John was a human wrecking ball as a lineman, Johnny Musso was, as Coach Bryant said, "a barrel full of guts on a football field." In the three seasons he played for us, I never saw Johnny get knocked backwards. After he was hit, you could count on him to fight forward for another yard or two or three or four. He was a special player.

With all that being said and remembering back to that meeting about personnel in 1969, we knew we were better, but hardly where we needed to be. Coach Bryant never discussed any thought of changing up what we were doing offensively, but there was a hint the wheels were turning in his head after our final game of the 1970 season, a 24-24 tie the Bluebonnet Bowl against Oklahoma.

The Sooners had gone to the wishbone offense, and I had learned first-hand how difficult it was to defend during our bowl game against Oklahoma. When we were flying back from Houston, Kirk McNair, our sports information director, was sitting near Coach Bryant and saw him pull out his yellow pad and start scribbling wishbone formations and plays.

Kirk thought Coach Bryant was just rehashing what had happened in the game and maybe he was, but knowing how acute his mind was, there is no doubt the man was contemplating a change of direction for our program.

Among the guest speakers set to teach intricacies of their football knowledge at our clinic that July was Darrell Royal, the Hall of Fame coach at Texas and one of Coach Bryant's closet friends in the coaching profession.

While Coach Royal was set to attend, there was another Longhorn coach who had been added to the agenda, not to speak at the clinic but to meet with our offensive staff, coordinator Emory Bellard, and the man generally given credit for being the father of the wishbone.

A few days before the clinic was set to begin, Coach Bryant came into our old staff room in Memorial Coliseum. If we thought we were going to sit around and discuss our responsibilities at the clinic, we were in for a surprise. A shock might be a better way of putting it.

Coach Bryant walked into the room and said in his gravelly distinctive voice, "We are going to switch to the wishbone offense. We are going to run it against Southern California in the opener in the Los Angeles Coliseum, and we are going to run it against Auburn in the season finale at Legion Field."

"We are going to sink or swim running the wishbone."

I think we were all too stunned to say much of anything, other than Defensive Coordinator Ken Donahue. Ken was one of the best football coaches ever, and he told Coach Bryant that he thought it was a mistake to try to change. Coach Bryant pretty much reiterated his line about sinking or swimming, told us that Coach Bellard was coming in to teach us the offense, and left the room.

When he left, Jimmy Sharpe, one of our offensive line coaches and one of my old teammates, started slinking down in his chair, gurgling like someone who was drowning. I think that pretty much was how most of us felt. This was going to be a challenge beyond all the challenges I'd faced as a player or a coach. Those boot camp days as a player seemed like easy days now.

One other thing Coach Bryant emphasized and we all knew he meant it, too: no one, and he meant no one, was to discuss our change with anyone, including our wives or best friends or anyone. The players, he said, would be told the same thing when they returned for August drills.

There used to be a Holiday Inn near the Indian Hills Country Club, and that's where Coach Bellard was staying. We got a meeting room there and our staff, which included Richard Williamson, Jimmy Sharpe, Jack Rutledge, John David Crow, Bob Tyler and me, would meet to learn the wishbone.

I won't go into all the technicalities of the offense, but after our first meeting, I knew why Coach Bryant was so taken with it. I must admit I felt totally comfortable with it as well. There were many keys to being successful in the wishbone, but the first one was having a skilled option quarterback running it, and no doubt we had our man in junior Terry Davis.

Terry was our top quarterback at the end of the spring and would have been the starter if we had started out in the pro-set that year, but he was just a natural at the wishbone. His footwork was just extraordinary, much like someone born to dance, like Astaire or one of those guys. Terry was meant to run the wishbone. That was one thing that made me at least halfway optimistic before the players reported the next week.

The other thing was Coach Bryant. He was dead set on returning the magic to Alabama football, and there were two things that all of us, who played, coached or worked for him had in common: we never wanted to let him down; and most importantly, we believed in him.

We were going to sink or swim with him and I know one thing: I was damned sure I wanted to swim.

14

THE NIGHT THE PRIDE
RETURNED TO THE TIDE

I don't know if a conversation that Coach Bryant had with John David Crow, his legendary running back at Texas A&M and our running back coach in the early 1970s, played a role in a re-shift in our fundamental philosophy, but it probably did. John David told Coach Bryant that our biggest problem was that we had gotten away from playing tough, physical football.

Our August drills in 1971 were not only tough and physical, but they were a learning experience for the players and the coaches as we implemented putting in the wishbone. I think it is worth noting that in all the years we ran the wishbone we never had a playbook. Every play, technique and blocking scheme was forever etched in my mind, and those of the offensive staff.

When we had a change on the staff, it was my responsibility to teach the new coaches the basics of what we were doing. That first year was a learning experience. As we repeated our plays, day after day that August, we thought we were getting better, but we were far from being a polished offensive unit.

During the final week of August, the SEC Skywriters came to Tuscaloosa for their annual visit to our campus. Back in those days, the media outlets would meet in Birmingham and fly to all 10 SEC schools, learning as much as they could about each school and its players.

The day before their scheduled trip to town, Coach Bryant told us in a staff meeting and the players in their meeting, that we would only be running plays out of the pro-I formation when the Skywriters were in town. Everyone had to reaffirm that there would be no leakage about our switch to the wishbone.

Before that practice, Coach Bryant said, "Mal, I want you to throw every damned down while they are here."

I think we about wore out the arms of our three primary quarterbacks --Terry Davis, Butch Hobson and Benny Rippetoe -- during those drills. A few days later the Skywriters released their pre-season picks. We were chosen to finish seventh in the conference and our only all-league picks were Johnny Musso and John Hannah.

One writer even wrote that he was reluctant to vote for Musso, because all Alabama does on offense is throw the ball!

By the end of the month, we had, like, six running plays and two passing plays, as we prepared for our trip to Southern California for a Friday night game on September 10, one day before Coach Bryant's 58th birthday.

No one gave us much of a chance of competing against the Trojans, much less winning the game. And, rightfully so. USC had thrashed us the year before 42-21 at Legion Field in Birmingham, and they had most of the same team back; and two of our best offensive players from that team, quarterback Scott Hunter and receiver George Ranager had graduated.

I would like to clarify one thing about the 1970 USC game. Talk about urban legend. There have been numerous stories and documentaries about Coach going to the USC dressing room after that game and bringing Sam Cunningham back into our locker room and saying, "This is what a real football player looks like."

I was there and it didn't happen. It wasn't unusual for Coach Bryant to go to a visiting locker area after a game and congratulate the other team if they beat us and he did do that after the game. But he never brought anyone back to our dressing room.

He often told us that after his Kentucky team beat No. 1 Oklahoma in the 1951 Sugar Bowl that Bud Wilkinson had come into the Wildcat dressing room and congratulated him and his team. Coach Bryant thought that was one of the classiest things he'd ever seen and said he was going to do the same thing and he did.

Coach Bryant paid attention to details. He assigned groundskeeper Herman

Shelton and his facilities folks to put up a tarpaulin around the field, so no one could watch us practice. He also had the University Police patrol the area and the managers stand by the fence and run off anyone who tried to watch practice. He even had the police go to an apartment complex across from the practice field and have the residents move away from the windows. Unless you were on the staff or a player, no one was admitted to practice!

Despite the fact we were coming off back-to-back five-loss seasons and being a double-digit underdog to the Trojans, there was the usual student enthusiasm about the season opener. On the Wednesday night before the game, the students had a pep rally on the quad and then they came to the practice fields.

We could hear them chanting and cheering outside the gates. Standing up in his tower with his bullhorn, Coach Bryant yelled at me to shut down the offense, and I did. And, then he told the managers to open the gates and let the students in. I think we were as mentally and physically prepared to play as any team I've ever seen. At our Wednesday night meeting, one of our new coaches, Brother Oliver, did his coke bottle trick. Let me say this about Brother, he was the absolute master not only at teaching techniques, creating turnovers and game planning; he was a great motivator.

He had learned this trick where he would take one of those 6 ½-ounce bottles, slam it against a bigger bottle, and break it. He stood before the players and said it didn't matter how much bigger and tougher USC was, it was all about the fight in a player's heart. Then he whacked the big coke bottle with the little one, and the players erupted in cheers.

The flight to Los Angeles was about as quiet as anyone can imagine. We were going out there on a mission, and there wasn't any wasted small talk or joking around. This was the ultimate business trip, and the level of concentration on what we had to do surpassed any team I'd ever been around.

On Thursday night, we were standing in the hotel lobby when USC coach John McKay came sweeping through to pick up Coach Bryant and take him to a party. Coach McKay was smoking the biggest cigar I'd ever seen, and I was standing there with some of our coaches thinking: He doesn't think we have a chance tomorrow night. I wasn't so sure either.

When we went out for warm-ups, we ran every play out of the pro-set. Coach Bryant even instructed a manager to go to the press box and tell our legendary announcer, John Forney, and his sidekick, Doug Layton, not to say a word about the wishbone in their pre-game report.

When John laughed and said our closest radio affiliate was in New Orleans that night, the manager replied, "Doesn't matter. Coach Bryant means it."

So, John never said a word either.

This was my first game as quarterback coach and the first I'd ever called plays. I can't begin to tell you how nervous I was. During our warm-up drills Benny Rippetoe took a snap, dropped back to pass and the ball went sailing out of the back of his right hand and almost hit me in the head.

I was seriously thinking, "I don't even know if we'll make a first down tonight against this team."

On the first play of the game, we put right halfback Joe Labue in motion, and Terry Davis handed off to Johnny Musso on a straight-ahead play that netted seven or eight yards. The Alabama wishbone days had finally begun.

Terry marched us down the field, and Johnny scored on a 13-yard run after taking a pitch. He did it in his usual style, getting hit on about the three and lunging somehow into the end zone. We had a 96-yard drive in the second quarter, and Johnny scored again, and we were up 17-0, but USC fought back, scoring twice to make it 17-10 at the half.

There would be no scoring in the second half, but each drive by both teams proved pivotal. Our much-maligned defense had a couple of turnovers in the second half, and we controlled the clock on offense. Late in the game we had fourth-and -one on the USC 28; and Coach Bryant opted to go for it instead of trying a field goal.

I called the same play that we had opened the game with, and this time the USC defense hit Johnny at the line of scrimmage, but he twisted and fought for three yards and a first down and our victory was secured, the 200th in Coach Bryant's career.

Someone asked me if there was jubilation after the game. All I remember was how relieved I was. I was as exhausted as our players.

It had been a physical, brutal hard-fought game. We had a pair of tough ends on defense, Robin Parkhouse and John Mitchell. We had actually stolen John away from USC. He was from Mobile and was a star in junior college in Arizona. Coach McKay had told Coach Bryant the best JC player in the country was from his part of the country but he was going to be a Trojan.

Coach sent Clem Gryska down to Mobile to offer him a scholarship and the next day, John was in Tuscaloosa. He was the first African-American to play for Alabama and would become our first black All-American and team captain.

Both of those players had great games that night but Robin took the most vicious hit I'd ever seen. They had a big tackle named John Vella, who blindsided him and literally flipped Parkhouse over. I thought he was dead.

A few plays later, Parkhouse was back on the field and knocked the ball loose from, of all people, Sam Cunningham. That stopped a Trojan drive in the fourth quarter and probably saved the game.

I do remember getting on the bus to head back to the airport. Terry Davis was sitting there with his head down, and all of a sudden he just raised his clenched fists together in an ultimate display of the ecstasy of victory.

When we got home, there were all kinds of stories about the students celebrating on the Quad, and on the downtown strip, and even in front of Bryant Hall. Even when we landed in Birmingham in the wee hours of the morning, there were fans lined up, yelling "Roll Tide!!!"

The next morning, Coach Bryant got a call from Darrell Royal who told him he'd listened to the game on the radio and congratulated him on the most improbable of victories. I picked up *The Birmingham News* and read the legendary Alf Van Hoose's story on the game.

He opened by saying, "Paul Bryant's coaching magic came back here in the Los Angeles Coliseum Friday night. And the sound of 'Rol-l-l-l Tide' is once again heard across the land. The pride is back at Alabama."

15

THE ULTIMATE
IRON BOWL

I'd be remiss in not talking about one of the most intense games I ever took part in, either as a player, coach or administrator. It was the Alabama-Auburn game of 1971, the "Sink-or-Swim Season."

As far back as I can remember, Auburn always had great players, and that year was no different. On Thanksgiving evening, two nights before the Iron Bowl, the Tigers' great quarterback, Pat Sullivan, was named the recipient of the Heisman Trophy during the halftime of ABC's telecast of the Georgia-Georgia Tech game.

I bet I've been asked a zillion times how emotional that year's Iron Bowl was, and if Pat winning the Heisman inspired us. We really didn't need any inspiration, because we were both unbeaten and untied entering the game at Legion Field. Plus Auburn, with Pat and his great receiver Terry Beasley had beaten us two straight years. Back in those days, we could only be on TV twice a year, and this one was the ABC game on Saturday afternoon.

To this day, it is the most viewed SEC game of all time, and by a large margin. I guess it was because it was the only game on TV, but the stakes were also high, especially with a Heisman winner and our own great Johnny Musso.

Coach Bryant liked to say, "I want to tell you something about football." Well, I'm going to tell you something about Paul Bryant football and the "gut checks" he stressed. I remember as a player and as an assistant coach, Coach Bryant standing before a team and talking about "sucking up your guts and laying everything you have on the field."

I think there was a certain badge of courage that was bestowed on a player who fought through adversity, overcame the odds and performed beyond everyone's expectations. Coach Bryant had done it as a player against Tennessee back in 1935. It is well documented that he broke a bone in his leg the week before but still found the intestinal fortitude to not only play but to excel in a 25-0 victory at Knoxville. Maybe that's the standard he set for all of us who were fortunate enough to endure the life's lessons he drilled into our souls.

On this late November Saturday, Johnny Musso displayed that mettle that Coach Bryant tried so hard to instill in all of us. During my years in football, I never saw such a performance like Johnny Musso's against Auburn in 1971. He had badly injured a big toe during the season, and we didn't think he'd be able to play against Auburn. He didn't practice all week and could hardly walk. I just didn't see how he could suit up, much less play.

Our trainer, Jim Goostree, worked around the clock with Johnny, keeping him in the whirlpool while the other medics massaged his foot. Goose, to his credit, was relentless and created a rubber foam and tongue suppressor cast that would fit in Johnny's shoe. We hoped beyond hope that it would work.

I met with Coach Bryant to discuss the game plans, one with Johnny and one without him. I don't think it ever crossed Coach Bryant's mind that Johnny wasn't going to play, but he knew we had to have a backup, just like we had a few weeks earlier when Johnny left the LSU game and didn't return.

At our workout at Legion Field on Friday before the game, Johnny tested the rubber molding during some drills. I doubt if it was comfortable, but you had to know Johnny. He was going to play.

I don't know if it buoyed our spirits, but I don't think it hurt any. As I said earlier, Coach Bryant called him a "barrel of guts on a football field." Against Auburn that Saturday, he had a game that should forever be etched in crimson lore. There have been backs who gained more yards and scored more touchdowns, but I seriously doubt any played with such grit. In my opinion, Johnny's play that day is what the tradition and determination of Alabama football is all about.

We continually attacked the heart of Auburn's defense with Johnny. He carried the ball over 30 times, which was unheard of from a wishbone back and gained

167 yards and scored two touchdowns. Rightfully, he was picked as the National Offensive Player of the Week.

If they voted on the Heisman like they do today, Johnny's performance against Auburn probably would have earned him that award, though he was such a humble man I doubt that recognition crossed his mind. Regardless of his physical condition, he had repeatedly taken handoffs and pitch outs from Terry Davis and attacked the Auburn defense with the resolve of the champion he was.

You couldn't stop Johnny for a loss or no gain. He just fought his way for the extra foot or yard or two yards. And, there was no day he did it better than on this overcast day in Birmingham when we won 31-7. When we needed three yards, somehow he got four, and when we needed four, he'd twist and fight for five.

We controlled the ball more than 42 minutes that day and an Alabama supporter in the state legislature made a proposal that in Auburn an hour should last only 18 minutes. Our performance that day pretty much set the tone for the rest of the 1970s. As dominating as our offense was that day, our defense was equal to the task as well. Probably better.

LSU had done a magnificent job of shutting down the Auburn passing attack the previous two years, and Ken Donahue had studied those game films with a passion to see what Charlie McClendon had done to stymie the Sullivan-to-Beasley combination. It didn't hurt that Brother Oliver had coached at Auburn before coming to Alabama that spring and had first-hand knowledge of how to defend them as well.

I remember vividly our great linebacker, Jeff Rouzie, who would later become a longtime assistant under both Coach Bryant and Coach Stallings, had a key interception that he returned to set up a touchdown. The relentless pass rush, led by our ends Robin Parkhouse and John Mitchell, stifled Sullivan the whole game. Auburn's only touchdown came on a halfback pass to Beasley. We had totally shut down the Tiger passing attack.

Another thing I'll never forget were fans running on the field after we had won. As we left the field, a young fan rushed toward Coach Bryant and stole his houndstooth hat while he was being interviewed. I'm sure it made Coach mad for a moment or two, but this game really captured everything he taught and believed in, so I'm sure he didn't worry about the lost hat for long.

Even though the loss to Nebraska in the National Championship game in the Orange Bowl was a downer, it should never diminish what the 1971 team accomplished. We played what most considered the toughest schedule in the country, and we beat a lot of teams with a lot more talent than we had.

It would be difficult to say if it was Coach Bryant's greatest coaching job, but I do think he'd say it was a year in which we learned how to win again and be among the elite. All I can say is that every player who ever wears that crimson jersey should learn a thing or two about Johnny Musso and what he found within himself to help beat Auburn that day.

In my opinion, it is what Crimson Tide football has been and hopefully will be about forever, individual players giving all that is within them to help their team become a champion.

16

THE MOST EXCRUCIATING LOSS OF THEM ALL

O ne Sunday morning after we lost a tough game, I walked to Coach Nick Saban's office, mainly just to let him know I was with him no matter the outcome of any of our games. He was really suffering that day, telling me while winning was great, there were times he felt more relief than joy in coming out on top. Losing was just torture.

I knew exactly what he meant. If you are a competitor, the losses live with you forever. The wins, for the most part, just seem to jumble together. During our great run during the wishbone era, we only lost a handful of games, but I remembered those few losses a lot more vividly than most of the wins. None hurt more than our loss to Notre Dame in the 1973 Sugar Bowl.

There is really no way to express the pain I felt. I know our staff and players felt it, too. Sometimes you lose because the other team is just better, like when we lost to Nebraska in the Orange Bowl. Sometimes you lose because you can't get your players' attention and they just aren't mentally ready to play.

Sometimes, you just do a poor coaching job and have execution breakdowns on the field that cost you a game, much like our loss to Auburn in 1972. We were clearly the better team and dominated the game but just seemed to figure out a way to lose it.

That Sugar Bowl in 1973 was different for so many reasons. First of all,

Notre Dame had a great football team with a great coaching staff, headed by Ara Parseghian. I can't express the respect that Coach Bryant and our staff had for the Notre Dame heritage and for that team in particular, but we felt strongly that we had a team that was special in every sense of the word as well.

We had really coasted through an 11-0 season and had the best offensive team we ever had during the wishbone era. Candidly, we could have set offensive records that would have stood for years. I usually don't get too upset when a sports writer says something I don't agree with, because that's just part of their business; but I wasn't too happy when I read an article a few years ago by a Birmingham writer claiming Coach Bryant had run up the score on people and pointed out some of the scores from the 1973 season.

I can tell you that in some of those games, we played everybody but the managers and water boys, and we could have scored triple digits if Coach Bryant had left in the second or third teams, much less the starters.

During the 1973 season, we beat LSU on Thanksgiving night in Baton Rouge, setting up the Sugar Bowl showdown with the Fighting Irish. LSU had a perfect record coming into the game, but we played well, hitting them a couple of times on long passes from Gary Rutledge to Wayne Wheeler. After that win, we moved up to No. 1 ranking in both major polls.

We didn't have much trouble in beating Auburn 35-0, and Notre Dame completed a perfect season as well when the Irish beat Miami 44-0.

When we started preparing for Notre Dame, I think every coach realized how special a team Coach Parseghian had put together. One day, Coach Bryant's old friend and USC head coach, John McKay, was in town and told us that Notre Dame was a lot better in person than they were on film. They looked pretty dang good to me on film.

One advantage we really felt we had offensively entering the game was the speed of our wide receiver Wayne Wheeler. He had been a sprint champion in Florida, and our track coaches were the ones who told us we ought to sign him as a football player.

Wayne was really the first receiver who put wings on the wishbone. He could fly, and we consistently hit him on the home run pass play during the 1972 and 1973 seasons.

Most Alabama fans, at least those who remember back to 1973, will never forget the opening play of the Tennessee game of that year when Gary Rutledge hit Wayne for 80 yards. We felt we had a real weapon to attack Notre Dame that night, but on the first play, Wayne pulled up lame and was really never effective the rest of the night.

It was a bad omen. So was the cold, rainy, slick day in New Orleans. The game was played in old Tulane Stadium on New Year's Eve, and the cold and rain weren't good for the wishbone either.

For whatever reason, we played uptight in the first quarter and fell behind 6-0, but we finally settled down and started exerting ourselves offensively. After Wilbur Jackson scored a touchdown to give us a 7-6 lead, Notre Dame's Al Hunter returned the ensuing kickoff for a touchdown and the two-point conversion gave the Irish a 14-7 lead.

During Coach Bryant's 25 years as head coach at Alabama, we only gave up two kickoff returns for six and that return by Hunter added to a night of unexpected breakdowns for our team. We scored a field goal before half and drove 93 yards for a touchdown in the third quarter to go ahead 17-14.

Then, probably the worst moment in my coaching career occurred after Notre Dame fumbled and we subsequently moved to around the Irish 20-yard line.

I think anyone who has ever coached in a big game will tell you that it's like a battle, a war. Woody Hayes, the old Ohio State legendary coach and noted military historian, once said something to the effect that football is the closest thing to war that there is, and I think he's right.

In a game and in a battle, there can be communication breakdowns that forever change the destiny of the winner. I was about to find out in the cruelest of ways.

We had third and about four to go for a first down. I was standing on one side of Coach Bryant and didn't hear Coach Bryant send Mike Stock into the game with our "gadget" play for that night, a halfback pass from Stock to quarterback Richard Todd. The halfback throwback pass to the quarterback was a play that Coach Bryant absolutely loved.

Well, I sent in another play and when it was relayed to Richard Todd, he naturally thought it was the one to use. Not only didn't we make a first down, but subsequently we missed the field goal as well.

Coach Bryant was some kind of fired up and mad at me. I can assure you that if you ever coached for the man, he fired you at least once on the sidelines during your career. He wanted to know what the hell had I done, and he fired me on the spot.

You talk about feeling sick and miserable. Adding to our problems that night was a fumble by Willie Shelby on our own 12-yard line, and Notre Dame scored to retake the lead 21-17. In the fourth quarter, we started our rally, going down the field and this time, Coach Bryant told me to "Run the damn halfback pass."

There was no miscommunication this time, and we ran it for a 25-yard touchdown pass from Stock to Todd. Then, like most of the night, we had another inexplicable breakdown, when we missed the extra point.

Even after Notre Dame kicked what would ultimately be the game-winning field goal, I think everyone on the sideline felt we were going to win, especially after Greg Gantt's punt backed the Irish in the shadows of their own goal posts.

The third-down play is one that will live in Fighting Irish lore and in Alabama infamy. It was a great call by the Notre Dame staff, a deep-out pattern from quarterback Tom Clements to little-used tight end Robin Weber, but our own defensive call really was perfect, too.

Leroy Cook, who would become one of the best defensive ends we ever had, had entered the game to replace our starter John Croyle, who had been injured earlier. Leroy was a ferocious pass rusher and appeared to have a clear shot at Clements, but he slipped on the turf. Regaining his footing, he leaped just as the pass was made. Pictures will show you the pass barely getting over Leroy's outstretched arms.

We also had a breakdown when one of our defenders was supposed to check Weber at the line of scrimmage and didn't. Those were two of the biggest "ifs" on that memorable play, at least from our perspective. If Weber had been checked, it's highly doubtful he'd been in position to make the catch. If Leroy hadn't slipped, it's highly unlikely the pass would have been completed.

Notre Dame would ultimately run out the clock and win one of the most memorable games ever, 24-23.

I can't begin to explain the overwhelming pain I felt after that game. Coach Bryant did his best to console the players and the coaches. He never mentioned my ill-fated call on the third down, not that I expected he ever would. But that play call is one that I never forgot. After the game, I went back to the old Roosevelt Hotel in New Orleans where we were staying, and went straight to my room.

My wife, Charlotte, was there and did her best to lift my sagging spirits. But her pep talk didn't do much good. I just stared out the window and thought of what should have been. There haven't been many days since then that I haven't thought about if I'd just heard Coach Bryant send in the halfback pass, the outcome of that game would have likely changed. It is a loss that has always haunted me.

After we beat Notre Dame in the 2013 BCS Championship game, some writers asked me if that made up for the 1973 game. I just smiled and told them it helped some, but in truth, it never erases the agony of that game.

It was the one loss that has lived with me throughout my career, the most excruciating one I ever experienced.

17

THE FIRST SUGAR BOWL IN
THE SUPER DOME

D uring the spring of 1975, we really felt like we had a team that was going to win the National Championship and Coach Bryant had made up his mind that he wanted to play in the first-ever Sugar Bowl in the newly finished Louisiana Superdome.

You have to remember that the SEC didn't have a bowl tie-in at the time, and Coach Bryant didn't think it was to our advantage for the league to have one, either. He liked the flexibility of deciding between the Cotton, Sugar and Orange Bowls so our players could participate in all the major bowls other than the Rose, which had its long-standing contract with the Big Ten and Pac-10.

One of Coach Bryant's best friends was Aruns Callery, who was on the Sugar Bowl committee. It had been well documented that the only reason Coach agreed to the 1973 Notre Dame game was because of Aruns. At the time, the Orange Bowl paid substantially more money, and Coach Bryant had been leaning toward going there.

During our annual spring game weekend, Aruns was in town from New Orleans and Coach told him then and there Alabama was going to the Sugar Bowl. I think it even caught Aruns off-guard, but he knew when Coach made up his mind, he wasn't going to change -- unless of course, we had a bad season.

It didn't start out well. Missouri beat us in the opener 20-7 on Labor Day night, and I have to admit that we were unprepared for the defensive schemes that Coach Al Onofrio's staff utilized in that particular game.

We had totally prepped on what they had done the previous season, and they made us look bad. If there is anything worse than awful, well, that was us that night.

I think the thought of the Sugar Bowl was about the last thing on anyone's mind the next two weeks as we prepared for Clemson, a game we would win 56-0. After that we marched over everyone, finishing the regular season with a 10-1 record.

About the only funny things about the Missouri game, in retrospect, were the telephone calls I got the next week from some of my coaching friends in the old Big 8, especially from Oklahoma coaches. Barry Switzer called and asked me, "What the heck kind of defense were they running?" Bud Moore, who had gone from our staff at Alabama to be the head coach at Kansas, was asking pretty much the same thing.

I told them we had done everything wrong imaginable and I hoped we were not that bad. As it turned out, Missouri finished 6-5 that year and lost its final two games – to Oklahoma and Kansas.

When it became evident that we were going to be extended an invitation to a major bowl game, Coach Bryant reconfirmed to Mr. Callery that our first choice was the Sugar, and he wanted to play Penn State and Joe Paterno.

Years later, I was visiting with Joe and he told me that he got a call one night in November of 1975 from Coach Bryant, asking if he wanted to play us in the Sugar Bowl. Joe told Coach Bryant that he'd love to go to the Sugar Bowl; but he hadn't heard a word from them and that the Nittany Lions were going to accept an invitation to the Gator Bowl the next day.

Joe just laughed, saying to me, "Coach Bryant said, don't agree to anything Joe. You'll hear from Aruns Callery of the Sugar Bowl tomorrow morning, and you'll get a bid.

"I didn't know whether to believe he could pull it off or not, but the next morning I received a call from Mr. Callery telling me the Sugar Bowl wanted Penn State, and I knew then just how strong Paul Bryant was."

The game turned into a defensive classic. Richard Todd had an MVP night in his final game, hitting 10 of 12 passes, including a long one to Ozzie Newsome to set up the only TD of the game, an option play to the left with Richard pitching to Mike Stock for the score.

It would be a play that would stick in my mind because we would use it again when we played Penn State in that unforgettable Sugar Bowl of 1979.

While Coach Bryant got quite a bit of attention that night for not wearing his houndstooth hat indoors and telling the press, "Mama told me to never wear a hat indoors," the thing I will always remember is Woodrow Lowe's dash to the Superdome.

We were staying at a downtown hotel that was probably a mile from the Superdome, and we loaded the buses headed to the stadium. Woodrow wasn't just a good football player; he was an all-time great linebacker and one of the keys to our defensive unit.

The elevator he got on was crowded, stopped so many times, that by the time he finally got to the ground floor, the buses were pulling out.

Well, the buses took off and Woodrow didn't make it, but he ran alongside the buses to the Superdome. Thankfully, we didn't have a police escort, so we had to stop at several traffic lights and Woodrow would always make up ground on the buses when we were stopped.

We were all hoping Coach Bryant wouldn't see him, because he had already suspended eight players for the game for being late for curfew, and we sure didn't want him suspending Woodrow. I don't know if Coach ever knew about it or not, but he never said a word. Woodrow got to the Superdome the same time as the rest of us.

Back in 2009, Woodrow was elected to the College Football Hall of Fame, an honor he richly deserved, and we shared a good laugh about his mad dash to the Superdome on New Year's Eve 1975. He just smiled, "Coach, that was one time I didn't need to go through warm-ups, because I'd already gotten all the exercise I needed chasing the team buses."

That Sugar Bowl was the last open one before the bowl coalition began its run. During the spring of 1976, Mr. Callery went to SEC Commissioner Boyd McWhorter with a proposal that the SEC and Sugar Bowl unite with the champion of the conference being the home team in New Orleans.

Dr. McWhorter told Aruns that he just didn't think it would ever pass because there was no way that Coach Bryant would agree to such a commitment. He added the caveat, "If anyone can convince Paul to do it, it's you, Aruns."

He did persuade Coach Bryant to agree to the SEC Champion going to the Sugar Bowl. "I've got to do what's best for the league, and not for me or Alabama," Coach Bryant announced when the decision was reached. "It's best for Alabama to be able to play in the other major bowls, but the SEC needs this tie-in, so I'm supporting it."

It was a magnanimous move on his part and probably elevated the conference and the Sugar Bowl to a higher level in the perception of college football across the country.

18

YOU HAVE TO LAUGH
WITH THEM

As much as I liked to hunt, there was one thing I'd never done, at least until the late 1970s, and that was kill a wild turkey. One March, Brother Oliver told me about a spot near where he grew up in Epes, Alabama, in Greene County, where he promised I'd get my chance. He was right, too.

Brother and I drove down to his favorite spot, and it didn't take long before I shot my first turkey. He was a big one, weighing about 20 pounds and having a 12-inch beard. During that time period, we knew we had the best group of players that we had ever assembled as a staff, and life couldn't seem to be much better.

My daughter Heather was in elementary school, and I couldn't wait to get home to tell her and Charlotte about my day away from football. I wanted to get the turkey mounted, as a so-called lifetime hunting achievement award.

I had this friend in Montgomery, Hoyt Henley, who was regarded as one of the premier turkey hunters around, so I called him to see if he could mount the turkey for me. He told me "Sure, when I have some time."

Well, I hadn't heard back from him the rest of the spring. So, when we were getting ready for August drills, I called him to see if he had made any progress. He told me not to worry that he'd have it done by the time we played our first game in Tuscaloosa, and he'd bring it to me then.

We played an afternoon game in Tuscaloosa in early October, and after the game I had gone over to the old Verner Elementary parking lot across from the south end zone of Bryant-Denny to see Frank McGough, one of our car dealers who always tailgated there. I couldn't stay long because I had to get back over to Bryant Hall where we had our recruiting dinner after the game. Well, who taps me on the shoulder but Hoyt. He told me to come over to a motor home where he had the mounted turkey.

My first thoughts were, I'm glad to be getting it but how in the heck am I going to get the turkey from here back to my car, which was parked by the old fire station directly by the south end zone. I was hoping Hoyt was going over to Brother's house after the game and would just leave it there. Then I'd figure out how to get it home, but Hoyt told me he was headed on back to Montgomery, so I had to come up with another plan.

I can tell you I didn't want to carry it back through the exiting football crowd to my car. It was mounted on driftwood board and it was not only heavy but cumbersome to carry. You can only imagine the looks and catcalls I got as I meandered back through the fans trying to get to my car with the turkey. The comedy was really only beginning though.

The turkey was too big to fit into my car because of the size of the driftwood board it was mounted on. I tried every which way to get into my car but it just wouldn't fit, so I walked into the fire station where I knew most of the firemen and asked if I could leave it with them until after the recruiting meeting. I was going to go home and trade cars with Charlotte, because hers was bigger and I figured we could get the turkey into her car.

That didn't work either. Charlotte and Heather rode with me back to the fire station, and again, we did everything to try to get the turkey into the car but it just wouldn't fit. One of the firemen told me that he was getting off work at 11:00 and that his son had a pick-up truck and we'd get it home that way, so I sent Charlotte on her way back to our house in Woodland Hills, which was about a 10-minute drive from campus.

Heather decided she wanted to ride with me and the turkey. They were taking off when the fire alarm goes off at the station, about 10 minutes before 11 p.m., and I'm thinking how am I going to get home now and how am I ever going to get the turkey home. The fireman said, "Don't worry Coach, just tell my son that I had to go to a fire. Tell him who you are and he'll get you and the turkey home."

That was a relief but when his son got there, we soon figured out that I was going to have to sit in the bed of the truck and hold on to the turkey or it would go flying onto the road. The way I was seated the turkey's head was staring out at passing drivers, which created quite a scene and quite a few more laughs, at least for the spectators of this comical event.

The fireman's son was driving so fast that the feathers were flying upward and I was trying to push them back down so I could bang on the back window to signal him to slow down before the turkey, Heather and I went spilling onto the road. Everyone was honking their horns at us, adding to the comic scene.

When we got to 15th Street where we would turn left next to Tuscaloosa High, we had to stop at the red light and I could tell the people in the car stopped next to us were getting quite a laugh out of me sitting there holding a stuffed turkey. The window slowly rolled down, and it was Dr. Richard Thigpen, who was serving as the interim President of the University, having replaced David Mathews who had left the University to go to Washington, D.C. to be part of Gerald Ford's Cabinet. Richard was laughing and said, "Mal, I didn't think we played well enough today for you to be out with a turkey tonight."

Several others in cars stopped when we were at traffic lights and one young boy, riding with his parents, rolled his window down and asked what in the world is that? I just said "A wild turkey." They all started laughing and drove away. To put it mildly, I was extremely happy to get home with my prized kill.

I think Heather was impressed with the prized turkey, but I remember Charlotte just rolled her eyes. I knew she was thinking about where are we going to put that new addition to the Moore collection? The next day in the coaching offices, I got ribbed pretty good about it too. It didn't take long for the news to travel around our circles.

Brother joked that he'd bet I wished I'd never been so determined to shoot a turkey. I said something to the effect that I don't know about that, but of all the people to see me riding in the back of the truck with my feathered friend, one had to be the President of the University. I guess it could have been worse. It could have been Coach Bryant.

Let me say this about Dr. Thigpen. Even though he only served as the interim, he was one of the most respected men on campus, and all of us in football regarded him as one of our most loyal supporters. I am thankful he had a great sense of humor as well.

You have to laugh at yourself, no matter your profession, and I had an even worse faux pas in front of Dr. Thigpen when we were traveling back from Seattle after we beat Washington 20-17 in 1978.

It was another pivotal game for us and helped position us back into the National Championship race that season. As I've said before, our football trips were all business, and this was another critical one for our team and for our season. Washington was coached by Don James, who had been on the Florida State staff back in the late 1960s, along with one of our former coaches Kenny Meyer.

Through Kenny, I got to know Coach James and he was one of the great coaches in college football, and would win the national title in 1991. For Alabama fans, he's probably best remembered for being the mentor to one Nick Saban at Kent State in the early 1970s.

The Huskies had a great team in 1978 and were defending Rose Bowl Champions. We had a real fight before finally winning 20-17. After a win like that, there was a lot of releasing of tension in the locker room and on the plane ride home. One of my old teammates, Tommy Brooker, who was serving as a volunteer coach with our kickers that year, was seated next to me. Dr. Thigpen was across the aisle.

When we were flying over Seattle, heading back east, the pilot dipped his wing, revealing the most beautiful body of water I'd ever seen. Tommy asked me if that was the ocean, and I said "No, that's pubic sound."

Dr. Thigpen just roared in laughter and it dawned on me that I had meant to say Puget Sound. Talk about embarrassing! Brooker started laughing, too, as did everyone who heard me. I laughed, too, but I wondered what in the world Richard Thigpen thought of me. Like I said, you better learn to laugh.

19

RECRUITING WINNERS

Recruiting has certainly changed over the years, but there is one thing that has remained a constant: you better recruit winners.

When I signed with Alabama, coaches could sign unlimited players to scholarships. That was a different time and place. I can tell you it was survival of the fittest then. Only a handful of players were even around after their freshman seasons.

The SEC, in an effort to address Georgia Tech's concerns about the number of players being signed, changed its limits in the 1960s. Then in 1973 the NCAA passed legislation, restricting the signing class to 35; and not long after that the number dropped to 30 and then 25. While the talking point was cost-containment, there was the prevailing opinion that it was done to equalize the game and bring parity.

I think the big irony is, for the most part, the same powers in the 1960s are still national powers fifty years later. It's just hard to erase the tradition of excellence.

I was the ultimate novice when I started out as an assistant coach and made my first rounds in recruiting student-athletes to Alabama. While I was probably as naïve as anyone possibly could be, I will tell you I believed in the school and the coach I was selling to the prospects.

I knew first-hand what competing and graduating from the University of

Alabama could mean to each football player I offered the opportunity to become a member of the Crimson Tide. My belief in the Crimson Tide name has never diminished either.

Coach Bryant assigned me to recruit from the central part of the state over to the Georgia line. During those years I met some of the finest people around, especially Dr. John Morgan. He was just a huge fan and became a dear friend to Charlotte and me. He would always sit with Charlotte at the bowl games, and I guess she did her best to keep him calm during some of those championship games we played.

I have to laugh about it, but he and Charlotte could talk on the phone forever. After a few minutes, I would run out of things to say and I would just hand the telephone off to her so she could spend the next hour conversing with Dr. Morgan.

Through the years I have made thousands of speeches representing the University, but the first one I ever made was in 1965 at the Holiday Inn in Lanett, Alabama. Dr. Morgan was a driving force in the local alumni office in the Valley area that included both the Alabama and Georgia sides of the Chattahoochee River. He set it up where Pat Dye and I would be the guest speakers.

Pat had the Georgia area to recruit and was coming down from Atlanta. I don't know if this was Pat's first speaking engagement or not, but it had to be one of his first, because he had just joined our staff that spring.

I was really nervous, because I had never spoken publicly before. It got worse when Pat called to tell me that he had gotten delayed in Atlanta and couldn't make it down to the meeting, so I was going to have to do a solo act.

Before the alumni meeting began, Dr. Morgan had invited me to his house to visit with some of the most prominent Alabama supporters in the Valley. He had this beautiful house and we were out on a breezeway where he had drinks and food for his nine invited guests, including me.

Well, the other eight visitors crowded around me, asking me all about the prospects for the team and about Coach Bryant. At least those were topics that were easy for me. Dr. Morgan had all kind of food already laid out on tables, but he rushed out there with this platter and sat it down in the middle of the table.

And he says, "Now Mal, this is caviar. I got it just for you!"

I had never seen caviar, much less tasted it. I was munching on some of the other food and so were the other eight men who were there. A little while later Dr.

Morgan came back over and said, "Mal, you haven't eaten any of the caviar."

Dr. Morgan put some on a plate and brought it over to me. Now I was in a quandary because I didn't even have a clue what to do next. There was this little knife next to the plate, so I sliced down into this mound and ate the caviar off the knife.

Dr. Morgan quickly ran over, grabbed another knife and some crackers, and spread the caviar on the crackers. Talk about embarrassing! And now I had to speak to them and the rest of the alumni group. All I could tell them was growing up in Dozier, Alabama, caviar wasn't one of our primary dishes. That's one recruiting trip I never forgot, though I don't even remember who I was scouting.

Who's the Boss?

There is one battle, though, that I'll never forget and that came eight years later when I was recruiting Johnny Davis out of Lanier High School in Montgomery. He was a special young man, an accomplished pianist, and one heck of a talented fullback. It was an all-out war to sign him because everyone wanted him and for good reason.

I felt strongly that Johnny was the ideal fullback for the wishbone offense. I believed you needed a big, strong athletic player there and Johnny certainly fit that description. I personally never liked to ask Coach Bryant to help out on a recruit unless I felt it was absolutely necessary, so I was hoping I wouldn't have to call on him to help sell Johnny and his family on attending the University.

I had been recruiting Johnny since he was a sophomore, which was unusual back in the 1970s, but he was that good -- and then some. On one trip to his house, I took a carousel projector with 100 or so slides in it. And I sat in one of his rooms and showed his mother pictures of the University.

There were pictures of everything from the dorm to the practice fields to buildings on campus, and I thought that would convince her Alabama was the best place for Johnny. But that still didn't sell her.

One of the many things I learned from Coach Bryant was that there was always a key person besides the player in recruiting, usually the mother. In this case, it was definitely Mrs. Davis.

We had one more opportunity to officially visit Johnny in his home. In a staff meeting, I told Coach Bryant that it was nip and tuck with Johnny, and I thought it might be best if he went with me to help sell him on the Crimson Tide. Raymond Perdue, who was one of our alumni in Montgomery, drove Coach Bryant and me to Johnny's house, and I introduced Coach Bryant to Mrs. Davis for the first time.

Coach Bryant and I sat on this little couch, Mrs. Davis sat in a chair facing us and Johnny stood next to the wall. Let me tell you, I don't think Mrs. Davis cared that much for football and didn't follow it either, but she wanted to make sure wherever her son went to college that he would fit in and have a chance to get an education.

I scooted up on the sofa and started my spiel on why Johnny should sign with Alabama. Mrs. Davis stopped me, looked right at me and asked, "Now, are you the boss, or is he the boss?" I almost fainted on the spot.

I said, "No ma'am, I'm not the boss. Coach Bryant, he's the boss and I brought him here just for you to meet the boss." Coach Bryant took over from there and when we were driving back, he said, "We'll get him." We did, too, and Johnny became one of our best fullbacks ever, starring on our teams from 1974-77.

Sometimes you have to be able to gauge a player on his future ability, too. Johnny Davis was a five-star prospect in an era before there were recruiting analysts saying who could and couldn't play.

Walk-ons Sometimes Beat the Odds

There were a couple of players, cousins Andy and Preston Gothard whom I recruited to the University who I guess would be considered projects in the modern recruiting world.

Andy was a few years before Preston, and played quarterback in Alexander City, which was part of my recruiting area. He was a huge Alabama fan and desperately wanted to come to Alabama. I candidly didn't think he could play quarterback for us, but at that time we had a lot of quarterbacks who ended up starring for us in the secondary and on special teams.

I was trying to get a mental picture of Andy playing safety in the SEC, because I honestly didn't think he could ever break into our quarterback rotation; but in the end, we decided not to offer him a scholarship. I know he was disappointed when I told him.

They used to have the Alabama high school all-star game that was played in late July in Bryant-Denny and I got Brother Oliver to evaluate him, too. Andy had a really good game but we still didn't have a scholarship for him.

On the Sunday after the high school all-star game, Andy came by my office at Coleman Coliseum, and I'll never forget closing the door and telling him that coaches weren't always correct in their evaluation; if he believed in himself and thought he could make the team, he ought to come to the University and walk on and prove himself correct and us wrong.

That's exactly what he did, too. Andy ended up playing quite a bit for us on the 1975 and 1976 teams. Not only did he earn a scholarship, but he would become an outstanding graduate coach for us while he was earning his law degree at the University. He asked Coach Donahue and me to be part of his wedding. I always felt a special affection for Andy, because he worked hard to live his dream of playing and contributing to the Crimson Tide.

In the early 1980s, I recruited Andy's cousin Preston to come to the University, again as an invited walk-on. He was from near Fort Deposit in Lowndes County and was playing at Lowndes Academy when I went to see him play. Preston was tall, just around 6-foot-5 and probably weighed just over 200 pounds.

There was just something about Preston that impressed me. I watched him play basketball, too, and while he didn't have great speed, he was extremely coordinated and had excellent hands. Most important, he was a tough, rawboned young man who I thought had the potential to play for the Crimson Tide.

Just like I had been compelled to tell Andy, I had the task of telling Preston that we didn't have a scholarship for him, but I would still like for him to consider walking on at the University and live in Bryant Hall with the other players. He would just have to pay his own way and earn a scholarship.

I visited with his folks and they agreed to let him walk on, so I felt like we had a future tight end prospect if Preston dedicated himself to doing the things necessary to compete at our level. I really liked him in those early practices, not only because he had soft hands and was tough, but was just a natural blocker as well.

That August, after one of those hot, two-a-day practices when no one else is on campus, he came into my office. He tapped on the door and closed it when he came in, and then he told me, "Coach, I want to go home. Can you call my father to come get me?"

He was a country boy who probably had never been away from home, and I did everything I could to dissuade him from leaving campus. I knew how he felt, too, because I had felt the exact same way back in 1958 when I was a freshman on the football team. I called Preston's father, and he tried to talk him out of leaving, too, but to no avail. His dad came and helped him clean out his room in Bryant Hall and they headed back home.

One day during the Christmas season of 1981, I got a call from Preston telling me he wanted to come back, so I went to see him when we had gotten back from the bowl trip. He was really having an outstanding spring for us, too, when he went up high to catch a pass and got nailed in the side by one of our linebackers.

The hit burst his spleen and he had to have an emergency operation to remove it. His mother wanted him to give up football, but he told her he was there to play. I'm sure he realized at that point that he was good enough to play for us.

He got even better in the fall of 1982, and I really thought he would be a future starter for Alabama. Before we left for the Liberty Bowl, and after Coach Ray Perkins had already been hired to become the head coach, I went to see Coach Bryant about Preston.

I said, "Coach, you know we have one scholarship available, and I hope you will consider giving it to Preston Gothard before we leave. I think he's going to be a hell of a player for Alabama."

Coach Bryant said something to the effect that I was right, and he was worried the new staff would waste it on someone else. He instructed me to go find Preston and tell him to come to his office. So, Preston was the last player that I helped get a scholarship for Coach Bryant and officially the last one signed by Coach Bryant.

That fall I was coaching at Notre Dame and didn't know anything about what was going on at Alabama. When I picked up a *Sports Illustrated* in October, I saw the picture of Preston catching the "touchdown that wasn't" in the final seconds against Penn State in 1983. That pass was the one he caught from Walter Lewis in the back of the end zone that would have given the Crimson Tide a victory, but the official on the spot incorrectly ruled him out of bounds.

Regardless of the call, I must admit I felt proud that Preston was getting the chance to prove he could play.

A few years later, I was in my den in South Bend and I had the television on Monday night football. Joe Namath was the commentator and I wasn't paying much attention until I heard Joe say, "Great catch by the Pittsburgh Steeler's

Preston Gothard. That's a good old Alabama boy."

I almost fell out of my chair. I had no clue that Preston was now playing for Pittsburgh. He would have a great run in the NFL as well. He's just one of those players that you have to tip your hat, because he was a man who believed in himself and hung in there through a lot of adversity. He beat the odds to become not only a great college player but an NFL starter as well.

When we played Penn State in Tuscaloosa in 2010, I thought it only appropriate to ask Preston to serve as the honorary captain for that game, letting him enjoy some of the limelight to make up for not being awarded the game-winning catch against the Nittany Lions in 1983.

Jon Hand

The last really can't-fail recruit I signed for Coach Bryant was Jon Hand out of Sylacauga in 1982. Jon was destined for future greatness because he had the size and athleticism, as well as being just one of the finest young men I ever had the pleasure of recruiting.

There was no doubt in Jon's case that his mother was a key to his recruitment. She worked for Avondale Mills in the textile business, and I called all over campus trying to find a connection. You have to remember you could use alumni to a certain extent in those days, and I found out that one of the executives for Avondale Mills was an alumna named Diane Bostick.

She was in the corporate office in New York, so I called her, introduced myself, and asked her if she would call or write Ms. Hand and tell her what a great place the University of Alabama was. She told me that she would, and she did.

Jon signed with us and became a star player in the ensuing years before going on to a distinguished professional career with the Colts and Eagles. In 1992, he was chosen as a member of the all-time Alabama team; and I was probably as happy about that recognition as Jon was.

When I got out of coaching and joined the administrative team, I went to New York for the annual National Football Foundation and Hall of Fame festivities. The University of Alabama has a substantial alumni base there, and at the time, one of the officers of the group had an office in the Empire State Building. During our trip, we went there to their annual Christmas party, where Hootie Ingram was going to speak for the department.

I was visiting with some of the people and this little woman walked up to me and tapped me on the shoulder and asked, "Are you Mal Moore?"

When I told her I was, she said, "I'm Diane Bostick. You asked me to help recruit Jon Hand."

I couldn't believe it. I was extremely apologetic, because I had never called her back or written back to thank her for her help. She went on to tell me that she had really not been that interested in Alabama football since she moved to New York. After Jon signed with us, she started going to all the games and had her picture taken with Jon and his mother after one of the games.

I know one thing: I always tried to be thankful and appreciative of all the people who helped me along the way. When I got back to Tuscaloosa, I wrote Diane a letter apologizing to her for not thanking her back in 1982, and told her how much I appreciated what she did for the University.

I guess the moral of these stories is that you better recruit winners. They may not always be the so-called can't-miss-stars, but a player that expects to win and wants to win helps make a championship environment.

20

AND THAT TEAM IS ALABAMA

Being part of three of the greatest runs in the history of college football, twice as a coach and then as an athletic director, is something I cherish. Frankly, it's quite humbling in retrospect to have played a role in watching the teamwork necessary among coaches, staff, players and supporters to reach such an elite status in the game that I've loved all my life and at the school that has been, along with my family, my life.

As the offensive coordinator in the late 1970s, we had our second run, finishing second in 1977 before claiming consensus championships to close out the decade. I know by the end of the '77 season Coach Bryant felt that team was as good as any he ever coached.

That team really came a long way, because we started out with a relatively inexperienced defense and suffered an injury in the August drills that very well may have cost us four consecutive national titles.

The injury was to Jack O'Rear, our senior quarterback, who had shared time with Jeff Rutledge during the 1976 season. Jack was similar to Terry Davis in that he was born to run the wishbone. He wasn't a great passer, but he excelled in running the option and he was one tough runner, almost like having another power running back.

If Jack hadn't gotten injured, we may have run the table in '77, leaving no doubt who the best team was; and from looking back on it, we probably would have been able to redshirt Steadman Shealy, which would have made him a senior in 1980 when we lost two tough games.

I think one of the best things we did as a staff was develop players and put them in a position that would help the team. Coach Bryant made a crucial decision in the spring when he moved Terry Jones from center to nose guard. TJ was a great center, too. We had learned early on in the wishbone years that you needed a big and quick center, and we had a string of all-stars, including All-Americans Jim Krapf and Sly Croom.

I think TJ was just as good, but I think he'd admit the player who took his place might have been the best center of all time, Dwight Stephenson. Terry excelled under the tutelage of Ken Donahue and went on to have a great career in the pros with the Packers as a defensive lineman.

While our defense was a work in progress, the offense was as good as we had ever had -- including that great '73 team, mainly because we had become so adept at throwing the football out of the wishbone.

Early on, we realized that we could get one-on-one coverage in the bone, and we had the incomparable Ozzie Newsome at split end during the 1974-77 seasons. I think the only game Ozzie didn't start during those four years was the season opener against Maryland in 1974, and I don't think it took too long before we inserted him into the lineup that afternoon.

We were deep, too, with two great fullbacks in Johnny Davis and Steve Whitman as well as really talented running backs led by Tony Nathan and Major Ogilvie. Dwight was not the only all-star on the line either. Bob Cryder and Lou Green were all-stars. Bob ended up being a first-round draft pick.

So, from early on, we didn't have much trouble moving the ball and scoring points. By mid-season, the defense had matured, and we really hit on all cylinders after we knocked off top-ranked USC in the Coliseum. By the last month of the season, we were just manhandling opponents on both sides of the ball.

I tell you, we could have set all kind of offensive records that year, but it wasn't our way of taking care of business. After we beat Woody Hayes and Ohio State in the Sugar Bowl 35-6, I have to admit I don't think we'd ever had a more proficient team.

That was a remarkable game in itself, because it matched two of the most fabled coaches in the history of the game. At the first press conference in New Orleans when both coaches appeared, they gave away posters of the two, and they literally had writers coming up to them, asking for their autographs. I doubt if that had ever happened before, and I sure doubt if it'll ever happen again.

Coach Bryant told the reporters "it was Alabama vs. Ohio State and not him vs. Coach Hayes." That's when he said, "Woody is a great coach, and I ain't bad." Candidly, from watching defensive tapes of the Buckeyes, we really didn't think they could stop us, either running or throwing. Jeff Rutledge had a great day and was named the MVP of the game, but our entire team could have earned that honor.

Lou "Mean Lou" Green was a star offensive guard for us, and he is still quite the character. He liked to watch pro wrestling, especially Dirty Dusty Rhodes, who had used his "bionic elbow" to knock out an opponent. During the season, when Lou thought (not the coaches) we had the game under control, he would get up and do his Dusty Rhodes' ugly elbow signal to the bench.

Let me assure you that didn't go over well with Coach Bryant. Dee Powell was one of our line coaches during those great seasons, and Coach Bryant told Dee to mark Lou down on his weekly grades every time he did "his damn elbow routine." Usually, Lou didn't do it until late in the game, but he got up on the first play of the Sugar Bowl and did his deal, signifying this game was over.

Coach Bryant wasn't happy, but Lou was right. We dominated the game from start to finish, but when the final polls came out; we were second to Notre Dame, who had beaten top-ranked Texas in the Cotton Bowl.

I think that win served as the players' motivation for the run we had the next two seasons which culminated in Alabama winning national titles. The 1978 season ended with us needing a major league assist from Auburn to even have the chance to play for it all.

Because of the SEC-Sugar Bowl rule, if there was a tie for the conference championship, then the team that had been mostly recent would have to go elsewhere. We were tied with Georgia for the conference lead late in the season, but Auburn tied them, giving us the chance to earn a Sugar Bowl berth.

Penn State, the top-ranked team, was set to go to the Orange Bowl and play Nebraska, but once it looked like we were going back to the Sugar Bowl, the matchup between the No. 1 Nittany Lions and No. 2 Alabama was set.

After watching tape on Penn State, I knew we were in for a war. They had the two best defensive tackle tandem that I ever coached against in Matt Millen and Bruce Clark. I knew points would be at a premium, because our defense had gotten better and better that year, and we felt we could limit the Penn State offense.

Even though we were No. 2 in the polls, we entered the game as a slight favorite. Coach Bryant made a prophetic statement to a small group of his friends in his hotel suite the night before the game. He told them that the game would come down to one or two plays, and he hoped like heck that Alabama was the team that made the play or plays.

I'll never forget how hard it was raining that day in New Orleans. You could hardly see the street when we pulled up to the Superdome and I guess I thought we sure were lucky that this game was being played in a dome.

As I said, I knew it was going to be a war and it was. My good friend, Keith Jackson, who was calling the game, once told me that it ranked as one of the two or three best games he ever called, saying it was like hand-to-hand combat on a football field.

No doubt, it was like two heavyweight boxers slugging it out for 15 rounds and never backing up. It was the most physical game I'd ever seen.

We had several chances in the first half to score but we bogged down in Penn State territory, and as expected, we were having a tough time blocking Millen and Clark. I tell you, I was disappointed because the game was going to be 0-0 at the half, and our defense had played lights-out for the first 30 minutes. We moved the ball effectively, but had failed to score.

Late in the first half, we were deep in Penn State territory but they intercepted a pass and nearly ran it back all the way. Thank goodness, Major Ogilvie didn't give up on the play and made a touchdown-saving tackle. Our defense stiffened again, and we took over the ball deep in our territory with under a minute to go in the first half.

Coach Bryant didn't have to tell me to run out the clock. That was a given. On first down, Tony Nathan gained a few yards. Joe Paterno called timeout, figuring Penn State would get the ball back with a few seconds left and possibly have a chance at a field goal. On second down, Jeff Rutledge handed off to Tony on a sweep to our right-- and lo and behold, he broke loose on a long run into Penn State territory, getting to the 30.

I wanted to take a shot in the end zone and Jeff threw a perfect pass to Bruce Bolton to give us a 7-0 halftime lead. All of sudden, we had all the momentum, but it didn't last long.

We missed another scoring opportunity, and Penn State converted a turnover into a touchdown and we were tied late in the third quarter. Then we made one of those big plays that turned the game.

Little Lou Ikner raced a punt back to the Penn State 10, and we were within the shadows of the goal line but facing a third down. I guess I momentarily remembered the 1975 Sugar Bowl when we scored on an option to our left, and I called the same play.

Jeff ran it to perfection, pitching to Major Ogilvie when he was getting hit, and Major did just a great job of bouncing off tacklers and getting us the touchdown. Of course, that set up the fourth quarter drama that included Don McNeal's and Barry Krauss' plays on the goal line stand, Murray Legg breaking up a late fourth down pass, and Mike Clements intercepting the final Penn State pass.

I've been asked often about our great defensive tackle Marty Lyons telling Chuck Fusina before the fourth-down play on the goal line, "You'd better pass." I don't know if it's true or urban legend. All I know is I was talking to our offensive staff about our next series, and never really saw Barry Krauss' tackle.

It was one of those games that lived up to its billing, too. Keith Jackson was right; it was just like two soldiers in hand-to-hand combat.

In the post-game interviews, Coach Bryant was asked if he thought Alabama deserved to be No. 1, and he replied in his own inimitable style, saying, "There's only one team that could have stopped Penn State on the goal line." After he paused and looked around the room, he finished, "And that team is Alabama."

Years later, I was talking about the game with Matt Millen, who had played on Super Bowl championship teams with the Raiders, and he told me, "Coach, one of those National Championship rings that you have still eats at me."

I had a similar talk with Coach Paterno, too. He told me of all his losses that one game still haunted him. I told him I knew that feeling, telling him that's how I would always think of our loss to Notre Dame five years earlier.

The following year, we ended the 1970s with a perfect 12-0 season, claiming Coach Bryant's sixth championship. We were really good on both sides of the ball that year, setting all kinds of records along the way.

After we beat Florida 40-0, coached by one of my old teammates, Charley

Pell, I thought we had perhaps the best overall team we'd ever had, but we suffered all kinds of injuries that day, and despite the romp in the score, we were a battered team for most of the rest of the season.

We limped into Legion Field a week later to play Tennessee, and we got off to an awful start that day. We were behind 17-0 and in deep trouble before we finally got the team settled down. Our backup quarterback, Don Jacobs, had a big day and helped us start our comeback.

We were down 17-7 at the half, and I guess all of us, including the players, expected Coach Bryant to give us a verbal lashing, but that didn't happen at all. I was at the chalkboard, drawing up the alignments Tennessee was using, and Coach said, "Mal, hurry up and finish."

I was trying to finish as fast as possible, but he repeated himself, and I knew what that meant. I just dropped the chalk and shut up. Instead of yelling and screaming at the players, Coach Bryant told them we had Tennessee right where we wanted them, and being behind was the best thing that could happen to us, because we'd find out what kind of team we had in the second half.

Talk about firing up the team. We went out and dominated, winning 27-17 and we could easily have scored late in the game, but we let the clock run out when we were near the Volunteer goal line.

A few weeks later, we beat LSU in Baton Rouge 3-0 in Charley McClendon's final game against Coach Bryant. During the wishbone era, no team gave us our offense more trouble on an annual basis than Charley's defenses. He had played for Coach Bryant at Kentucky and had starred in the Wildcats' stunning win over Oklahoma in the 1951 Sugar Bowl.

We knew it was going to be a typical, physical game but we sure didn't anticipate the rainstorm and mud bath we encountered in Tiger Stadium. Major Ogilvie played with an injured foot, much like the Johnny Musso game against Auburn in 1971. Somehow, someway, Jim Goostree had gotten Major well enough to play.

On one of the first offensive plays of the game, we ran the option to the short side, our bench, and I saw Major steam rolling straight toward Coach Bryant and me. I thought for a second, "Please let him hit me and not Coach Bryant." It didn't work out that way. He ran over Coach Bryant, but thankfully didn't hurt him too badly.

It was another game we dominated but we fumbled around, especially deep in LSU territory. Allen McElroy made a third-quarter field goal for the only score. In a National Championship run, you know you are going to have to survive and move on. We had done just that.

After the game, Coach McClendon was asked if he thought Alabama was the best team in the country. Earlier in the season, his team had lost in the final minutes to Southern California. Charley said, "Alabama is the best defensive team I've ever seen and their offense isn't too shabby." He was right.

At season's end, we had the largest differential in SEC history between yards gained and yards given up. It was almost 300 yards a game, a stunning statistic. Before we could pat ourselves on the back and think about winning a championship, we had to prepare for an 8-2 Auburn team that was loaded with outstanding personnel.

The Iron Bowl was almost a disaster. I think we lost four or five fumbles, and most of them were in the third quarter and we saw a two-touchdown lead vanish. Midway in the fourth quarter we were down 18-17.

When we took over on our 20, we had another fumble on the first play, but Major recovered the ball; and we then went the length of the field to secure the win on a championship drive. Steadman Shealy showed great leadership that you need from your quarterback, because he basically told the players we were going down the field and nothing was going to stop us. I know he had a key pass to Keith Pugh, and Steve Whitman had a big run, too.

Not only had Steadman engineered a drive that would be remembered forever; he had scored the winning touchdown as well.

By the time we earned a Sugar Bowl bid, we had gotten healthier, so we went to New Orleans feeling confident, even though our opponent, Arkansas, was a more than formidable opponent. Arkansas was coached by Lou Holtz, who two years earlier had embarrassed Oklahoma in the Orange Bowl.

Coach Bryant always liked to tell the team who we were going to play in the bowl before it was officially announced. When he told the team that we were going to be playing Arkansas in the 1980 Sugar Bowl, he started bragging on Lou Holtz, calling him, "the hottest commodity in coaching, and the most innovative, brightest young coach around."

When he ended his talk, Coach Bryant looked around the room and finished, "I love to play smart coaches, and we're going to hit them like they've never been hit before." I think we won the game right then and there. We knew they'd make a coaching call that would make them a big play, but at the end of the day, we were going to physically and mentally beat them down.

We employed a double wing for that game, and Steadman Shealy ran it flawlessly. Let me say this about Steadman, he had unbelievable quickness and was another quarterback born to run the option. He had a severe knee injury in the spring of '78, and I don't think he was ever quite the same, but he was still special and was the spark-plug of that '79 team.

Major Ogilvie was the MVP of the game, scoring on a long run and setting up a TD on a punt return. I think Steve Whitman scored on a run, and our defense once again just dominated, much as it had all year. We had one of those once-in-a-generation offensive lines, too, with tackles Jim Bunch and Buddy Aydelette, guards Vince Boothe and Mike Brock, and center Dwight Stephenson. Our tight end, Tim Travis, was a blocking machine. Bill Jackson was a great back for us. Keith Pugh continued our tradition of having a big-play wide receiver.

After the Sugar Bowl, we were unanimous National Champions, the last of Coach Bryant's career.

It was just one of those teams that wasn't going to be denied under any circumstance. It had a special character and determination to overcome any obstacle in its way. I know we had some more talented teams, but not many had the will to win like that 1979 group.

21

THE ERA ENDS

There were all kinds of signs in 1980 of the inevitability that the end of the Coach Bryant's reign as the head coach and athletic director at the University was nearing an end. I don't think many of us wanted to accept it. I know I didn't.

During that summer, Charley Thornton, the assistant AD for sports publicity, called Ken Donahue and me and said he needed to meet with us. Cloaked in secrecy, he told us that Coach Bryant had suffered a stroke but was going to be okay. Coach wanted a private meeting with his coordinators in his hospital room.

Dr. Phillip Bobo, who was one of our team doctors, and our trainer, Jim Goostree, had taken Coach Bryant to Druid City Hospital. Despite the effects of his sudden attack, Coach Bryant had insisted on walking into the building. His health might have been failing him, but not his dominating presence.

Our annual summer media fling was coming up, and Coach Bryant instructed us on what to say to preview the offense and defense to the media. Charley would handle the press on why Coach Bryant was absent.

Naturally, our foremost concern was Coach's health, but he told us he'd be back and ready for the August drills. Reflecting back on those final three years, I have to admit that there was a noticeable change in Coach Bryant, and it probably impacted our performance on the field.

We had started losing recruits to our rivals as well. Schools were using Coach Bryant's age against him, telling the prospects that he wouldn't be there for their full four or five years, and they needed to play at a school with more stability.

Privately, Coach Bryant and I had discussions about the future of our offense as well. I think we both knew that the sweeping rule changes that had been first passed by the NFL and then on the college level were opening up the passing game to a level we'd never seen before.

In particular, the holding rules were changed dramatically, which benefitted pass protection. Then there were the moving in of the hash marks, and the restrictions on what defensive backs could do in checking receivers. I don't think there is any question that if Coach Bryant had been younger or in a healthier condition where he could have stayed on past the 1982 season, we would have adapted to the rules.

There was one other factor as well. Because of all the success in the passing game on the NFL level, players were starting to drift towards teams that stressed that aspect of the game. Although we were still in the era when athletes stayed their full four years in school, it wasn't rocket science to know the time frame was short before they would start leaving early. With the ever escalating NFL salaries, the days of recruiting and selling just your school were ending. Now players were starting to look at who could put them in the NFL.

I'd be remiss in not mentioning that in his final year the University upped Coach Bryant's salary to $100,000 in order to help him on his retirement. I think Coach Donahue and I were making about half that. When the Supreme Court struck down the NCAA's control of television, salary changes were in their initial stages as well.

During those final three seasons, we had a few games that reminded me of our dominating days of the 1970s. We beat Tennessee handily in Knoxville in 1980, 27-0, in a game that our offensive line so battered the Volunteer defense that our center Steve Mott was named the "TV Player of the Game."

In 1981, the year in which we were trying to help Coach Bryant become the winningest coach, we beat Mississippi State in Tuscaloosa 13-10. If there was a game as physical as the Penn State Sugar Bowl, it was that one. Our great safety Tommy Wilcox intercepted a pass near the goal line to help Coach Bryant near the record win. That win was No. 313, one shy of the record held by Amos Alonzo

Stagg.

When we beat Penn State at Beaver Stadium to tie the mark, we really looked like our old selves. That was the game in which Coach told me to call plays like we were two touchdowns behind, much like he had instructed Ken Meyer to coach against Nebraska in the 1966 Orange Bowl. We really thought we had an advantage in the passing game that day because of our two great receivers, Joey Jones and Jesse Bendross. Walter Lewis was spectacular, and we won 31-16, although the game wasn't really that close.

Penn State had been unbeaten and was probably on its way to a spot in a National Championship showdown until we beat them, handing them their only loss of the season. It was the first of a 10-game series, and we had to fly in and out of Harrisburg to get to State College. On the bus trip in, we got behind oxcarts driven by Amish families and it took more than three hours to get to our hotel. I'll never forget Coach Bryant saying if he'd known it was this hard to get to Penn State, he'd never have scheduled this series. It would be his only trip there.

A couple of weeks later when we beat Auburn to enable him to set the record, it was another game that I think the players and coaches felt more relief than anything else. We had not played particularly well that season, or even in that game, so I guess I was just thankful it was over.

After we lost to LSU at Legion Field in 1982, I think Coach Bryant really felt it was time for him to call it a day. He was apologetic to the players and to the coaches, feeling like he had let us down. I think we all felt just the opposite, that we were the ones who had let "The Man" down.

A few weeks later, he told me that he was stepping down, and that I would get an interview to replace him. I'm not sure of all the coaches who interviewed, but I know Gene Stallings, who was with the Cowboys at the time, did and so did Ray Perkins.

I met with the President of the University, Dr. Joab Thomas, in his office and I outlined to him why I thought I should take over for Coach Bryant, who had decided to remain the Director of Athletics.

After my interview, I went to the bowling alley, where Heather, now 13, was with some of her friends. On the way home, she quizzed me, and I told her that I really thought I had a legitimate shot at the job. I told Charlotte the same thing.

Years later, I would find out that Charlotte had told Heather that she didn't think I had a chance at the job, and she was correct, not because she doubted my ability to do the job. She didn't think I would play the political game to get the position. Coach Perkins, who was with the New York Football Giants, took over right after Coach Bryant announced his retirement on December 15, 1982.

We had one last game together, the Liberty Bowl in Memphis. Although Coach Bryant didn't mention it, I think his sense of history was the reason we were playing there against a talented Illinois team. Obviously, Coach Bryant's first bowl game at Alabama had been the Liberty, and he wanted to close out like it all started.

Let me tell you, those last few weeks were a blur, filled with continual choke-filled moments for all of us.

At our last practice in Tuscaloosa, he gathered the players and staff around, and gave a short talk. We knew he was walking off those fields he loved so much for the last time. I don't know if I cried that day or not, but I know my heart was broken.

After Ray had taken over, I told Coach Bryant that I didn't care to interview to stay on, because I knew that Coach Perkins would likely be running his own offense, I also felt it was a time for a new beginning for me.

Even though I was disappointed I had been bypassed for the Alabama job, I really thought I was destined to become a head coach, and I got a call from West Point about the head job there. Army had gone 4-7 and Ed Cavanaugh had been relieved of his duties, and I really felt I had an excellent chance of becoming the next head coach there.

I had already started talking to a few coaches about going with me, including Murray Legg, a bright young defensive coach for us who had not been retained by Coach Perkins. A few weeks later, I would get a call telling me that Army was going to hire Jim Young, so that dream, too, was gone.

Through the years, I had turned down a few offers for head coaching positions, including the Fresno State job. Coach Bryant had warned me that he didn't think I would fit in well there and it would be a bad mistake, so I decided to decline taking the Fresno job.

While I was naturally looking for another coaching job at this juncture, I was also intent on helping Coach Bryant go out a winner, just as he so richly deserved. When we got to Memphis, I think it really began to sink in that this was the end.

Accepting it wasn't easy on anyone, including all those fans who had become so attached to the man who had represented the ideals they embraced: winning and winning with class.

One day we were in our staff meeting room in a suite that overlooked the Mississippi River. Coach Bryant pointed to the bridge that crossed over into Arkansas, and he told us about when he was a player and the times that he and his legendary teammate, Don Hutson, had thumbed rides back home to south Arkansas. He talked about the times he couldn't get a ride and crossed over from Tennessee by walking across the bridge. Those were riveting moments for me, and I am sure for the rest of his staff as well.

Our final practice was the toughest, though. He gathered the players, coaches and staff around him, and he choked up talking about how proud he was to have had the opportunity to be the head coach at Alabama and how much he appreciated and loved all of us.

It was the most emotional I'd ever seen him, and everyone was crying. I tried not to break down, but when I looked over and saw Ken Donahue sobbing, I couldn't hold it any longer. Ken Donahue was one of those old, tough coaches who had played for General Robert Neyland and had been with Coach Bryant since 1964, the same year I came back.

There was never a coach who lived that could outwork Ken-O and none tougher than he was either. He was a rock, unemotional in the best of times and in the worst. On this day, he couldn't hold back. I couldn't either. Every player, coach and support person there was crying unashamedly.

It was frigid that night in the Liberty Bowl and the game see-sawed back and forth until the final minute of play. I remember Craig Turner diving into the end zone for the final touchdown and Peter Kim scoring the final point. I remember Walter Lewis making big plays.

I remember remarkable defensive plays by Russ Wood and Robbie Jones to help win the game.

I remember Jeremiah Castille having one of the best games any player had ever had for the Crimson Tide, intercepting three passes and knocking the ball loose from a receiver on one of the hardest hits I ever witnessed.

I remember that slow stroll to the dressing room. Coach Bryant, shoulder-to-shoulder, with his players, walked slowly off the field for the final time. I had no idea what he meant to all of us, players, fans and rivals, maybe because when you are a part of it, you become insulated and unaware of his immense power and influence on the game that had made him such a legend.

I'm proud to think I played a small role in that magnificent run, and to reminisce and know I was there for 24 of the 25 years, well it makes me feel humbled in a way I can't describe in mere words. I'm just thankful I was lucky enough to be there with him and at the University that I love.

22

JANUARY 26, 1983
THE SADDEST DAY OF MY CAREER

The month of January 1983, was one of the most difficult and transitional times in my professional career. I had been passed over for the head-coaching job at Alabama and had apparently been the runner-up for the position at West Point.

Although coaching football was really the only vocation that I knew and loved, I had braced myself for the reality that my career in athletics was basically over. I had talked to Benny Nelson, an old teammate of mine, and loyal friend, about going to work with him up in Huntsville.

I had gotten some feeler calls about assistant jobs, but I wanted to explore other options, and mentally, I was preparing for a new life outside football. I also had some opportunities in the Mobile area and decided to go down at the end of the month to at least check them out.

The coaching convention that year was in Los Angeles, and I chose not to go, even though Coach Bryant had told me and the other assistants who hadn't been retained by Ray Perkins that he would pay our way and do his best to help us get a job. I know Murray Legg and Bryant Poole went, but I decided to stay home and try to make some career changing decisions.

I knew I was going to have to uproot Charlotte, who had grown up and lived in Tuscaloosa all her life, and Heather who was 13 at the time and doing well in school.

A few days before I was going down to Mobile, Coach Bryant called and told me he wanted to go to lunch. I picked him up in front of Memorial Coliseum, and asked him where he wanted to go. I'll never forget him saying that he wanted vegetables, but there wasn't a place in town that could cook vegetables like his mother.

Coach Bryant told me that he was headed out to Las Vegas to do a television show on the upcoming Super Bowl between the Washington Redskins and the Miami Dolphins with his old friend and Michigan State legend, Duffy Daugherty. He talked about how proud he was of Bob Baumhower, Don McNeal, Dwight Stephenson and Tony Nathan, who were all stars for the Dolphins that year, but that was about all he said about football.

When I dropped him off, he told me he'd see me when he got back to Tuscaloosa, and to always know he was there to help me. I watched him slowly climb those steps up the Coliseum and I drove away.

The morning of January 26, a Wednesday, was raw, cold and raining. I had a meeting in Mobile that morning and I drove over to a coffee shop to grab a cup of coffee and a hamburger. The lunch rush hour had already passed, and I sat in a booth in a basically empty building, sipping coffee and probably feeling sorry for myself.

There were two ladies working behind the counter, and I heard one of them say she just heard on the radio about "The Man" dying this morning and they both started crying. I didn't have a clue what had upset them so much. I just stirred my coffee, wondering what the heck I was going to do with my life, and how I was going to support Charlotte and Heather.

After I paid for the coffee, I went outside, I wanted to make a call to Billy Neighbors in Huntsville, where he'd moved after he retired from the NFL to become a stockbroker, before I went back to the hotel where I was staying. There were no cell phones then, so I climbed into a telephone booth right outside the coffee shop, found a quarter in my pocket and called Billy to check on a stock that he had sold me.

I thought I heard Billy sniffling and I asked him what was wrong. He said, "Mal, you haven't heard, have you?"

"Heard what?"

"Coach Bryant died this morning."

I don't remember saying another word. I don't remember hanging up the telephone or even leaving the phone booth. It was the saddest moment of my career.

I just leaned up against the aging brick wall of the coffee shop and cried.

After cancelling my room, I headed back north. Between the raindrops and the tears, the ride was probably as treacherous as any I ever had. Driving back alone to Tuscaloosa from Mobile that afternoon was painful.

The first thing I did when I got into town was to drive to the Bryant house to see Mary Harmon. I don't remember a lot of people being there yet, and Paul Jr. answered the door. It was an emotional scene for both of us, but I always remember the composure and grace of Mrs. Bryant during this most sorrowful moment for all of us who loved Coach Bryant.

Two days later, January 28, they had Coach Bryant's funeral. I'd be totally dishonest if I didn't say I was disappointed that the coaches who hadn't been retained weren't included on the manifest to ride the team buses to Birmingham for his burial. I know that the other coaches felt like I did. We had been there with Coach Bryant until the end and we should have been offered the dignity of being there for his final interment, but that was not the case.

It was left up to us to make our way to Elmwood Cemetery for his burial. You know you hear a lot of people talk about all the dignitaries who were there. It was a virtual Who's Who of football, a walking Hall of Fame of coaches and players.

But, that's not what I remember. They were Coach Bryant's peers. It was Coach Bryant's people who lined up on what is now Bryant Drive and the other streets of Tuscaloosa to say their final good-byes that left an impression on me that words can hardly describe. From mothers with infants to school children to grandparents to businessmen to common laborers, there were thousands of his people there to say good-bye.

I'll never forget driving down the interstate from Tuscaloosa to Birmingham and seeing endless miles of cars and trucks pulled over to the side of the freeway. From truck drivers to doctors to lawyers to farmers to every type of blue-collar and white-collar worker imaginable, they stood as one on both sides of Interstate 20/59.

They were of all colors and I'm sure of all creeds and religious backgrounds, too. The overpasses were filled with banners and mourners, most of them tearfully saying good-bye to the man who had pulled a plow and fought a bear to become the ultimate example of what determination, perseverance, dedication and belief in oneself symbolizes.

At the cemetery, the two people I remembered seeing were his old friend from the Sugar Bowl, Aruns Callery, and his loyal friend, driver and bodyguard Billy Varner. Mr. Callery knew everyone across the country, from janitors to Presidents, including John F. Kennedy.

He said, "Mal, I've known two men who were charismatic, one was President Kennedy and the other one was Paul Bryant. And, whatever John Kennedy had, Paul had more of it."

If there was anyone there that day with a more forlorn look than me, it was Billy Varner. I don't remember what Billy said, but I always could remember him telling anyone who asked about Coach Bryant: "He's the only man I've known, the only man I've ever heard about, who was just as comfortable eating pheasant under a glass with the President of the United States as he was being around the common folk.

"He'd asked me to pull into a service station to get some gasoline. And, he would lumber out of the car and eat cheese crackers, drink a soda pop, talk with the mechanics and the men who pumped the gas. That was who Coach Bryant was."

I had lived virtually my entire adult life as a player and coach for Paul Bryant. I think it finally hit me that day that this man was the most beloved figure in the history of this state. There was only one Paul William Bryant, and I felt lucky to have walked in his footsteps. He was one hell of a man.

23

SUNDAY MORNING CALL

Early on the Sunday morning after Coach Bryant's funeral, I was sitting at my house, drinking coffee with Charlotte when the telephone rang. On the other line was Gerry Faust, the head football coach at Notre Dame.

I'd met Gerry at some point, probably at a coach's convention, but I was hardly friends with him. Frankly, I had no idea he had an opening on his Fighting Irish staff. When he asked me if I would like to come to South Bend for a few days to discuss being his running backs coach, I told him I would be on the next plane.

The old saying about when one door closes, another one opens – well, that is what certainly happened to me. I'd pretty much given up hope of ever coaching again at that point, but it had been my whole professional life, and I didn't want to give up on it.

Before I headed to Birmingham to catch the airplane for my flight to Chicago and then into South Bend, I told Charlotte that if Coach Faust offered me a job, I would seriously consider taking it. I really didn't make a decision without her blessing, and she assured me that she was all in favor of making the move.

I think we both felt that it would be best for me to leave Tuscaloosa, which was why I had explored opportunities outside football in both Huntsville and Mobile. Notre Dame intrigued me for the obvious reasons, its prestige as a University, its football tradition and the people who worked there.

When we had played the Irish when I was an assistant for Coach Bryant, I had never met a classier group of folks. I guess I felt strongly that I could adapt well to South Bend, and it would be a nice reprieve to be competing outside the Southeast area. Then there was the Coach Frank Thomas aspect as well.

Coach Thomas had played quarterback for Knute Rockne and starred on the Notre Dame baseball team. I know how much Coach Bryant had respected and admired Coach Thomas, and a lot of his coaching think-tank came from things Coach Thomas had first learned during his years as a player for the Irish. And, Coach Thomas had passed his knowledge to Coach Bryant when he was a player and young assistant coach.

When Coach Faust offered me the job as running backs coach, I accepted, but the offer was contingent on one stipulation: that I would stay with him unless I got a head-coaching job. I gave him my word that I wouldn't leave Notre Dame for another assistant job.

During my three years in South Bend, I lived up to my word. I had learned at an early age from my parents, and had it re-enforced during my years with Coach Bryant, that your word is your bond. I had several calls from some high profile coaches and programs about accepting assistant jobs elsewhere but told them about my commitment to Notre Dame.

Both Charley Pell and Galen Hall called me at different times about openings they respectively had at Florida, and Barry Switzer called me asking if I would be interested in coming to Oklahoma. Under different circumstances, I would have readily agreed.

I really can't begin to say how much respect I had for Gerry Faust. Even during the most difficult times we would undergo during the 1983-85 seasons, I never heard that man say one negative word about anyone or anything, especially Notre Dame, a school he cherished. I can gladly look back on those years and remember them fondly because of Gerry Faust, the other coaches, the Notre Dame administration, the fans and especially the players who competed their hearts out for the staff and the school.

When I first got to campus, I lived in a hotel while Charlotte and Heather stayed in Tuscaloosa to finish out the school year. During that time, I did my best to learn as much about the University as possible. Probably the one thing that surprised me the most was the respect that everyone there had for Coach Bryant, which certainly made me feel even more welcome.

On one of my first days on the job, Gene Corrigan, the athletic director, asked me to come to his office to visit. When I got there, I saw this autographed picture of Coach Bryant behind his secretary's desk. She told me that she had asked Coach Bryant for it, and he had obliged.

Gene was taking me around the facilities. When we went into Heritage Hall in the Athletic Convocation Center, he showed me the Notre Dame trophy case, which was quite impressive, as you can well imagine. Right in the center of the trophy case was a hand-written letter from Coach Bryant to Father Theodore Hesburgh, congratulating Notre Dame after that memorable 1973 Sugar Bowl.

I thought the world of everyone on the coaching staff, but I had known linebacker coach George Kelly for years and our friendship thrived when I joined the staff. After work one day, he asked me if I wanted to join him at a neighborhood gathering place, Pat's Pub.

When I walked in there, I saw pictures of Notre Dame players and coaches all over the wall. But right in the middle, and with a light shining on it, was a picture of Coach Bryant with the inscription, "Notre Dame misses you too, Bear."

While we didn't have as much success on the field as we would have liked during those three seasons, we did beat our archrival Southern California rather easily all three years, twice in South Bend and once in the Coliseum.

After the 1985 game, one that we dominated 37-3, we were really celebrating in the locker room, because it probably was our most complete game the entire time I coached there. During our postgame bedlam, here comes Father Hesburgh wearing a houndstooth hat.

I said, "Father, you look mighty handsome in that hat."

He smiled and said, "Mal, Paul gave me this hat and autographed it to me, too."

Sure enough, he showed me the inside strap with a personalized autograph from Coach Bryant to Father Hesburgh.

There were a couple of other games at Notre Dame that really stand out to me: the 1983 Liberty Bowl against Boston College, and the 1984 game when we played LSU in Baton Rouge.

The Boston College game became known as "The Vatican Bowl" because it featured two of the most prestigious Catholic universities in the nation. We had a most formidable opponent in the Eagles and their superstar quarterback Doug Flutie.

I knew that Flutie had led Boston College to a victory over Alabama late in the season, but I was too busy studying Boston College defensive personnel and schemes to pay much attention to Flutie before we got to Memphis. One day at lunch, I asked George Kelly about the BC offense and he told me that Flutie was going to be more than a handful, and that he was better than advertised. And he was.

That night, though, we really overpowered them with our running attack and escaped with a 19-18 victory. I was so proud, not only because we had won, but two of my backs -- Allen Pinkett and Chris Smith -- both topped the 100-yard rushing mark. Allen earned the game's MVP after scoring two touchdowns.

After the game, amid the euphoria in the winning locker room, I saw an old familiar face, Jimmy Bryan of *The Birmingham News*. He was there covering the game, and Jimmy asked me if I ever thought about Coach Bryant. I told him,

"Every day, and this trip back to Memphis had really been emotional for me."

I have no words to describe my feelings on that trip, returning to Memphis a year after I had been there with Alabama for Coach Bryant's final game. It was an eerie sensation walking on that field and being flooded with memories of him and all that had taken place in the ensuing year.

I was mighty proud of our effort that night and how the Notre Dame team had responded in an underdog role and upset Doug Flutie and the Eagles.

When we played LSU the next season, Bill Arnsparger, one of the greatest defensive coaches of all time, had really turned around the Tiger program. LSU was ranked in the top 10 and undefeated when we traveled to Baton Rouge to play them in late October. None of our players had ever played in Tiger Stadium before. I told them how crazy and rowdy their fans were going to be.

We had our great runner, Allen Pinkett, back in '84, and I had told him that he was in for the experience of a lifetime, and playing the game in Tiger Stadium was the easy part. By the time the players had weaved through the mob of LSU fans who were yelling and screaming "Tiger Bait" at them, I was already in the locker room. I just smiled at Allen when he got there.

He told me, "You were right Coach. This is crazy."

I didn't tell him that the best part was yet to come: going on the field before the game when they had the cage with the real Mike the Tiger waiting at our entrance. Let me tell you, that can be intimidating, but I always felt at Alabama, and that day at Notre Dame, that all that commotion and the tiger roaring only inspired our teams.

We had some great leaders on that team, too, and one of them was defensive lineman Mike Golic, who went on to become a nationally recognized radio personality. I think Mike brought an LSU cap with him and was wearing it when the players were walking through the throng of fans. Then he tore off the cap and stomped on it. That really stirred them up even more!

I was telling some of the coaches about the 1973 Alabama-LSU game and we had played on Thanksgiving Night in Tiger Stadium. The students had thrown oranges at Coach Bryant when we had our pre-game walk around the stadium. In his own inimitable style, Coach Bryant picked up one of the oranges, peeled it and started eating it. He always thought the best way to settle the crowd down was to show they couldn't intimidate us. Of course, I don't think anything could intimidate Coach Bryant.

Well, they didn't scare Notre Dame that afternoon. We upset LSU 30-22 and Allen Pinkett had a great game for us in the process, scoring the touchdown that in essence clinched the victory.

During the course of the next season, it became apparent that Coach Faust's contract would not be renewed, and once again I would be searching for new coaching opportunities. With that being said, I wouldn't give anything for those three years in South Bend and being part of the Notre Dame football program.

I really felt that the new coach, Lou Holtz, would be inheriting some really good players and even better people, including future Heisman Trophy winner, Tim Brown, and a long-time NFL quarterback, Steve Beuerlein.

After I took over as athletic director at Alabama, Steve came to Tuscaloosa and played in our annual fundraising golf tournament for scholarships. We auctioned off a helmet that was half Notre Dame and half Alabama with his autograph on one side and Cornelius Bennett's on the other. I was coaching in St. Louis when that famous tackle took place in 1986, so I didn't see it until I watched it on video years later.

No wonder Steve never talked about it!

24

CHARLOTTE'S FALL

After Coach Gerry Faust was relieved of his duties at Notre Dame, I again thought about leaving the coaching profession, although it was really the only thing that I knew. It wasn't long before I got several calls about assistant jobs at other schools, but I was more interested about going into pro football. That opportunity seemed possible after Gene Stallings became head coach of the St. Louis Football Cardinals.

Kenny Hatfield, who had become a top-notch college head coach at the Air Force Academy, had returned to his alma mater, Arkansas, to replace Lou Holtz. He called and asked if I would be interested in working on his staff. I was just intrigued with the possibilities of moving into the NFL, and I wanted to see if I had a chance of joining Coach Stallings, so I turned down the opportunity to talk to Coach Hatfield about going to Fayetteville.

Of course, I enjoyed a long and trusting relationship with Coach Stallings, dating back to my freshman year as a player for the Crimson Tide, and then serving as an assistant under him, helping out with the defensive backs on the 1964 National Championship team.

Actually, Coach Stallings and I had renewed our friendship in the spring of 1985 when he was on the Dallas Cowboy staff. He had flown into South Bend, checking out some of our players first hand and I had the opportunity to show him around Notre Dame.

I really looked forward to that opportunity of transitioning into professional football, coaching the elite players and competing against the very best in the sport. Two of my old colleagues at Alabama, Dee Powell and Bobby Marks, both former teammates and assistants for Gene, probably helped sell Coach Stallings on offering me a job on his staff as the tight ends coach.

Coach Stallings had earned a reputation as being one of the top defensive assistants in the NFL, serving from 1972-85 as a coach under Dallas Cowboys' legendary Coach Tom Landry. Having spent most of his career serving along with Coach Bryant and Coach Landry certainly gave Gene a unique perspective on the game.

Of course, he had won a conference championship as the head coach at Texas A&M back in 1967 and subsequently became Coach Bryant's first former player to win against one of his teams when the Aggies beat Alabama in the 1968 Cotton Bowl.

There was little doubt that Coach Stallings incorporated the same confidence level that helped ensure the successes of both coaches Bryant and Landry, but there was one missing link, or obstacle so to speak, in St. Louis that he hadn't faced at either Alabama or Dallas. St. Louis just didn't embrace football like his other stops in his professional career.

I felt the same way. At Alabama and Notre Dame, success in football was not only paramount but it was expected. When I'm asked to give examples, I always think back and laugh about having to practice on the outfield of old Busch Stadium in St. Louis. To say our facilities were subpar by NFL standards would be an understatement to say the least.

The baseball Cardinals ruled supreme in every aspect, including pretty much dictating our practice schedule when the two seasons overlapped, which usually meant there were going to be conflicts into mid-to-late-October.

Let me say this: I am not taking anything away from the baseball team, their loyal fans and their fine management. They just enjoyed a luxury that was never afforded the football team. There just wasn't the same level of commitment.

Not only did we have to share the same facility with the baseball team, but our managers had to go out every day before practice and put tape on the artificial surface in the outfield to mark up a playing field for us. To say it wasn't an ideal situation for a pro football team would be an understatement. Heck, even at Dozier High we had a practice field for the football team. That wasn't the case in St. Louis. During the 1987 season, my second and final one in St. Louis, the baseball Cardinals were on their way to the World Series against the Minnesota Twins, and if we were normally back page news in the city, we became even less noticeable during the pennant race, playoffs and World Series.

I'll never forget the baseball Cardinals returning to Busch Stadium to practice after losing the first two games in Minnesota. They were in an angry mood. They started taking batting practice and they had a big, strong first baseman named Jack Clark, who just laced a screaming liner that almost decapitated half the coaching staff. That ended our practice that day.

I don't think there was any doubt after that that the team owners, the Bidwell Family, would make the rumors of the team moving to Arizona become a reality. There were some moments of levity, though, especially in 1987 when the baseball Cardinals hosted the Los Angeles Dodgers in the National League Championship Series. Tommy Lasorda, the manager of the Dodgers, had a reputation of being quite a character. I'd never met him, but I would that afternoon when Los Angeles started warming up for batting practice.

Coach Stallings came over to me and said, "Mal, go down there and tell that coach that we are about to wrap up in the next five or ten minutes and then they can have at it."

So, I go walking through a maze of Dodger baseball players looking for the famed manager. I went up to Tommy Lasorda, introduced myself, and told him that we were wrapping up and Coach Stallings would appreciate it if he'd wait a few minutes before they started.

Tommy said he wanted to meet Gene Stallings and walked back out to the outfield with me. The two of them struck up a conversation, and there was little doubt that Tommy Lasorda was just as congenial as advertised. He said he always wanted to take a snap from an NFL center, and the next thing I knew he was under center and throwing passes to our wide receivers.

The players and coaches loved it. Being a former major league pitcher gave Tommy the opportunity to show off his left arm. It wasn't long before he said that was enough, and he invited our players to come take some swings in the batting cage. Several of them trailed after him toward the batting cages and had their pictures taken with him. That was one fun day at practice for all of us.

Years later when I became athletics director at the University, one of our softball assistants, Alyson Habetz, told me she was long-time friends with Tommy Lasorda and he was coming to Tuscaloosa to watch the team play. I got to renew my friendship with him, and he was just as convivial as ever, laughing with me about that day at the combined football/baseball practice in St. Louis.

There weren't many days like that, though. We had a really good offensive team during that time period, especially with quarterback Neil Lomax, wide receivers Roy Green and J.T. Smith, and tight end Jay Novacek. Unfortunately, we just didn't have the defensive personnel to really compete with the best in our division, which included the New York Giants, Washington Redskins and Coach Stallings' old team, the Dallas Cowboys.

I think our whole situation as a staff really started unraveling after that first year when Coach Stallings and the rest of us on his staff were excluded from having any real input into the draft. We were exiled from the war room when the picks were being made.

As a staff, we really wanted defensive line help and I think we were pretty unanimous in feeling that Jerome Brown, a super talented lineman from Miami, was a player that would elevate us to a much more competitive level. Jerome was represented by Robert Fraley, one of my quarterbacks at Alabama, and we let Robert know that Jerome was the player we wanted.

The frustration of having the management bypass Brown and select a player in a position where we felt we didn't need help, quarterback Kelly Stouffer, probably accelerated the feeling that there really wasn't a commitment to winning.

Our assessment about the situation proved true, too. Jerome, who would die tragically a few years later, became one of the best, if not the best, defensive linemen in the NFL for the Philadelphia Eagles, while Stouffer never agreed to contract terms with the Cardinals and ended up playing a handful of games for Seattle as a backup.

Despite the disappointments of losing and the prevalent sense that the team would indeed move to the Phoenix area by 1988, I have to say I enjoyed my time in St. Louis. There were great people there and I had the unique opportunity to meet and become acquaintances with two of the city's most legendary figures, announcer Jack Buck and one of the great baseball players of all-time, Stan Musial.

We made a legitimate run for the playoffs in '87, which included a win over Dallas and the defending Super Bowl Champion, the New York Giants. When Lomax, Green and Smith were injured, our offense lost its effectiveness and our chances of making it into the post-season were sidelined without them.

When the season was nearing its end, we got word that the Bidwell Family had reached an agreement to move the team to Phoenix, so Charlotte and I began making preparations to move once again.

Heather was still in high school and when we moved to Missouri, we wanted to be in the best school district possible. So we bought a house in Chesterfield where she attended and eventually graduated from Lafayette High School.

During March of 1988, I moved along with the rest of the staff to a hotel in Tempe, where a new practice facility with all the amenities you would expect for an NFL team was being built. Charlotte and Heather were going to stay in Chesterfield during this transition, enabling Heather to graduate from high school and giving us time to sell the house. That task, like most of the other ones around the house, was left to Charlotte.

It would be a twist of fate that would forever alter all of our lives.

One afternoon Charlotte had shown the house to some prospective buyers and after they left, she had walked to the back where we had a swimming pool. There was a hose by the pool and Charlotte picked it up to water the azaleas.

Then a haunting moment occurred. Charlotte tripped on the hose, shattering her leg. That was bad enough, but when she was trying to regain her balance during the fall, she hit concrete deck next to the pool and then fell into the water. Clinging to the side of the pool, she gasped to breathe and held on, trying not to drown.

Heather was at home, and heard her mother scream as she fell into the pool, desperately calling for help. It would be the beginning of the most difficult period of my personal life. Heather managed to get help before the situation became deadly. When I received word of Charlotte's injury in Arizona, Charlotte was undergoing emergency surgery to repair her severely injured leg, which would keep her hospitalized and in rehabilitation for weeks.

The trauma of almost drowning, the lengthy surgery, and the probability she may have hit her head during the fall started an ominous decline in Charlotte's health that wouldn't subside until her death in January, 2010.

Reflecting on those days, I think it is safe to say that Heather and I were both in denial about the degree of Charlotte's memory problems. I first began noticing mental lapses when Heather enrolled at the University of Arizona in Tucson. When Heather was at home, Charlotte would ask her to balance the checkbook and help her with small details like that.

That might sound insignificant, but Charlotte was extremely intelligent and had always handled those household tasks for the family. She earned her master's degree from the University of Alabama in education and had specialized in helping special-needs individuals. She was not only smart but an accomplished lady.

After Heather was born, Charlotte retired from the Tuscaloosa County Education System where she was the supervisor of all special education instructors, she became a full-time mother, having to handle most of our child-rearing without the help of a football coach-husband. Such was the life of a football coach's wife during those years I had been an assistant at Alabama and Notre Dame.

It was understood that coaching football not only meant endless hours in the office or the practice field, but also pounding the highways searching for potential recruits.

Charlotte had really been the foundation in my life away from football, and I just didn't want to admit how concerned I was about her declining mental clarity. Frankly, I refused to believe just how serious her problem was and how heartbreaking it would become for all of us in the Moore family.

There were other signs of Charlotte's problems that continued to concern me, primarily the long moments that she seemed to be disoriented, or have to be reminded who someone was. I guess I was just hoping she would return to her old self.

It was a bittersweet time for me; I enjoyed coaching and living in Arizona, but as the losses mounted and the slow deterioration of Charlotte's mental acuteness continued, my spirits plummeted. Those events would lead me home to Alabama, and ultimately, away from the coaching profession.

The one thing that I had learned to love about coaching in the pros was the free time that I never had as a college coach. For the first time, I had been able to be at home more frequently, have the opportunity to watch Heather grow up in her teen years, and spend more time with Charlotte.

On the football field, the new environment in Arizona momentarily seemed to infuse some much needed hope into the Cardinal organization. There was little doubt the community embraced the team in a way St. Louis never had. Midway through that season, we were 7-4 and battling the Philadelphia Eagles and New York Giants for first place in the Eastern Division.

After we beat the Giants in early November that season, it certainly appeared the Phoenix Cardinals were playoff-bound but we didn't win another game the rest of the season. It didn't help that our quarterback Neil Lomax once again got hurt during the stretch run.

Our 1989 season seemed to be a rerun of the previous season, except this time, Coach Stallings would be dismissed in November after a victory over his old team, the Cowboys. When Gene was let go, we were 5-6 and didn't win another game. I am not trying to make excuses, but when you have a lame duck situation like we had, it is just difficult to keep all the coaches and players focused. We were just a team going through the motions during the last five games of the season.

At the end of the year, I was again facing uncertainty in my professional career. I had made up my mind that I would prefer to stay in professional football in some capacity, particularly with the Cardinals. I visited with the Bidwells about the possibilities of staying on as a scout or in a front-office job.

I really didn't want to uproot Charlotte and move, particularly with her debilitating situation. Plus, I didn't want to move away from Heather during her college days. Sometimes, fate has a different path for us, though.

I really hadn't followed college football that closely during my days with the Cardinals, other than observing some players who were potential additions to the franchise. When I flipped through the channels on New Year's Day, I watched Alabama lose to Miami in the Sugar Bowl. Never in my wildest imagination did I guess that in a few days I would be returning to Tuscaloosa.

During that time frame, Coach Stallings seemed to be high on the list to go the Naval Academy as head coach, and I doubt if he ever dreamed his path would wind back to Alabama. When Bill Curry accepted the head-coaching job at Kentucky, I got a call one night from my old roommate and close friend, Richard Williamson.

Richard told me that he was high on the list to become Coach Curry's replacement, and wanted to know if I would join his Crimson Tide staff. Although my first choice was not to coach in college again, knowing the rigors of being on the road to recruit, I told him that I wouldn't hesitate to work with him.

Let me say this about Richard Williamson. He was one heck of a football coach and had done a remarkable job of making Memphis State relevant back in the late 1970s. He seemed to be on the fast track, but some of his players got into trouble off-the-field, which derailed all that he had accomplished. Afterwards he had gotten into pro ball, and would go on to become one of the most respected assistant coaches in the business.

When I got a second call from Richard, he really thought he was going to get the job. He pretty much had assembled an all-star cast to be on his staff, including our old teammate and defensive guru, Brother Oliver.

A day or so later, Richard told me that Alabama was going in another direction. That direction was Gene Stallings, who offered me a job to serve as his assistant head coach. I was returning to Tuscaloosa seven years after I left. Never did I expect to return to Alabama to coach, but it was a blessing to me. No doubt, I also hoped returning to her old hometown would help Charlotte regain some of her diminishing memories.

25

COMING HOME

oming back to Alabama to coach certainly wasn't a priority for me, because I really never thought that opportunity would arise again. Frankly, I had rarely gone back to Tuscaloosa since leaving there in 1983, but arriving on campus in January 1990 elicited a rush of emotions and memories.

I was indeed back home and for the most part, it felt really good. But I had the lingering reasons to pause, mainly Charlotte's continual mental decline. I hated to face the reality that her fall had caused permanent memory lapses and uncharacteristic behavior. At times, it was difficult to worry about my job, because I was constantly concerned about her.

Nevertheless, I had a job to do, and there were several noticeable team deficiencies that the new staff had to address, principally hitting the road at such a late date and trying to sign a few players in a short period of time.

Our roster was pretty much depleted at quarterback with only returning starter Gary Hollingsworth and a junior who had never played, Danny Woodson, among our candidates. So, I immediately began the task of trying to find quarterbacks to bring in for the fall. We signed two quarterbacks from the Anniston-Oxford area, Jason Jack and Steve Christopher, and there was a player in Trussville who I had been told might be a prospect, Jay Barker.

Auburn had apparently been interested in bringing him in as a defensive back, but I liked his arm, even though he was really raw at the time. I recommended to

Coach Stallings that we sign Jay, and we did. It would begin a remarkable career for him.

I want to say this about the situation we inherited in 1990. First of all, I know it is much easier to take over a program like Coach Bryant did in 1958 or Nick Saban did in 2007, when the team is down and you can start the building process. In 1990, Alabama was coming off a season in which it shared an SEC title and had, at one time, been ranked No. 2 in the country. There had been long droughts for Alabama when both Coach Bryant and Coach Saban assumed command, but obviously that wasn't the case when Gene took control.

From watching videos on the 1989 team, I was impressed with the job that Coach Curry and his staff had done. Having spent the previous four years in the NFL, I knew that there was only a handful of what you would term pro-type players on that team. Unfortunately, for us two of them, John Mangum and Keith McCants, were headed to the NFL for the 1990 season.

There was also a definite change of philosophy from Coach Curry to Coach Stallings. We were going to be a tailback-oriented offense under Gene, and we were going to be tough, mentally and physically. There is little question that the common thread between respective coaches Bryant, Stallings and Saban, is they believed in the same system for winning. They were going to make their teams mentally and physically tougher than their opponents.

After the spring of 1990, we felt we would have a quality football team on both sides of the ball with one major caveat: we really could not afford to lose a single player in order to be really good. That was an undeniable fact that unfortunately would prove to be our major bane for the season.

Fans like to talk about the injuries we sustained in those early losses with tailback Siran Stacy and wide receivers Craig Sanderson and Prince Wimbley going down in successive weeks, but our problems actually began that summer when our starting left tackle Vince Strickland was ruled ineligible by the NCAA.

He had taken classes at a junior college a few years earlier, and it was ruled that his matriculation to the junior college counted against his years of eligibility. It was quite a blow because he was a quality player. It forced us to move a freshman, Matt Hammond, into the starting role. It was really unfair to Matt to be thrust into that role at such an early age, particularly in a pro-set offense where that position is so critical. Matt would get better and better and start for four years, but those first few games in 1990 were a real test for him.

Those first few weeks were extremely frustrating. We gained almost three times as many yards as Southern Miss, yet lost the game on a late field goal. When Siran went down with a season-ending knee injury, our offense would never be the same either. After ensuing losses to Florida and Georgia, accompanied by the losses of Sanderson and Wimbley, we had a season that really was on the brink. Gene and our staff, I think, did a great job of not only holding it together, but winning some key games along the way.

Probably none was more important than the win over Tennessee in Knoxville. That was the game that ESPN Analyst Lee Corso said would be comparable to a high school team playing a college team. Our players heard those remarks that morning at the team hotel. I don't know if they needed any more motivation but that may have given it to them.

I can tell you how depleted we were from a depth situation. We knew our best chance to win was in the kicking game, to shorten the game by controlling the clock as much as possible, and making Tennessee go three and out as often as possible. In the staff meeting, line coach Mike DuBose said defensive end Eric Curry wasn't going to be able to play because of an injury.

Defensively, we were going to have to play with the same players the entire day with the exception of when Brother Oliver called the nickel and dime formations, and Whammy Ward and Antonio Langham would come onto the field.

Offensively, our situation was the same. We were down to two freshmen tailbacks Chris Anderson and Robert Jones. The only area where we really seemed to have any depth was at fullback, where we had two outstanding players in Kevin Turner and Martin Houston.

Tennessee was absolutely loaded with an all-star cast of players that had played a flawless game the week before in routing Florida 45-3. No one gave us a chance, except our coaches and players.

I'll never forget arriving at Neyland Stadium, because some of our coaches weren't allowed through the gates. Coach Stallings didn't take too kindly to this. When he saw what was happening, he started chewing out some of the gatekeepers. As he liked to say, "I gave them a comeuppance." He did, too.

It's funny, but I think it was at that point our players started to believe. They saw their coach ready, so to speak, to go to war and that's what they did that day. Offensively, we did our best to pound their front, make first downs and control the clock. The defense, repeatedly stopped Tennessee, and Phillip Doyle won the game with three field goals, including the dramatic 47-yarder at the final gun. There were other great plays in the kicking game, with the blocked field goal by safety Stacy Harrison (setting up the game winner) and a fumbled kickoff caused by Whammy Ward's violent tackle.

It had been a long time since I had seen such absolute joy and happiness in a locker room. Seeing that cigar smoke wafting up in the air and hearing the players sing was special to me. After the game, our senior center, Roger Shultz, made the statement, "We ought to pay property tax in Knoxville because we owned Tennessee." I don't think Gene liked that too much, but on this particular Saturday, I don't feel like many of us worried about it. It would really be the beginning of that remarkable run in 1991 and 1992.

Of course, beating Auburn in the season finale at Legion Field was special, too, because it ended a four-year streak. None of our seniors had ever been a part of beating the Tigers, and it was personally gratifying for me to see players like Gary Hollingsworth and Lamonde Russell -- and those senior linemen, Roger Shultz, Trent Patterson, Terrill Chapman and Chris Robinette be part of something that special. I would have hated it for them to leave Alabama without having won over Auburn.

There was a lot of controversy that year about the bowl situation. The Fiesta Bowl was feeling pressure because of the State of Arizona's vote against allowing Martin Luther King's birthday to be an official holiday. Of course, the Fiesta Bowl had nothing to do with that controversy, but unfortunately became embroiled in the consequences of it.

Certainly, there was no unanimity at Alabama about accepting a bid either, but Coach Stallings wanted to go, especially because of having coached there the previous two seasons. I did too, not only because of my affiliation with the Cardinals in 1988 and 1989, but because Heather was still in school at the University of Arizona, and had been the Fiesta Bowl queen the year before and was the outgoing queen which made it really special.

Ultimately, the game was anything but fun. Our coaching staff had spent most of that December on the road recruiting, which would prove beneficial in the long run. When we got to Phoenix, the unusual happened: it rained and rained, which I think hampered us badly, not only in preparations, but also in getting our playing legs back in game-condition.

We were a step slow all day and Louisville was just a lot better that day than we were. One of my old coaches, Howard Schnellenberger, was the head-man at Louisville, and I knew his name had been in discussion for the Alabama job in 1982, 1986 and 1990. Howard was one heck of a football coach, too, so I know beating us so easily had to be especially rewarding to him. It was the proverbial "long day at the office" for us.

Our right tackle, Terrill Chatman, broke a leg, and on the plane trip back, he had to lie on the floor in the front of the plane on some blankets. If it was a tough trip home for most of us, I can't even imagine what Terrill had to endure.

That first year was over. It had been an interesting one, with the lows of difficult losses and the highs of memorable wins over Tennessee and Auburn. Heading toward the spring, I think there was renewed optimism, especially after the signing class that included one of the most dynamic players I would ever coach, an all-purpose back from Birmingham, David Palmer.

26

THE CHAMPIONSHIP SPIRIT

When I reflect on our 1991 and 1992 seasons, I can't help thinking about how those two teams had developed a pair of common characteristics of a championship team: the belief in their ability to win and a championship spirit that is hard to define.

Of course, our only loss during those two years was 35-0 to Florida in Gainesville in the second game of the '91 season, and other than the final score, it really shouldn't have been that surprising. We were still seeking an identity at that point, as well as breaking in a new quarterback, and basically a new offensive line as well.

Danny Woodson won the quarterback job in the spring, showing an ability to do some really remarkable things on the field. We were running some option packages early in the year, because we felt with Danny, and a healthy Siran Stacy, along with his top backup, Derrick Lassic, we had the ability to make some explosive plays.

The game against Florida really got away from us in the second half after Woodson was injured, and we had to turn it over to Jay Barker, a redshirt freshman who was seeing his first extensive duty. It was a rude introduction into SEC football for him. It would serve him well, though, during his magnificent stretch as one of the winningest quarterbacks in college football history.

After the 35-0 loss in Florida, we knew it was imperative to get the ball into the hands of our freshman receiver and kick returner, David Palmer. He had been nothing short of sensational in August drills, excelling to a point that then-sophomore cornerback Antonio Langham joked after a practice, "Palmer can do things on a football field that Michael Jordan wishes he could on a basketball court."

We turned David loose the next week on Vanderbilt, and our streak of victories that would extend to November 1993 began. One of our most important wins that year came when we beat Tennessee 24-19 at Legion Field. It was another physical, typical "Third Saturday in October."

I'll always remember one run that Siran made in the second half. He was bent over with four or five Tennessee players on his back and just bulldozed them off and kept running to set up a touchdown. It gave us a lead that we would never relinquish. I think that run epitomized what I think Alabama football was all about, a player fighting with all his heart to make a difference.

When we were getting ready to play Mississippi State a few weeks later, I did something I usually didn't do. I picked up the SEC statistical page and saw where Danny Woodson was leading the conference in passing efficiency. I was proud of him and how much progress he had made during the last year and really thought he was on the verge of doing some great things for the Crimson Tide.

Against the Bulldogs, he wasn't playing well, and we turned it over to Barker in a game that we needed a late goal line stand to win. The next day Coach Stallings had to suspend Danny for the remainder of the year for breaking a team rule, leaving all the quarterback duties to Jay.

As our tailbacks combined with the fullback tandem of Kevin Turner and Martin Houston, our offense became even more dependent on those players. In the LSU win, Siran and Kevin each rushed for more than 100 yards, marking the last time that an Alabama fullback would top the century mark in a game.

When we beat Auburn 13-6 to end the regular season, thanks to a long run by Kevin on a pass from Barker; and an absolutely brilliant TD rush by David Palmer through a maze of Tiger players, I thought that team had come about as close to playing up to its potential and its strengths as any I had ever been around.

I wish I could say I remember a lot about the Blockbuster Bowl win over defending National Champion Colorado, but that was the game I got waylaid on the sidelines in the hardest hit I had taken since Lee Roy Jordan hammered me during a scrimmage back in '62. I don't even remember who ran over me and delivered a second-quarter knockout blow; but I do vividly recall David Palmer putting on his show, earning MVP honors in leading us to a 30-25 victory over the Buffaloes. When the final polls came out, we were ranked No. 5, and I think we all knew deep down inside that we would be extremely difficult to beat in 1992.

If I had to pick out one championship that meant the most to me, it would be that 1992 team for several reasons. First of all, it was the Centennial Season of Alabama football. The theme for the season for the Crimson Tide was "Century of Champions" and I know I felt a special pride in wanting to ensure Alabama had a championship season.

Also, it was the first year of the Western and Eastern Divisions in the Southeastern Conference, and I felt it would only be just for Alabama to play in the first SEC Championship game. Alabama had won the league's first ever SEC title back in 1933 and had been the first to claim a bowl victory as well.

We were No. 8 to start the season, which was probably where we should have been rated. It wasn't important where we started; it was important where we finished.

Jay Barker was still just learning the quarterback position and still had some erratic moments as he continued his maturation as a college signal-caller. Looking back on the 1992 season, I can say that when Jay was on, we were a pretty doggone good offense. When he wasn't, we tended to struggle.

Regardless, we knew we were so strong defensively that if we didn't turn the ball over and played field-position football, we were going to be hard to beat. The objective was not to lose the game, or probably a better description: not give it away. It was a sound and professional approach that Coach Stallings instilled in the team. More importantly, it worked and worked well.

While our football team was getting better and better each week, my own problems at home with Charlotte continued on a downhill spiral. She simply wasn't getting any better.

Back then, we always had one road trip where the wives of the coaches would travel with us. In 1992 Athletic Director Hootie Ingram picked the Tulane game at the Superdome for the annual wives' weekend.

While we would win the game 37-0, it was a trip that I would remember for other reasons. First of all, my old friend, Aruns Callery of the Sugar Bowl, was on his death bed, and I ran by his house on Saturday morning to say my final good-byes.

I just couldn't imagine playing a game in New Orleans without Aruns being in the stadium. He'd been there with the Crimson Tide during some of our more exhilarating wins and saddest losses. I couldn't help but think of how his friendship with Coach Bryant had set in motion some of the most legendary games in the history of college football.

Charlotte's memory lapses really got worse that weekend. On the Friday night before the game, Charlotte was going with the other wives to a dinner party in the French Quarter and literally got lost in the hotel. Thankfully Ann McCorvey and Ann Ross, the wives of my fellow assistants Woody McCorvey and Randy Ross, found her and help shepherd her around the rest of the weekend.

Even more disheartening, Charlotte saw our old friend Dude Hennessey in the hotel lobby and didn't recognize him. It was a most troubling moment for me, and it probably really hit home then that she just wasn't ever going to be the same. After the Tulane game, we got ready for Tennessee in Knoxville. All we heard at home and on the road was the persistent question: "Who have you guys beaten?"

The day we were beating Tulane, Tennessee lost it first game of the year, falling to Arkansas, a team we had beaten 38-11. At Neyland Stadium, some fans were yelling at our coaches asking them that question and Coach McCorvey said, "Well, at least we beat Arkansas."

We beat Tennessee that day, too, 17-10, in a game that we should have won by a larger margin, but we accomplished what we needed to and headed into the home stretch of the schedule, unbeaten and climbing in the polls.

The next week we had Ole Miss for Homecoming, facing a strong Billy Brewer coached team. Joe Lee Dunn was his defensive coach, and he really liked to pressure on just about every down. Our offensive staff knew that Jay would really have to be good or we could be in serious trouble. Ole Miss had the second best defense in the SEC, so the burden was really on Jay to have a good game.

In probably his best game of the year, Barker continually hit Palmer, Curtis Brown, Kevin Lee and Prince Wimbley, effectively ruining the Rebel blitz in a 31-10 win. We threw for nearly 300 yards, which was quite a bit for us in our tailback-oriented offense.

By the time we got to Baton Rouge to play LSU in Tiger Stadium, we had climbed to No 3 in the polls, but the news got even better that afternoon. During our 31-11 win over the Tigers, we got the word that top-ranked Washington had lost to Arizona, which meant we were going to be No. 2 behind Miami in the next vote of the major wire services and the coaches poll. While that certainly felt good, our next game against a tough Mississippi State team in Starkville offered little consolation.

Jackie Sherrill was the Bulldog coach, and I think everyone knew that playing there on a Saturday night was going to be anything but easy. While I don't think there was any question we had the better football team, there was another variable that played a significant role that night: a gusting wind that whipped through the stadium. It really was a factor in the third quarter when Bryne Diehl's punts just seemed to be knocked down in midair, giving Mississippi State a field position advantage, and the Bulldogs capitalized on it.

Entering the fourth quarter, we were down 21-20 but we finally had the wind at our back. Like a championship team, we made the plays. Michael Proctor's field goal gave us the lead back and then George Teague seemed to take over the game. His interception started a touchdown drive that ended when Chris Anderson crossed for six, and on the next State drive, George picked off another pass. It had been a typical tough SEC game and we were just happy to leave Starkville with a win.

Our game against Auburn was on Thanksgiving Day, the second time in my career that we had played the Tigers at Legion Field on the holiday. Back in 1964, when I was helping Coach Stallings with the secondary, we beat Auburn 21-14 in a game that Ray Ogden returned the second half kickoff 108 yards.

This game wouldn't have quite the dramatics, but there was the added drama from Auburn's perspective. Head coach Pat Dye announced his resignation that morning. There certainly was a lot of emotion on the Auburn side because of it, too. I'd been friends with Pat since 1965 when he joined our staff. It's never easy leaving the profession that has been your life, and I know it was really tough on Pat. I would learn that lesson the hard way the next season.

Antonio Langham's third-quarter interception return for a touchdown pretty much ended the day for Auburn. We were just so dominating on defense; we felt the only way we could lose was to turn the ball over.

Our great defensive bookends Eric Curry and John Copeland dominated throughout the afternoon, and we pounded their defense with Martin Houston leading us in rushing. With the 17-0 win, we were undefeated, ranked No. 2 in all the polls, and still really hadn't won anything at all. The first ever SEC Championship game would determine the league winner, and Florida presented a most formidable foe.

That inaugural game, as well as the second SEC Championship contest, was played at Legion Field, and we were really lucky to escape with a 28-21 victory. It was bitterly cold that afternoon, and much like the Mississippi State game, the third quarter almost proved to be our downfall. There were several key moments that are often forgotten and one that probably was never really reported.

After we scored a touchdown to go up 20-7, we had back-to-back personal foul penalties as well as a procedure penalty, forcing Michael Proctor to attempt the extra point against a stiff breeze from 46-yards out. While Michael made some key field goals for us during his career, his long-distance extra point may have saved the day for us. Frankly, I don't recall ever being in a game or even watching a game where a kicker had to make an extra point from that distance.

If anyone thought we had the game under control, Florida had different thoughts. An injury to our outstanding linebacker, Lemanski Hall, certainly didn't help matters. Not only was Lemanski a great defender, but he helped us get lined up properly, too. After he left the game, we really struggled the rest of the quarter. The situation got so bad that Brother Oliver, who was calling our defenses in the press box, told our linebacker coach Jeff Rouzie to find out if Lemanski could go at all, because we needed him just to get us lined up properly.

When Lemanski went back into the game, Florida didn't move the ball very well again, but by that time, the score was 21-21. There still weren't any overtimes in college football then, but the SEC had adapted the system that is used today to be utilized in case that game ended in a tie.

Thankfully, that didn't happen. We finally got a long run by Derrick Lassic to switch field position, but a penalty stopped our drive late in the fourth quarter. Before Florida took possession, Brother told Antonio Langham to squat behind the receiver, because he felt Gator quarterback Shane Matthews was going to throw a curl on first down.

I don't know if Brother had a premonition or not, but it worked. Man, did it work. Not only did Antonio pick off the pass but he weaved through the Florida defenders for what proved to be the winning touchdown. It marked the third straight game that he'd scored a touchdown. They were all critical in our drive to the National Championship game, and for his efforts against Florida; Antonio had the distinction of earning the first ever SEC Championship game MVP honors.

The next afternoon, it was announced officially that we were going to play top-ranked Miami in the Sugar Bowl for the National Championship. This game had all the makings of being another epic one as well. Not only was Miami the defending champions, the Hurricanes were on a 29-game winning streak. That topped our own mark of a 22-game win streak by seven.

I couldn't help but think back on all those historical games that the Crimson Tide had played in New Orleans during my years at Alabama. I'll never forget the statement that one of our great linemen on the 1978-79 National Championships, Byron Braggs, made, "The only thing better than winning the National Championship in New Orleans on New Year's Day is celebrating winning it in Tuscaloosa on January 2."

Our 1992 team had earned that opportunity to experience what Byron was talking about, too.

The odds makers didn't give us much of a chance, but this game was going to be played on the field and we believed in our team. It was going to be a special time for the Crimson Tide.

Here I am in my high school uniform with teammates Maurice "Pee Wee" Dozier (13) and Bobby Hollis (21). I'm wearing my first number, 22.

Elementary school, circa 1950.

Posed action shot from 1959.

I'm on the run behind a block by Billy Richardson during the 1959 season.

My bride Charlotte and me in 1968.

This picture was taken with Charlotte and Sugar Bowl rep and good friend Aruns Callery in 1975.

On the sidelines with Coach Bryant in 1977.

Sending in a play with Don Jacobs in 1979.

To Coach Moore,
Simply, the
greatest coach I've
ever had. Also a
great man who installed
in me the values of
loyalty and pride.
I will never forget you
coach.

Allen
1985

Here I am with my star running back at Notre Dame, Allen Pinkett, 1985.

On the sidelines with Gene Stallings and Danny Pearman in 1991.

With Charlotte in the front seat we enjoy her final National Championship parade in 1993.

One of my first priorities as AD was to start planning for new facilities in 2002.

Wearing a hardhat as the north end zone expansion begins, 2005.

I always loved poetry, especially reading to my grandchildren Anna Lee and Cannon.

Condoleezza Rice was our special guest at the 2005 Tennessee game along with her colleague from Great Britain, Jack Straw.

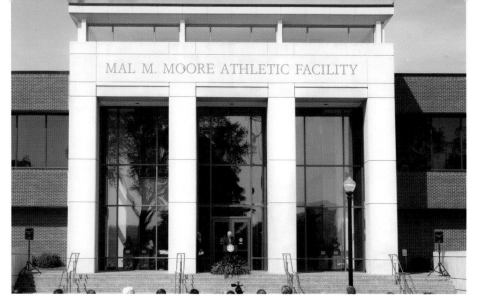

I had few greater honors than having the football complex named in my honor in 2007. Here I am addressing the crowd.

I had most of my family there for the dedication, including all my siblings as well as Heather and her family.

My brother Frank was my childhood idol and his son Chuck played a key role in the hiring of Nick Saban.

Addressing the audience at the press conference introducing Nick Saban.

One of the greatest moments of my career was turning over the podium to Nick that January morning.

Addressing the news media after the Nick Saban introductory press conference.

Celebrating the SEC Championship win over Florida signaled the return of Alabama football to the top.

After the win over Texas to clinch the National Championship, my administrative assistant Judy Tanner and I are having some fun on the field at the request of my grandchildren.

Terry Saban was all smiles at the unveiling of the statue commemorating Nick as one of our championship coaches.

I always loved bird hunting and took time off in 2010 to do just that.

Having Presidents like Dr. Judy Bonner and Dr. Robert Witt helped return Alabama to the top in every way possible.

Paul Bryant, Jr., and I share a laugh leaving football practice in 2011.

My old teammate Bill Battle congratulates me after my induction into the State of Alabama Sports Hall of Fame, 2012.

The incomparable Joe Namath and I enjoy a sideline view before a game in 2012.

Heather, my grandchildren Cannon and Anna Lee, and son-in-law Steve Cook join in celebrating the 2012 SEC Championship.

Heather and I enjoy some time together at Times Square in New York City during one of visits for an award ceremony.

My good friend Archie Manning, who supported me in getting the John Toner Award, visits with my grandson Cannon, and me before the 2012 Hall of Fame banquet.

Here I am accepting the Toner Award at the National Football Foundation and Hall of Fame dinner in 2012.

27

SUGAR SWEET

When we started preparations for our Sugar Bowl showdown with Miami in December, I think there was not only an excitement among our players but a prevailing feeling among our staff that we were destined to win, not because of some pre-ordained fate, but because we felt we were the better football team.

If you have ever played or coached, you know what an absolute grind it is to survive an SEC schedule and that year, six of the seven conference teams that earned a bowl bid returned home winners. There weren't any easy pickings in the conference that year, just like there aren't any now. When you play in such a competitive league -- where the teams and their fans take so much pride in their schools – each game is an event. We had survived and moved on.

In my opinion, we had played tight against Florida in the championship game, maybe because we knew a National Championship showdown was at stake. I think our staff felt it was incumbent that the players not get caught up into all the hype in New Orleans. Miami had become the most dominant program in college football and the Hurricanes had a reputation of baiting opponents into a war of words. We wanted to do our talking on the field on January 1.

Offensively, we knew that we needed to add some new wrinkles and lessen the pressure on Jay Barker. I asked the offensive staff for their input and ideas on what our best plan of attack would be against the great Hurricane defense. One of our offensive line coaches, Danny Pearman, suggested we add some trap plays because of the way that Miami liked to attack. There was also the added element that we felt the traps would take advantage of the quickness of our top two backs, Derrick Lassic and Sherman Williams.

So in practice, we started out by pulling our right tackle Roosevelt Patterson, not only because he was a great blocker, but because he had the athleticism and quickness to make some things happen for us. We also put in traps where we could get our two off-side linemen in front of the plays on our sweep packages.

Going to New Orleans, we really felt good about our game plan. Nobody had run the ball on Miami in 1992. Shoot, for that matter, no one had run on them in a decade. We were determined to change that on New Year's night.

Let me say this about that coaching staff: Gene Stallings was surrounded by coaches who had championship pedigrees, and I personally think there is little substitute for having been around teams that knew how to win, and win titles. A lot of times, football fans speculate how great a coach or team is by their statistics. Really though, the only true mark is in winning and losing. And when I say winning, I'm talking about championships.

Our 1992 staff had coaches that had been winners as players and coaches, including Brother Oliver, Jeff Rouzie, Mike DuBose and Jimmy Fuller. I always considered Danny Pearman and Woody McCorvey as part of the Paul Bryant coaching tree because they had been with Danny Ford at Clemson, and they knew how to win. So did Larry Kirksey and Ellis Johnson.

Heading to New Orleans, my biggest concern was not losing the game. I really felt if we didn't turn it over much and limited our breakdowns, we were going to win. Let me add this, I don't think I'd ever seen Gene Stallings so confident going into a game. I know when reporters kept asking him about us being eight-or-nine point underdogs; he repeatedly answered that he wouldn't trade our team for theirs. That wasn't just coach speak either.

Our players and staff opted to drive to New Orleans on our own that year and arrive on Christmas Day. I rode down with Brother Oliver and Danny Pearman, and we talked about what we needed to do to win the game. Brother and I had been in too many of these games not to have had some type of feel for what the emotional level would be. We agreed that the key was minimizing our mistakes and keeping our players from getting too uptight.

I also felt that when we did make a mistake, which inevitably is going to occur in a game of this magnitude, the main thing the coaches had to do was keep the players calm, poised and confident.

During my career, I had learned so many lessons from Coach Bryant, not only on the football field, but in life as well. One thing he instilled in his players and coaches was this constant: when you have a bad play or get a questionable call, you have to move on to the next play. Players and teams that dwell on something negative that has just happened will let their emotions obstruct what they have to do on the next sequence of plays.

I had to make sure Jay Barker provided the leadership to the rest of the offense to move on to that next play. You can't minimize the importance of remaining strong in the bad times. Being strong is something that is easy to do when things are going your way.

Another important element in our preparations in New Orleans was to remain focused on what we had to do on New Year's night and minimize the distractions that are simply a natural part of visiting the "Crescent City". I think Coach Stallings and the staff did a really good job in explaining to our players that they didn't need to get into any smack contests with Miami players.

That was one of the Hurricanes' ways of disrupting their opponent, and I know some of our players had to just about bite their tongues to keep silent that week, particularly some of our secondary players. Miami's great receiver Lamar Thomas said at a press conference, "Alabama's cornerbacks (George Teague and Antonio Langham) don't impress me one bit. They're over rated. Real men don't play zone defense and we'll show them a thing or two come January 1."

If our defense needed any more inspiration, I don't know why. Same for our offense when one of their defensive ends, Kevin Patrick, said Miami had the best defense in the country and they'd intimidate us.

Coach Stallings and the rest of the staff never rehashed those remarks with the players. Our job was to continue to make sure our game plans were solid as we practiced that week at Tulane University, and on December 31 at the Superdome. There was no doubt, though, that our players had had enough of the Miami bravado. We were coiled and ready to play.

While we had added the trap packages to our offensive schemes for the Sugar

Bowl, Brother and his defensive staff had created some looks that they felt would confuse 1992 Heisman Trophy winner Gino Torretta, including bringing all 11 defenders up near the line of scrimmage. It might have seemed like a dangerous ploy, but our secondary personnel were so talented and well coached that there was little doubt that it would create confusion to the offense.

If there was any part of the week leading up to the game that proved problematic to me, it was trying to attend to Charlotte. She had ridden down with some of the other coaches' wives a few days after the team had reported to New Orleans.

Although she hadn't officially been diagnosed with Alzheimer's, I had reached the sad conclusion that she had to be afflicted with that dreaded disease. It was almost like watching a person revert in years to a childlike existence. I didn't even know if it was safe for her to be at the game among a sellout crowd. I worried how she would react to the crowd and the noise level in the Dome.

Regardless of my personal problems, I had to focus on the game. When we arrived at the Superdome, I had that old adrenaline rush from having been here when we had clinched National Championships in 1978 and 1979.

Seeing that swarm of Crimson Tide fans at the gates on Poydras Street to greet the team only added to my expectation that tonight Alabama was going to return to its rightful place in college football. How could it get any bigger, especially considering we were concluding the celebration of marking a century of Alabama football?

When we went out for our warm-ups, I have to admit, I couldn't believe the crowd. The Superdome was already packed with 76,000 fans, and it seemed more than 95 percent of them were wearing crimson. It was an absolutely amazing sight and environment.

I exchanged the courtesy good-lucks with a couple of Miami coaches that I had known for quite a while: their head-man, Dennis Erickson, and their defensive coach, Tommy Tuberville. Dennis had played quarterback for Jim Sweeney, so we certainly shared a common bond there. Coach Tuberville had gotten his coaching start under one of our old graduate assistants, Larry Lacewell, who had gone on to become a legendary defensive coach at Oklahoma and Tennessee. In 1992, Lace had become the player personnel director for Jimmy Johnson and the Dallas Cowboys.

Larry was at the game, and when I saw him at the hotel, I asked him who he was pulling for, Alabama or his old assistant. He said, "Mal, if they cut me open, I would still bleed crimson. Don't ever forget that I'm the second best coach ever to come out of Fordyce, Arkansas, and my mother thought I was better than Coach Bryant!"

When we finally kicked it off and had played a few series, I felt my original instinct was correct and that the only way we would lose was if we gave it away. Utilizing the trap plays, and with fullback Martin Houston blowing up Miami's linebackers, Derrick Lassic and Sherman Williams continued to rip off big yards.

Miami wasn't having much luck moving the ball at all. Our only problems were a pair of interceptions and a celebration penalty that wiped out a touchdown for us.

Regardless, two Michael Proctor field goals and a touchdown run by Sherman gave us a 13-6 halftime lead. My only disappointment was we should have been up by at least another score.

The third quarter was one of the most dramatic in Alabama history, particularly plays made by George Teague. We had gone up 20-6 on a run by Lassic, set up by a Tommy Johnson interception, and then Teague made two game-winning type plays. Brother called one of his plays where we had everyone up close to the line of scrimmage and George picked off a slant and ran it back for a touchdown.

Bob Griese, the great quarterback from Purdue and the Miami Dolphins, was calling the game with Keith Jackson for ABC-TV and he made the comment, "George Teague knew the pass route better than the Miami receiver."

Later in the quarter, Miami hit their only really big play from scrimmage when Torretta connected with Thomas. I was standing next to Coach Stallings, assuming that the Hurricanes had just scored and preparing for our next offensive sequence when I heard Gene yell, "We have the ball!" Even when I watch the replays, I can't believe George caught Thomas, much less stole the football from him.

Even though the play was wiped out because we were offside, it didn't negate the fact that Miami was still backed up in the shadows of their own goal line instead of lining up to kick an extra point. After that point, all we wanted to do was run the ball and play the clock game. The only way we could lose was to just give it to them. And, we weren't going to do that, and we didn't.

To say it was a joyful dressing room is an understatement. Our outstanding center Tobie Sheils probably summed it best for our offense when he said, "Miami thought they were going to intimidate us. We intimidated them with our running attack. We took it to them."

Our whole line, including tight end Steve Busky, had done a great job that night. Our tackles, Rosey Patterson and Matt Hammond, our guards Jon Stephenson and George Wilson, joined Tobie in taking it to the Hurricanes. They sure hadn't been intimidated.

I was happy for all of our players, but especially George. I had played with his father, Butch, on the 1961 National Championship team, and George had suffered one of the worst foot injuries imaginable in a gun accident. He joined his father Butch in having a National Championship ring, a rare accomplishment in any family.

That season had been so special because not many people really gave us our due respect except for a Tucson, Arizona sports writer Corky Simpson, who had voted us No. 1 every week from the pre-season to our 34-13 win in New Orleans. In his column after the game, Corky wrote: "Vindication isn't mine, it's Alabama's. As the only voter in the AP top-25 poll who picked the Crimson Tide No. 1 every week, I took my share of flak from around the country, but that's part of the game. I stuck with those kids from Alabama because they gave me no choice. How do you bail out on a team that refused to lose?"

I said after the game and will always believe it: You don't earn a football tradition over a few years. You earn it by sustaining it over the decades. The Alabama championship legacy dated back to Rose Bowl wins under Wallace Wade and extended through Coach Thomas and Coach Bryant.

That night in New Orleans, the Crimson Tide had answered its critics and proved what it means to be a champion.

28

MY FINAL YEAR ON THE FIELD

During the 1993 season, a year in which we were coming off our National Championship run, I was 53-years-old and my entire life had centered on my faith, family and football. Although I didn't want to consciously admit it, I was in the midst of a year that would forever change the course of my life.

First of all, I knew we would have challenges on the football field. We lost some dominating players from the championship team, but with that being said, there was one thing our staff knew how to do: win football games. That is a quality that might be hard to define but the truly great coaches possess that attribute. Men like Coach Bryant and Coach Stallings did it their way, and didn't much care what the naysayers had to say about it. Nick Saban does it that way, too, and it sure seems to work for him.

I heard Gene say if he had run the team like the fans wanted him to in 1992, we would have lost three or four games, and that's probably true. One thing I knew going into 1993 was that we could ill afford many serious injuries. I just wasn't sure that we had the quality depth to sustain what we accomplished in 1992.

Well, unfortunately for us, we had a season that included some devastating injuries that restricted the play of quarterback Jay Barker, receiver Kevin Lee and running back Sherman Williams. Then there was the ordeal with Antonio Langham when he was ultimately declared ineligible for his dealing with an agent.

By the time we finished the season, we were pretty much limping to the finish line. So was I. Sometimes, I think back and wonder how I made it through the trials and tribulations of that season. I really think it had to be the faith that had been instilled in me by my family during my formative years in Dozier.

Charlotte had continued her rapid downward spiral. It had become almost overwhelming at times to try to coach and to serve her as best I could. She had become almost helpless. I not only had to physically feed her, but I had reached the point where I now had to bathe her and lead her from room to room in the house.

I got the team doctor to see her and met with her two or three times. He said he wasn't sure if she had Alzheimer's, but did recommend a neurologist, Dr. Gene Marsh. I'll never forget Dr. Marsh saying, "Coach, she definitely has Alzheimer's and it is going to be a life-changing experience for you."

I really had no idea of how true that remark would be. People would ask, "Why don't you put her in a nursing home?" I always answered, "I feel it is my responsibility, because she's my wife and Heather's mother. I love her and it's my job to take care of her for as long as I physically and mentally can."

Every day, I would rush home at lunch, prepare her something to eat and drive her around a little, too. She loved to ride in the car and that seemed to keep her smiling. By late October, she had really gone down. We were playing Ole Miss in Oxford, in a game that is probably best remembered for David Palmer replacing an injured Jay Barker and putting on a show that had Heisman voters buzzing.

Sadly, what I remember most was getting off the team plane and calling home. Charlotte didn't answer and I began to panic and started calling some of our neighbors. I finally reached one of the neighbors and she went to the house and found Charlotte just staring ahead. I don't think Charlotte ever answered the phone again.

By then, I knew I had to have someone stay with her, and I went through 12 to 15 women before I finally got one that Charlotte liked. Rarely, did she remember my name and she hardly asked about Heather. That just broke my heart, because she loved Heather more than anything in the world.

During that 1993 season, we had an open weekend, and I was out in the yard, doing some work. I saw some of our neighbors, laughing on their way to dine out on a Saturday night. That made me sad. I knew Charlotte and I would never be able to do that again. I think that's about the only time I ever got mad, because I realized that I had lost my wife.

It was also the day that I came to the realization that I had to deal with her disease 24-hours-a-day, seven-days- a-week. I knew I was doing a disservice to the Alabama football program because I wasn't able to put all of my heart and soul into the Crimson Tide.

There were a couple of other episodes that pushed me to begin discussions with Coach Stallings about stepping aside. Charlotte seemed to find some solace in watching television. This calming effect didn't ease my mind much, but it did make me feel she was safe while I wasn't home.

One day she was watching some program. I don't know if it was a soap opera or some old rerun of a drama from yesteryear, but what happened on the television became real to her. There was a gun fight on the show and it became reality to her, and she fled the house. One of my neighbors called me, and I rushed home, leading her from the street back into the house. That's when I started hiring the ladies to stay with her.

There was another occasion when one of the assistant athletic directors asked me to go lunch just for me to get a few moments break. I told him when we finished I wanted to drive by my house and check on Charlotte. When we got there, she had cut out four pictures of football players from a media guide. She had placed them by coffee cups and was having a conversation with the pictures.

It was certainly a moment that just tore me up and expedited my decision to give up my responsibilities as a coach.

Hootie Ingram, the Director of Athletics, called me to his office one morning and told me that if I wanted to give up my coaching job, he would create a position for me on the administrative side. We talked about me moving into a fundraising role, something that our department had been restricted from doing by university policies.

I think Hootie, as well as most of our administrators, felt we were well behind our sister institutions in the SEC in this area, and that we were falling behind in the world of keeping up with the competition, mainly in one realm: new and updated facilities.

When Ray Perkins had been athletics director and created "Tide Pride," he created a concept which would prove to be one of the most beneficial and successful ticket enhancement programs in college athletics. When Tide Pride was implemented in 1988 under Steve Sloan, the President's Office determined that Tide Pride would be the only fundraising program for athletics.

Early on, I am sure that made sense. But, as the years went by, the need for monies to build and maintain facilities increased. It had become painfully clear that our chief competitors were leaving us behind on the "facilities' war."

So, I was enthusiastic about this potential opportunity with the knowledge, though, that I would be leaving the one job that had been my whole professional career. It was not just a profession to me, but something I loved. Walking away from those practice fields, the players and the coaches, was not easy. And, that's an understatement.

By the time we were preparing for North Carolina in the Gator Bowl, it was pretty much known within the football complex that this would be my final game. I really can't correlate it to how I felt when I walked off that field at the Liberty Bowl in 1982. I will say that I was emotionally drained from a year that had started with a parade celebrating another Crimson Tide championship and ended with my wife being debilitated by her memory affliction and a team crippled by injuries and falling short of winning a championship.

I really think our offensive staff did an outstanding job of piecing together a game plan for the bowl. It centered on our backup quarterback, Brian Burgdorf, and he had an outstanding game in leading us to a 24-10 victory over a very strong Tar Heel team.

I remember Brian breaking loose for several long runs on the quarterback draw and hitting our fullback Tarrant Lynch and wide receiver Chad Key for touchdowns. The one to Chad was in the fourth quarter and pretty much clinched the win for us.

While we had our setbacks that year, I want to say this: our all-purpose star David Palmer had about as good a season as any player that I ever had the privilege of coaching. Woody McCorvey is the one who really coached him, but I liked to tell David that I was the one helping him get the ball.

He had exactly 1,000 yards receiving, had rushed for 300 more, passed for 300 more and returned kicks for another 300 or so. In the game I talked about earlier, Jay got hurt against Ole Miss, and we put David in at quarterback. He basically won the game by himself. Against Tennessee, he caught a pass to help set up a touchdown in the final seconds and raced into the end zone with the two-point conversion that tied it up at 17. He finished third in the Heisman, but I don't know of any player who was more valuable to his team.

When we were leaving the Gator Bowl Stadium that night in Jacksonville, David told me he was probably going to declare for the draft, and I told him I wished he'd reconsider because he could have a very special senior season.

I didn't tell him that I had already made my decision to leave the coaching profession. I guess in some twist of irony that when we left the Bowl game, cranes were already lined up outside the Gator Bowl stadium ready to raze it and start the process of building a new one. Maybe I thought that it was just an omen from above that tomorrow would also be a day when I started rebuilding a new life, too, though I admit I didn't eagerly look forward to what may lie ahead for me.

29

THE GENESIS OF THE CAPITAL CAMPAIGN

After I had left the playing field as a coach and joined the administrative team in January of 1994, I started visiting other campuses around the SEC, which was probably the first time I became aware that other schools had really surpassed us in the arms race for facilities.

During that time frame, athletic dorms had been outlawed across the country. Bryant Hall -- once called the finest facility in the nation by *Sports Illustrated* -- had really started to deteriorate. I think the same could be said for most of our athletic facilities. Like I said before, the University had a policy that limited the department's ability to raise money to the Tide Pride donations, which hardly filled the coffers with enough money to maintain the current facilities much less update them or replace them with new ones.

When Glenn Tuckett, who had served as interim athletic director for a year, announced he would be leaving in the summer of 1996, I really wanted the AD job and pursued it. One of my primary concerns was the fate of Bryant Hall, which was in total disrepair, but sitting in the center of campus.

We were still using it as our academic center for athletics, but that was where the old recreation room had been, and it was small, outdated, not functional and certainly not conducive to inspiring our student athletes to achieve success. I was going to meet with the selection committee late that spring. Before I did, I visited with Paul Bryant, Jr., and posed to him my idea of converting Bryant Hall into an academic center for all Alabama student-athletes.

He liked the idea, and I presented it to the committee that week. A few weeks later I traveled to Gainesville, Fla., to meet with Dr. Andrew Sorensen, who had just taken the president's job at Alabama. He had been the provost at the University of Florida, and he had yet to make the move to Tuscaloosa.

I felt strongly about our facilities situation, but I felt equally convinced that the athletic director needed an extensive background at the University, or at least the SEC. Let's face it, the job was tough enough on someone who knew the strengths and weaknesses of the school and its fan base. I just didn't think a so-called outsider would ever be able to reunite the splintered fan base, much less understand the complexities of the Alabama supporters, in order to raise the monies to elevate the Crimson Tide back into a position of prestige.

Also, I knew that football was clearly the lifeline of our program, because it provided the financial means to support all other sports team. Dating back to the days of Dr. George Denny, football had been a unifying element for the entire student and alumni base as well.

A few weeks later, Dr. Sorensen arrived in Tuscaloosa. His first major move was to hire Bob Bockrath from Texas Tech as athletics director. Dr. Sorensen's decision was disappointing because Coach Stallings had talked to Dr. Sorenson that morning and told Gene that I was the leading candidate. In truth, I don't think I was ever seriously considered.

In all due respect to Bob, I don't think he ever grasped just how important the football program was to the University. I'm not going to put Coach Stallings' thoughts into words, but I'm convinced Gene believed that there was no longer any administrative support to have a top-notch football program when he decided to retire.

Coach Bryant always told us that a football program cannot be successful without total support of the President and the other key administrators. It was the beginning of the end for Gene's successful run as head coach.

Early on in Bockrath's administration, we talked about the facilities situation, and he also seemed to feel we had fallen behind our competitors. I broached the topic of converting Bryant Hall into an academic center, as well as other problem areas, facility-wise, in our department. I'm not sure if that particular proposal resonated with him or not. I do know that neither the President nor the Athletic Director seemed too keen about the east side expansion of Bryant-Denny Stadium that had been initially proposed by Hootie Ingram in 1994.

That proposal had already been implemented in 1995 with the agreement to move the sorority houses on the east side and the relocation of the old fire station on Bryant Drive. Plus, the necessary utility work had already begun, so the project was already a go and there was no turning back.

I guess what really hit home to me, though, was when an old friend, R.C. Slocum called to tell me that he and some other members of the Texas A&M Athletic Department were touring schools to look at their football facilities. I had known R.C. for years and at the time he was the head football coach at Texas A&M.

Although he had never coached at Alabama, R.C. had followed the Crimson Tide football team during Coach Bryant's years, and there had been a lot of Alabama-Texas A&M connections throughout the years as well. Anyway, the Aggie entourage came to Tuscaloosa after visiting North Carolina, Tennessee, Florida and some other high profile universities.

What they saw was disappointing: a small outdated weight room, an old-fashioned locker room with metal cages that looked more like a high school than a major college, leaks all over the place, and carpet that hadn't changed since the football complex opened in the mid-1980s.

Coleman Coliseum was just as unimpressive, the only major update since it opened in 1968 was the annex for basketball practice and gymnastics accommodations. Bryant Hall looked like a building getting ready to be put on the condemned list; our softball team played at a local recreational park; there were no seats at soccer; our golf team couldn't recruit at the old University Pritchett facility east of campus; and our tennis stadium was dilapidated to say the least.

There was little doubt that R.C. and the Texas A&M folks were not impressed with what they saw. There were only two ways to fix the problem: convince Dr. Sorensen we needed to have the ability to raise money and then educate our supporters on how bad the situation really was.

The University commissioned a survey, which clearly showed that our alums and supporters had absolutely no interest in contributing any money as long as Bob Bockrath was the athletic director. Adding to the dilemma was the amount of money that the University was extracting from athletic department funds on an annual basis.

Plus, we were the only school in the SEC not receiving a dime from student activity fees. Some of our chief rivals – such as Georgia, Tennessee, Florida and LSU were getting as much as $4 million a year in activity fee money. We were getting nothing.

Money was being taken from the athletic department to offset the University's proration problem, as well. Our money had to go into the University's Capstone Foundation; and we had to pay an eight percent fee to use our own money.

One of the biggest misconceptions among our supporters was that our student-athletes go to school for free. Nothing could be further from the truth. For the 2010-11 school year, the athletic department paid the University $14 million in tuition and fees for our athletes to attend school, and while the costs weren't that high in 1999, they were still substantial.

Morale around our program was at its lowest point since the 1950s. Having two disappointing football seasons coupled with the danger of a real and imminent fiscal crisis didn't help matters either.

30

BECOMING ATHLETIC DIRECTOR

The summer of 1999 proved to be an unsettling one for the entire football program. Rumors had surfaced on a Birmingham radio call-in show back in May, implying that head football coach Mike DuBose had been inappropriately involved with another University employee. During that time, Mike was traveling around the state playing golf and raising monies for his charity organization. He happened to be in Dothan when he addressed the situation for the first time.

He told the press gathering there that there was no truth to the rumor, and that it had been detrimental to the families and to the football program. Everyone thought that was the end of the issue, but in late July the *Orlando Sentinel* broke a story that Alabama would have a "Clintonesque" scandal become public in the near future.

It was late July, right before the beginning of August drills when Mike went to Athletic Director Bob Bockrath and confessed that the rumors were true, which set off a chain of events that would certainly alter the department and change my life in the process.

Although I wasn't involved in the discussions or privy to what took place, rumors circulated that Bob had gone to President Sorensen to determine if the indiscretions deserved immediate termination.

There is no question that a number of prominent individuals wanted Mike relieved of his duties immediately. I know several board members were upset with Dr. Sorensen and Bob Bockrath for not informing them of the situation before it hit the press.

Rumors were rampant that a change was imminent, or at least an interim coach would be installed to lead the team through the upcoming season. In one conversation, Paul Bryant, Jr. asked, "If Mike is let go would you be interested in taking over the team for the upcoming season?"

Paul wasn't on the Board of Trustees, but obviously he had received calls from people wanting to know what was going to happen. I still had to take care of Charlotte on a daily basis, and there was just no way that I felt I would be able to concentrate my efforts on being the coach, even knowing it would be a three-month deal.

Some prominent people wanted to ask Coach Stallings to serve as the interim Coach. Of course, there were also persistent rumors about a member of the 1999 staff assuming the job for the remainder of the school year. I was told that if they did pick a staff member to be the interim, it would likely be Neil Callaway.

The Board of Trustees held an August meeting in Birmingham. Although it was closed to the public, the press gathering there was substantial. One rumor circulated that if a vote was taken, the President, AD and head coach would all be gone by the end of the day.

I am not sure what happened, although I understand there was a protocol issue that did not allow a vote to take place at that time. No one was dismissed that day, but there was a 40-day period of evaluation placed on Mike, which coincidentally would come the Monday after our game with Florida in Gainesville.

While there'd been no changes, that didn't stop the rumor mill that changes were on the horizon. There was little doubt that Bob was viewed negatively by a large segment of the Crimson Tide fan base. Dr. Sorensen wasn't getting many rave reviews either. As I mentioned earlier, that spring, the survey on fundraising had not been very positive for either one of them. Conversations about Bob being fired as athletic director accelerated as the football team prepared for the 1999 season.

Even though we were coming off 4-7 and 7-5 seasons, there was a genuine optimism that we had the personnel to have a strong squad, if we could maintain some type of internal decorum. We started off the season looking like we had the chance to be a special football team, especially after opening the year with a win over Vanderbilt in Nashville and Houston in Birmingham. The next week would be tumultuous in more ways than one.

We were playing at Legion Field again, this time against a Louisiana Tech team that employed an explosive offensive team, but one that was limited defensively. They had given up something like 500 yards rushing the week before, so it seemed that with an offense featuring Shaun Alexander at running back and Chris Samuels at left tackle, we would be okay offensively.

On Friday before the game, rumors about Bockrath being let go intensified to a point that it was all over Birmingham, especially at the team hotel, the Sheraton. I wasn't there but another department member called and told me what was being said, leaving little doubt that there was substance to the rumor.

Before I drove to Birmingham for the game, I stopped at a friend's house to have a cup of coffee. This particular friend told me point-blank that Bob was gone, and if I were interested in the job, I had better begin putting together my game plan.

It was certainly a surreal moment when Bob came to the game, headed to the press box at Legion Field and was intercepted by Dr. Sorensen, who informed him of his decision to relieve Bob of his duties. Bob just turned around and left.

To say the game was a disappointment would be an understatement. I had gone down to the end zone to watch the last few minutes of play, and Dr. Sorensen came up and stood beside me to watch. He never said a word about Bob's firing.

We watched together as Louisiana Tech made the day even darker by throwing a touchdown pass right in front of us to win in the final moments of the game.

That was September 18. All I could think about was how disappointed I was for the coaches, team and University. There wasn't a lot to celebrate, especially since the team had a very good Arkansas squad coming to Tuscaloosa the next weekend.

Dr. Finus Gaston was named the interim athletic director on the following Monday. Soon after, Dr. Sorensen announced a committee would be in place to make a recommendation to him on the replacement for Bob.

There had been a lot of talk that Lee Roy Jordan would be a candidate for the job, because he had been prominently mentioned both when Steve Sloan and Hootie Ingram had been hired. I talked to Lee Roy and he was pretty adamant that his time had come and gone; however, he was determined to play a role in who was selected.

I know Lee Roy called Dr. Sorensen and volunteered to be on the committee, with the stipulation that the committee would have real influence, rather than acting as a a rubber stamp group. There had been other committees picked to interview candidates and make recommendations for various other jobs on campus, and the President had ignored their endorsements. I knew Lee Roy would never be a part of such a committee.

Obviously, I wanted the opportunity to take over the department, and I wanted to be totally prepared when I had the chance to visit with the committee. There were a lot of people who helped me, supported me, and gave me good, sound advice on presenting a plan that would unify the supporters of the program, prepare the department for the 21st Century with modernized facilities and a united athletic department. I felt confident I could do those things and restore respect for the Crimson Tide.

Meanwhile on the football field, our team started its return to respectability with an upset win over Arkansas. More important was the match-up with Florida and Coach Steve Spurrier, who had pretty much had his way against us during the 1990s.

It was also the week of the end of that 40-day moratorium, during which a decision would be made about Mike's future. It was strongly rumored that if we lost, he would be gone. Several media members even questioned our players about it in the days leading up to the game at Florida Field.

I had to stay home and take care of Charlotte and wasn't at the game. Instead, I watched it at home with her and it was one of the most memorable games for Alabama in several seasons, particularly with the Gators being undefeated and ranked No. 3 in the country.

On the Friday before the game, I had been in Birmingham and had lunch with my old friend Coach Pat James at his barbecue place in Hoover. He asked me about the game, and I told him that I had a good feeling. I'm not sure about gut feelings, but that one was on target, as was our quarterback Andrew Zow that Saturday afternoon.

Zow picked Florida's vaunted defense apart all day, but we didn't have much luck slowing down Florida's offense. Shaun Alexander scored late to tie it in regulation and did it again in overtime. With the score tied at 39, we missed the extra point attempt, but Florida got a penalty. On his second attempt, Chris Kemp made the extra point to win it 40-39. I wished I had been there, but the immense pride I felt for everyone made it up for it.

After the victory, there was no more talk about a coaching staff shake-up and the team continued to respond, winning over Ole Miss and setting up a key game against Tennessee, the first in Tuscaloosa since 1930.

The Volunteers were defending National Champions but lost to Florida earlier in the year, setting up a game that would figure prominently in the SEC championship races for both divisions. We had a chance to take a lead when Shaun Alexander dropped a sure TD pass from Andrew Zow. It was the start of more disappointments, with both Shaun and Andrew sustaining injuries in the second half. It was a tough game to lose, especially in face of the injuries and with a difficult stretch of games ahead of us.

It was also a time that I lost an old friend and colleague, Jim Goostree, who had served with distinction as the long-time athletic trainer for Coach Bryant and then as associate athletic director in the department. Losing an influential supporter like Jim certainly was something that left a void for me personally, especially with the search for Bob Bockrath's replacement heating up.

A number of former players and coaches were vocal in supporting me, which made me feel good. I also felt confident that my own plan for the department would enable me to demonstrate to the selection committee that I was the right person at the right time for the job.

Besides Lee Roy Jordan, our faculty athletic representative, Gene Marsh, and board of trustee member Dr. John England were on the committee and supportive of my efforts to become the director.

At one point during the search, the rumor broke that Dr. Sorensen was having clandestine meetings with other candidates at the Atlanta airport. One television crew from Birmingham was on the scene when Sorensen arrived and asked him if it were true he was there to interview candidates for the AD job. He denied that was the purpose of his trip, but he turned around and immediately caught another flight back home without ever leaving the airport.

That particular action sparked Lee Roy to call Dr. Sorensen and tell him that if the rumors were true, he would resign from the committee. Those secret interviews stopped. Lee Roy was just as tough off the field as he was on it, and that's saying something!

I met with the committee in early November, but there was no immediate action taken by the President to hire anyone. Frankly, I knew Dr. Sorensen really didn't want to hire me, even though I had support from the selection committee. Later, he would tell me he had never seen as many letters of support as I received from the Crimson Tide supporters.

Meanwhile, the football team rallied nicely, beating Southern Miss and LSU, but we lost a number of key players to injuries that day. The next Saturday, on an overcast afternoon in Tuscaloosa, we beat Jackie Sherrill's Mississippi State Bulldogs 19-7 to clinch the title, the first time we had ever won a Western Championship at Bryant-Denny.

It was an exciting time for me as well, because I was hearing that I was going to be offered the job as Athletic Director and the football team was favored to beat Auburn for the first time at Jordan-Hare Stadium.

On Friday, November 19, 1999, Dr. Sorensen offered me the job and I accepted. The next day the Crimson Tide made history by defeating the Tigers 28-17 at Auburn. It was a victory that was typical of so many other Crimson Tide wins of the past, with the team rallying in the fourth quarter behind the running of Shaun Alexander and the blocking of Chris Samuels, which set up a rematch with Florida in the SEC Championship game in Atlanta.

The next Monday, we had a press conference to formally announce that I was the new Athletics Director, which began a roller coaster ride that would be replete with exhilarating highs and extremely disappointing lows.

Certainly, it started out on a high when we completely dominated Florida in the championship game, winning 34-7. That earned us our first Orange Bowl berth since the 1974 season and our first major post-season game since the 1993 Sugar Bowl. It would be our last premium bowl game for almost a decade. We would sustain a series of setbacks that would have pretty much sunk any other school.

Tom Brady, the Michigan quarterback that night in Miami, continued to lead the Wolverines back when it appeared we had the game under control. Ultimately, we lost in overtime, 35-34, in a game we played without the best lineman in the country, Chris Samuels.

Despite that loss, the enthusiasm in and around our program was back at a high level. I started my first full year as Athletic Director with confidence that we would remain a national power for years to come. Little did I know the nightmare, I was getting ready to experience.

31

LEARNING THE JOB AMIDST
THE NIGHTMARE

In retrospect, I can truthfully say that I really didn't fully understand or appreciate the role of running a comprehensive athletic department when I began serving as Athletics Director. I had been used to dealing mainly with football. All of a sudden, I'm in charge of 20 sports and a variety of areas, such as compliance, ticketing, promotions, information, media and facilities that weren't new to me, but the depth of work each entailed was.

I spent those first months and years doing my best to educate myself in each area and trying to make each department the very best it could be. During the first part of 2000, there were areas of the football program that bothered me. I learned as a player and assistant under Coach Bryant that the off-season was critical to building and maintaining success.

There was obvious discord between Mike DuBose and his staff. The increasing tension among the coaches should have served as a warning signal that the upcoming season would be a letdown for everyone. It certainly showed in the opening game against UCLA at the Rose Bowl in Pasadena. In front of a capacity crowd, including more than 30,000 fans dressed in crimson and white, our performance was disappointing to say the least.

About the only thing the fans had to cheer about was a punt return for a score by Freddie Milons in the first quarter. It was the only time we would lead and certainly the only time we looked like the third-ranked team in the country.

That defeat revived questions as to whether Coach DuBose was the man for the job, and it would only worsen in the upcoming weeks, culminating with the disastrous homecoming upset at the hands of upstart Central Florida. I was being bombarded with complaints about the direction of the program and a decision had to be made about Mike's future. I spent many a sleepless night hoping and praying that I would make the best decision for the University.

There was little question that the players were splintered. The coaching staff was probably even more divided than the players. There was plenty finger-pointing going on. Players blamed other players and coaches. Coaches blamed other coaches and players. They were all blaming Mike for the ultimate demise of the 2000 team.

The Central Florida game was played on October 28. By Halloween Day, I made the decision that we had to make a change for the good of the program. I visited with President Sorensen first, and he agreed that Mike needed to be fired. I also visited with Paul Bryant, Jr., who had just joined the Board of Trustees, to inform him of my recommendation.

I drove to Birmingham to consult with board member, John McMahon. We met in the parking lot at the Summit, where I told him I thought it best we make the move, and he agreed. Two things I wanted to make sure of were that I had their blessings, and that I would be given the authority to hire the next coach.

Having spent my entire career in coaching, I felt my experience would be an asset in finding and hiring a football coach. I would learn it would be an excruciating and difficult process. Letting Mike go was not easy, either. I had known him since we recruited him back in the early 1970s, and Mike had been a standout defensive end for us during the 1972-74 seasons.

I coached with Mike DuBose on those 1990-93 teams, and he was also an excellent teacher and motivator as an assistant coach. Under different circumstances, I think Mike would have been a successful head coach at Alabama. I can't speak for Mike, but he probably wasn't ready to be a head coach at a high-profile school when he was hired.

I've often been asked why the decision to make a change was made with three games remaining to be played in the season. My answer was always the same. I felt that Mike had lost the trust of his players and staff, and an immediate change was necessary, to make sure we sent the right signals for the future of the program.

I felt the timing would enable me to start the process of hiring the replacement and we could get someone in place immediately after the conclusion of the Auburn game, starting the process of uniting the players and the fan base.

When I told Mike of my decision, he asked me if I would give him one more year to help turn it around. I told him the decision had been made, and there was no turning back. Our next game was against LSU in Baton Rouge under the Tigers first-year coach, Nick Saban. We hadn't lost to LSU in Tiger Stadium since 1969, and though we really played well that day, we lost 30-28.

While the team was losing its SEC finales against Miss. State and Auburn, I was working overtime trying to hire the next coach. Then another threat appeared as a dark cloud on the horizon, a rumor that the NCAA was investigating us for violations dating back to 1998. Frankly, I knew this might prove to be problematic in hiring a coach. Never did I dream how deep the problem was, and the impact it would have on our program for the next five or six years.

That being said, there were two coaches atop my radar screen: Virginia Tech's Frank Beamer and Miami's Butch Davis, both of whom had outstanding credentials and championship pedigrees as head coaches.

Coach Beamer had been prominently mentioned back in 1996 when Coach Stallings had retired. He played at Tech for Jerry Claiborne, a protégé of Coach Bryant both as a player at Kentucky and an assistant coach at both Texas A&M and Alabama.

I flew into a small town outside Blacksburg and met with Coach Beamer and his wife at a local hotel. We discussed the job at length, and I felt he was interested. I don't know if Frank officially withdrew his name from consideration because I also wanted to talk to Butch Davis, or because of the rumor of an investigation into our program. One thing I know is that Coach Beamer is a class act and had fought an uphill fight to elevate Tech after taking over a probation-riddled program.

During that time, I was also consulting with Larry Lacewell, who was the director of player Personnel for the Dallas Cowboys. Larry was an old friend of mine, who had started out as a graduate assistant for us back in 1961.

Larry had gone on to a long and successful career as one of the premier defensive coordinators in college football at Oklahoma and Tennessee. He also had been an extremely successful head coach at Arkansas State. Larry was a football man and had traveled to virtually every campus looking for players for the Cowboys.

Larry was familiar with Butch Davis, who had coached for Jimmy Johnson at

Miami and then with the Cowboys, Larry recommended him as a "can't-miss" head coach. I flew to Miami and met with Butch and had several other conversations with him, and I felt he was also genuinely interested in the Alabama job,

During the process, rumors about us receiving a letter of inquiry from the NCAA circulated around the college football world. Once he found out about the letter, Coach Davis called to say that he was pulling out of consideration for the job. He had been through a tough situation with Miami, trying to rebuild the program after it went on probation. He was adamant that he didn't want to fight those battles again.

With Beamer and Davis out of the picture, I spent a lonely and sleepless night trying to decide on which direction to go. I talked to Coach Lacewell again and he recommended I check out TCU Coach Dennis Franchione, who had been the architect of rebuilding the long-dormant Horned Frog program back to one of national prominence.

I called both Coach Stallings and Lee Roy Jordan to ask if they knew Dennis and what they thought of him, since they lived in the Dallas area and would know if he would be a good candidate for the job. Both told me that they didn't really know him but liked the way he coached and what he had done with the TCU program.

One of my old coaching friends, football legend Darrell Royal, told me that if he were hiring the next coach for the Longhorns, the man he would hire would be Dennis Franchione. That was high praise indeed.

I was also in contact with John David Crow who had left the AD job at Texas A&M a few years earlier. John David talked to Fran at length about Alabama job. Arizona State had already offered him its job but Fran let us know that he wanted to talk to me before making a decision.

After getting permission to talk to Dennis, I flew into Dallas and met him and his wife Kim at a local hotel. I instantly liked Fran, and we talked at length about the Alabama program, including the pending NCAA investigation and the possibility that we might be handicapped with scholarship losses.

I think Fran wanted me to offer him the job that night, but I told him that I had to fly back and see Dr. Sorensen and consult with some board members before I could do anything. I told him that I would contact him the next day no matter what.

In my talks with Coach Fran, I did tell him, "Fran, the worst thing you can do is take the job and then leave in two years, if we go on probation." He told me I had nothing to worry about, that he would be in it for the long haul.

When I got home late that night, my front yard was packed with media representatives. Satellite trucks were lined up on the curb, wanting to know if I had hired a coach. I learned then about tracking tail numbers of airplanes and how the media had known about my meeting with Coach Fran in Dallas. I told them no comment because no decision had been made, but I told them I would have an answer by the end of the weekend.

I again had a sleepless, restless night, because I didn't know if I was betraying our former players by hiring someone without a connection to Coach Bryant. There was one other coach out there who I wanted to talk to, Mike Riley, who was then the head coach of the San Diego Chargers and had been quite a success on the college level at Oregon State. Southern California was trying to hire a coach as well and he was at the top of their list.

Mike was one of our former players and the nephew of long-time Alabama assistant coach Hayden Riley. Mike had been a teammate of Ozzie Newsome back in the 1970s, and Ozzie told me he thought Coach Riley was a quality candidate and should be considered.

There was one problem with Mike – his contract with the Chargers locked him into another year there, so he was in no position to come to Alabama even if offered the job. The next morning I got up early and headed to the President's office to ask Dr. Sorensen's permission to offer the job to Coach Franchione. He agreed. I immediately called and offered the job to Fran He accepted on Friday, December 1. I really thought that our football program would be in good hands for as long as I served as Athletics Director.

Unfortunately, the next two years would turn into a recurring nightmare for the University and me. People liked to say that we should have done this or that, but hindsight in reality, is just that. It's hard to turn back the clock and have a do-over in real life.

One morning I got a call from Dr. Sorensen about the University officially receiving a letter of inquiry from the NCAA. He also told me that I would pretty much be excluded from the process because one of our boosters and an old friend of mine, Logan Young, was being accused of illegally recruiting defensive lineman

Albert Means of Memphis.

I don't know how many times I was asked why we signed Means, with all the prevailing rumors swirling about him. That's a valid question that I can now answer: we should have never signed him. But I will also say there were rumors about other players, including some from our own state who signed elsewhere. Rumors are part of recruiting. I deeply regret not being more alert to the problem, and I offer no excuses.

I will say I was extremely disappointed that the SEC Office contacted most of the member institutions and told them not to sign Means due to the rumors. No one at the University of Alabama ever received such a call from the Commissioner's Office. I wish we had.

While the NCAA ultimately found Logan and others guilty of improprieties, and we were handed one of the harshest penalties ever meted out by the governing body. All of us affiliated with the Crimson Tide were forced to begin the process of healing our wounds and straightening out our program.

And I say this, not only from a compliance standpoint, but also from an attitude one as well. For years, we had lived off our name and a reputation of doing things the right way. All the while, we had become lax in so many areas, including how we recruited and being complacent in letting our facilities become outdated. I knew we had to make a step forward in facilities before we could ever be competitive at the highest levels; not only in football but in all of our sports.

During those seemingly endless, depressing days of the investigation and the subsequent penalty phase, I suffered a heart attack. I was making coffee for Charlotte and me when the attack began. I drove to the hospital and was immediately treated for a heart attack.

Sitting in the hospital bed at Druid City Hospital in Tuscaloosa, I had to make some tough decisions personally as well. I finally came to the realization that I was going to have to move Charlotte from our house into an assisted living facility. I could no longer handle that chore while trying to serve as Athletics Director, especially at a time when I had to be strong in trying to rebuild our program and our integrity.

If I had any second thoughts about my decision to move Charlotte to a nursing home, those thoughts were quickly reinforced by my brother, Frank, and my friend Paul Bryant, Jr. Both told me I had to do it for my own health, and I knew they were correct.

Dr. William Hill actually pulled Heather aside and told her that if we didn't put Charlotte under professional care that I would be dead in nine months. I had cared for Charlotte the best I could for 13 years, but now there was only one choice and that was to put her in the LaRocca Nursing Home.

Never did I know how challenging the next few years would be. It seemed like every day I was dealing with bad news, but I never wavered in my belief that the sun would shine on Alabama again.

I really thought Dennis Franchione had the ability to be a long-term solution for our program, and we did have some mighty fine moments on the field during the 2001 and 2002 seasons. But the crippling penalties and Fran's obvious interest in the Texas A&M job delayed my goal of getting Alabama back to the top of the college football hierarchy. Our aging facilities were a continuing problem that had to have my immediate attention.

32

DEALING WITH FACILITIES

When I was hired in the fall of 1999, my initial focus was to do something about our facilities problem. In order to do that, I knew I had to have complete support from the University, our alums, and supporters to move us forward. It was a daunting task.

I drafted a letter to Dr. Sorensen, requesting that the University not take any money from the department for five years. Reluctantly, he agreed. Soon after that, I met with him about allowing us to have a capital campaign to raise money for facilities. We were relying on ticket sales, Tide Pride donations, and conference TV and bowl money to fund just about everything in our department. We had reached a critical stage in our athletic existence.

Dr. Sorensen rejected the recommendation. I went back a second time and then I had to present the plan to the 12 deans on campus, not once but twice. There was a certain degree of apprehension here as well, mainly because they felt it might negatively impact donations to their respective colleges at the University. They were also concerned about this being an annual campaign, but I assured them it would be a one-time deal, for facilities only.

Finally, after several years of pitching the concept, we got approval. Then, there was the other rising obstacle in our way, the NCAA investigation into our football program that would result in stiff penalties. I had no idea how this might impact our ability to raise money. When the penalties were announced in February

2002, it was one of the most devastating moments of my professional career. Just one month later, we would announce our capital campaign. It was another sink-or-swim time for us.

After eight years of trying to get permission to raise money, the Crimson Tradition campaign began.

No Expert in Fund Raising

I was naive enough to think I could go out, along with our athletic development director Bill Farley, and raise $100 million. Bill had come to Alabama from the University of Oklahoma in the late 1990s. I know he was eager to finally move forward. For the record, the only other person assigned to our campaign was Bill's administrative assistant, Telisa Blanton.

I had no background in fundraising, other than when I was an assistant coach and was asked if I had any contacts with prominent supporters. The University was celebrating its sesquicentennial back in 1981 and a capital campaign initiative was underway.

Dr. John Blackburn was in charge of development then, and he called me one day and asked me if I knew Jim Wilson in Montgomery. I was the football recruiter in that area, and I had met Jim but I really couldn't say that I knew him very well. I made the mistake of telling Dr. Blackburn, "Sure I know him."

Well, Dr. Blackburn asked me to visit him and ask him if he would make a donation to the University for the 150th Anniversary. I was thinking, "What in the world have I gotten myself into now?"

First of all, Jim had grown up in Montgomery and played high school football with Bart Starr, before going to play college ball at Tulane. Nevertheless, his family was still predominately Alabama fans, and his son, Jim III, would not only attend the University but become a member of the Board of Trustees and a great friend.

I set up an appointment with Jim and went by his office in downtown Montgomery. When I got there, the receptionist told me that Mr. Wilson had just stepped out, but for me to go into his office. A couple of minutes later, here comes Mr. Wilson. I probably did a double-take; because he was a lot older looking than I had remembered.

He started asking me all about the football team and Coach Bryant, and we really had a great visit. Then, he asked me how he could help me, and I told him about the anniversary and asked if he would consider making a donation to the

University. He just started laughing and told me that I had the wrong Jim Wilson that he was the first one and I needed to visit his son, Jim Jr., who ran their business.

Talk about being embarrassed. I trudged down to the second Jim Wilson's office, where he was meeting with his lawyer, who he hurried out. Jim started asking me about the football team and Coach Bryant. When he asked me what he could do for me, I started my spiel again, and he pulled out a checkbook. While he's writing a check, he asked, "How's our defense going to be this year?"

When I got the check and saw he was donating $100,000, I thought, "Man, fundraising wasn't so hard." Leaving there, I was thoroughly embarrassed that I had gone to the wrong office and I can always envision that entire office meeting together and laughing about that rube from Dozier, Alabama.

From that experience in 1981, I guessed wrongly that Bill Farley and I could raise the 100 million easily. Soon, I was soliciting help from Jeff McNeill and Pam Parker from the University's Development Office. They were not only friends but reaffirmed what Bill had told me. Their cogent advice was simple: form a committee and make sure you have half the money you need pledged before you ever announce it publicly.

They also said that I needed an outside person to serve as the committee chairman and, of course, the person I turned to was Paul Bryant, Jr. At the time I was on the board of AmSouth Bank, and Paul's office was in their building downtown on University Boulevard.

After the meeting, we went to lunch and I told him in more detail about the Crimson Tradition Campaign. We were standing outside by his truck and I told him this is something that Coach Bryant would want us to do. Thankfully he said yes, and just like that the campaign that would have a lasting impact on Alabama athletics officially began.

The first official meeting of the Committee took place in the lobby of Bryant Hall. It would prove to be a turning-point in the education of some our key donors about where we stood facility-wise at the University. Joining Paul Bryant, Jr., Bill Farley and me that day were Dr. Sorensen, Bud Moore, Angus Cooper, Tom Patterson, Owen Aronov and Randy Billingsley.

Bud had played and coached with me at the University before going on to become the head coach at Kansas, and then a successful businessman in the panhandle area of Florida. Angus had been a good friend of mine for years and had been a rock solid supporter on the Board of Trustees.

Tom graduated from the University's engineering school and became successful in a number of business ventures, including Daxco, Inc. Owen had become the principal driving force in Aronov Realty Management in Montgomery. Randy was another former player who had become an ultra-successful businessman in Mobile.

After I took them on a tour of the building, they were flabbergasted at the decline of what was once a showcase. Paul had no idea that Bryant Hall was in such poor condition. Bud Moore was even more direct, saying, "I don't know how we've recruited anyone to come to Alabama with a facility like this."

I really think that was a kick-start to the entire Crimson Tradition Fund. These influential supporters had seen first-hand where we stood. And we didn't stand in a very good place! Tom Patterson was so moved that he became one of the first major contributors, pledging a million dollars for the computer service area in Bryant Hall.

Owen Aronov was quick with sage advice after the meeting, "Whatever we do, let's build above the other schools, not to their current level, or in a few years we'd be right back where we are."

One day during this process, I called R.C. Slocum in College Station to tell him that we had gotten approval to raise money for facilities and some of our staff was interested in coming to Texas A&M to look at how they had done their VIP seating area in their expansion at Kyle Field.

I'll never forget what he told me, "Mal, I'm glad to hear that. When we came to Tuscaloosa to look at your facilities a few years ago, I didn't want to tell you how disappointed I was. I thought we'd be going to Alabama, the home of the Crimson Tide, to see the crown jewel of facilities. What we saw were the worst athletic facilities I'd seen in years."

That was like having a fist slammed into my gut, but it also reaffirmed what I knew. We had to upgrade our facilities if we were ever to re-establish our football program as one of the premier program in the nation.

On March 4, 2002, in the media room in the football complex, I was joined by the Crimson Tradition Committee to announce the launching of the $100 million campaign for facilities. It had been a long time coming -- more than eight years to be exact. I was determined we would build facilities that would make every

Crimson Tide supporter proud.

This announcement came only a month or so after we had received harsh probation penalties for violations that had occurred in 1998-2000. While the penalties were devastating, they also served as a clarion call that we needed to right our ship in all areas.

33

HIRING AND FIRING MIKE PRICE

The Sunday after our end of season Hawaii game on December 1, 2002, Sylacauga native and television star Jim Nabors hosted the entire Alabama delegation at his house overlooking the Pacific Ocean in Honolulu. It was a beautiful setting and a great evening. Although the rumors persisted about the Texas A&M job coming open for Fran, that evening's party seemed to ease my concern that Fran might be interested, even if he was the Aggies' top target.

Everyone seemed completely relaxed and feeling the reverie of the setting as well as the victory over Hawaii that had ensured us a 10-win season. Just before we returned to Tuscaloosa Monday, the news broke that my old friend, R.C. Slocum, was indeed out at A&M and that Fran was the Aggies' choice to replace him.

Certainly, there was a lot of restlessness among everyone affiliated with the University, including the coaching staff and players. That Tuesday night, Fran came to my house to meet with me and three of our board members: Paul Bryant, Jr., John McMahon and Angus Cooper. We addressed all of Fran's concerns, and I really thought at the conclusion of the meeting, he was going to remain as our head coach. He even suggested we drink a beer to toast the occasion.

Unfortunately, the next morning, Wednesday, December 4, everything changed. Fran told me that he was going to College Station just to see what they had to offer. That afternoon, around 3:00 p.m., he called to tell me that he had accepted the Aggie offer. When I asked him if he was going to come back and address the team, he simply said "No." Carl Torbush, the defensive coordinator, and I had that unenviable task of breaking the news to the football squad.

The players reacted with disbelief and total disdain for Fran. It was like a scene out of a movie, and not a good movie either. We had to get our security personnel to the football building because some of the players were ripping up pictures or anything that referred to Fran. I can't emphasize enough, though, the positive impact that the assistant coaches had during this time of turmoil.

Virtually every one of them came to see me personally; some with tears streaming down their faces, telling me that they didn't want to leave Alabama. They also engaged the players and told them to remain committed to the Crimson Tide no matter who the new coach would be. The loyalty of these men to Alabama and our players was something that I will never forget.

Try putting yourself in these coaches' shoes. This was a difficult time for them, too. These assistant coaches knew they were leaving Tuscaloosa, but they showed enormous class by the way they left and the way they did their best to calm the players.

I know in one situation that offensive coordinator Les Koenning called running back Santonio Beard and told him that he was making a big mistake by considering leaving school and entering the NFL draft. There were many other similar moments during this complicated week.

In situations like this, you just have to persevere. My goal was to quickly hire the best replacement possible, and my immediate attention focused on Frank Beamer. For the third time in a six-year period, Frank's name was being mentioned as a possible candidate to become the head coach at Alabama.

There really wasn't anything not to like about Coach Beamer. Frank's integrity, hard-nosed approach to the game and success at Virginia Tech made him an ideal candidate for our job.

I talked to him that Wednesday night and immediately offered him the job. I knew that he was extremely interested, but he told me he really didn't want to discuss it until after his game on Saturday at Miami. Although it was only a few days for me, they were long ones, with sleepless nights. In the era of instant news, I was beleaguered about what was happening by the press.

Everything was on hold until I talked to Coach Beamer on Sunday. I felt good about him accepting the job. One night, during the wait, though, I received an unexpected call from Mike Price at Washington State, telling me that he was interested in the job. Mike and I had been friendly through the years, dating back to the time he had coached under Jim Sweeney, my old boss at Montana State.

Washington State had just won the Pac-10 Championship and was preparing to play Oklahoma in the Rose Bowl, which was quite an achievement, considering the disadvantages the Cougars had compared to some of the other powers on the West Coast. I told Mike I appreciated the fact he was interested, but I had already offered the job to someone else.

On Sunday, December 8, Coach Beamer called me from his hotel room in Miami. It was not good news. He and his wife had stayed there after the game to discuss all the pros and cons of accepting the Alabama job, and he decided not to accept it. It was back to the drawing board.

One of my old teammates, Curtis Crenshaw, called from Tampa Monday morning and encouraged me to check out South Florida's head coach, Jim Leavitt. Jim had built the South Florida program from scratch into an up-and-coming Division 1-A program. Another one of our old players, Dewey Mitchell, also expressed support for Coach Leavitt, and everyone I talked to praised him as a coach, including highly successful Kansas State coach, Bill Snyder.

I flew to Tampa and met with Coach Leavitt. I really liked him, feeling he had many of the ingredients I thought necessary to be successful at Alabama. During this time, I was in touch with a lot of people in the football family, including Ozzie Newsome, the General Manager of the Baltimore Ravens. Ozzie was still extremely high on his old Alabama teammate Mike Riley.

I had talked to Mike during the search in 2000, but his contract with the Chargers pretty much negated him as a candidate then. During the ensuing two years, San Diego had let Riley go, and he had become an assistant with the Saints. This time, though, he became a principal target of mine for the job. After visiting with Mike in New Orleans, I really felt like we had our man. We discussed his coaching staff, the offenses and defenses he would employ, even the strategies for the kicking game. He told me that he wanted to talk to his wife that night but if I offered him the job, he was going to be the coach at Alabama.

The next day, I contacted Mike to officially offer him the job, but he asked for a couple of days to think about it. I told him that I would give him 24 hours. The next day I called and he asked for more time, and I told Mike that it was probably best if I just withdrew the offer.

That Wednesday night, December 11, one week after Fran had taken the

Texas Aggie job, I called Mike Price to see if he was still interested. He was down in Orlando for the annual awards banquet where the recipients of most of the prestigious honors in college football are announced. He was in line for the Coach of the Year award.

Mike told me he had always wanted to coach in the SEC and would love to talk about the job. So I sent the school plane to Orlando to pick him up and bring him back to Tuscaloosa. He stayed at the North River Yacht Club and on that Friday morning I drove him around campus, the football complex and the football stadium. There were satellite trucks everywhere, so we never got out of the car at the football complex. I just waved at some of the media reps, and they never knew I had Coach Price in my car.

The final choice in 2003 came down to Mike Price and Jim Leavitt; and I decided to offer the position to Coach Price. I really thought that Mike Price was a good hire at that time for Alabama. I knew he could coach. Winning two conference titles at Washington State was a tribute to his coaching skills, and his innovative wide-open offense was something that I felt would help us through our probationary period.

Coach Price's teams were moving the ball up and down the field against Southern California, when no one else in the country could, and with players, certainly not on the same level as the Trojans. I thought he would bring excitement and enthusiasm to our team and be able to relate to them in a way that we desperately needed.

Mike was set on bringing most of his offensive staff with him, but he eventually hired Joe Kines as the defensive coordinator. Joe came back to Alabama from Florida State, where he was the linebacker coach. At first, it looked like Carl Torbush would remain as the defensive coordinator. He had gone to Texas A&M with Fran, but Mike had several lengthy discussions with Carl about remaining on at Alabama. Ultimately, he decided to go with Fran.

In all my years in athletics, I've never seen a group of young men take to a coach like our 2003 squad did to Mike Price. There was a genuine respect, player-coach relationship, and there certainly was a lot of enthusiasm on the practice fields during spring drills that March and April.

Unfortunately, everything changed dramatically in early May. My first cousin, Jane Moore, who had attended Alabama, had gone on to a long and distinguished career as a professor at Auburn. She had also become the Tigers' faculty athletic representative.

On May 2, she was to be honored when the new softball stadium at Auburn was dedicated and named after her. She had requested that I make some remarks at the dedication, so on that Friday I headed to Auburn.

Our assistant AD for media relations, Larry White, called me on my cell and alerted me to press inquiries about Coach Price's conduct at an adult entertainment club in Pensacola on Wednesday night. Mike had gone to Pensacola to play in a celebrity golf tournament.

Ironically, I was supposed to be on that trip to attend the golf outing but had to cancel to attend a funeral. Our star track athlete, David Kimani, had tragically died earlier in the week and I needed to be there with our coaches, athletes and staff.

Larry's call was the first indication that we might have trouble ahead. After the function in Auburn that Saturday, I started driving back to Tuscaloosa and Mike called, telling me he needed to speak to me about this situation. I told him I'd be back in a few hours and to meet me in my office.

One thing I learned from Coach Bryant was that in order to really have a successful athletic program, you have to have a strong university president who is totally supportive of the program. Dr. Robert Witt had only been at Alabama a short time, but he had already made quite an impression on everyone affiliated with the University. I had to call him to let him know that we might have a problem, and I explained what I knew at the moment, and that I would report back to him as soon as I knew more.

After Mike told me his story, I called one of my closest advisors who fortunately, was close by at Sewell-Thomas Stadium watching our baseball team play Arkansas. I asked Mike to repeat his story about the event in Pensacola to both of us. My adviser didn't mince words and basically told Mike that he was in deep trouble if this story was reported in the mainstream media. I agreed and told Mike that was my feeling, too.

Basically, Mike told me the story about going to the strip club, having too much to drink and waking up to find a waitress, sleeping on a couch. I told him that I had to update Dr. Witt about it, and the President would want to meet with him. When Mike asked me if I thought he could lose his job, I told him that it would basically be up to Dr. Witt. I also told him whatever you do, tell President Witt the truth; which is what Mike did.

Before we had a meeting with Dr. Witt, I called Larry White to join us at the football complex. He echoed our opinion that Mike's behavior could indeed jeopardize his employment at the University.

I called Dr. Witt and he said he wanted to meet with Mike as soon as possible, and we immediately headed to Rose for a meeting that would certainly define the future of the University's football program.

When we were leaving the president's office, Dr. Witt told me that he would handle this situation in the way he felt best for the University. It was another week of anguish and anticipation. While a Board of Trustees meeting was called at the Bryant Conference Center for Saturday, May 10, to determine Mike's final fate, Dr. Witt told me that if the Board didn't accept his recommendation he would leave as President. It was an emotional time, with everyone being torn apart by this incident.

On the Friday before the decision was to be finalized, I got to my office and there were at least 15 football players there waiting to see me including three of the team leaders, guard Evan Mathis, quarterback Brodie Croyle and running back Shaud Williams, who would eventually become the captain of the 2003 team.

It was one of the most heart-rending meetings in which I ever took part. There were tears and anger. The players supported Coach Price 100 percent and they made that perfectly clear to me and everyone else. The common theme was forgiveness. I'll never forget Brodie Croyle telling me, "Coach, we've forgiven Coach Price. I hope the rest of you will. And I will guarantee you this, if it was Coach Fran, there wouldn't be a player here supporting his staying."

That was the kind of impact Mike had on his players in the short time he was here. During this time, Dr. Witt pulled me aside and told me that it wouldn't affect our relationship if I supported Coach Price, but that he had made the decision to terminate him. In the board meeting that morning, he made his recommendation, which was unanimously accepted and approved.

In the lobby of the hotel, Dr. Witt called Mike over to deliver the news, and despite Mike's pleas for a second chance, the decision had been made. It was time to search for yet another coach.

NAVIGATING CHOPPY WATERS

After Coach Price was dismissed on Saturday, May 9, 2003, I met with Dr. Witt about formulating the plan to hire the next coach. At the same time I told him that if he felt it was in his best interest and the best interest of the University, I would offer him my resignation as well.

Dr. Witt assured me that he wanted me to remain as athletics director and together we would form a team that would help strengthen the football program at the Alabama, no matter how long it took.

Certainly, considering all the variables we were dealing with, including probation and the fact the new coach would not even have the advantage of going through spring training; I felt strongly that the next head coach had to be someone who had a background with the University or at least in the Southeastern Conference.

The new coach would have to have an understanding of the choppy waters we would have to navigate. I think both Dr. Witt and I understood this all too well, although I have to admit some of our fans couldn't accept how the NCAA penalties would impact the overall performance of the team.

Hiring a current head college coach in May really was never a possibility or a consideration. I also felt that hiring an interim was not the solution either, although I gave it some initial thought, especially since two of Coach Price's staff members, offensive coach Sparky Woods and defensive coordinator Joe Kines, had been head coaches.

I also looked immediately to the NFL. We had three quality assistant coaches in the NFL who fit the criteria of being alums and having the understanding of Crimson Tide football: Mike Shula, Sylvester Croom and Richard Williamson. I talked with each one of them on the phone before Dr. Witt and I personally went and visited with each of them.

Dr. Witt clearly demonstrated his total commitment to the entire University and to the football program and athletic department. He insisted on participating and assuring each candidate that I had his full support, which was especially meaningful to me. We developed a special bond.

Although Dr. Witt never sought the spotlight or the headlines, his leadership, in my opinion, propelled the University of Alabama into a position of national prominence, both academically and athletically. I don't think anyone understood the need for our facility revitalization more than he did. He also knew how important it was to recruiting. That was easy to see by what he did for the entire University.

All over campus old buildings were being razed and new ones constructed. Importantly, he was attracting elite students and overseeing the dramatic rise in student population. His impact on the entire University should never be ignored or understated. All I can say is that I had immense personal pride in having the opportunity to not only work for him but to watch his master plan thrive.

One of the first things Dr. Witt did at Alabama was attend a Crimson Tradition meeting, which was the backbone of our fund-raising drive for athletics. During the meeting, he stopped everyone, pulled out a check and wrote a donation to the committee right then and there. His understanding of our mission and being a contributor to it showed his genuine interest in restoring the University to the highest level in all areas.

So, we began our quest to hire a new coach. I really thought this would be my final head coaching hire. We met with Richard Williamson and Sly Croom separately at a hotel near the Atlanta airport. Both were impressive and wanted the job.

There is no one who has ever coached with Richard or against him who won't tell you that he is just a superb football coach and a man of unquestioned integrity. I had played and coached with Richard, so I knew he was a quality candidate. He had been a head coach at Memphis State and Tampa Bay, so he had experience as a head coach, and there was no one in the NFL who didn't recommend him as a man who could do the job.

The biggest concern with Richard was his age. He was 62 at the time, and the prevalent feeling was that the University needed a younger person at this particular point and time.

As far as Sly was concerned, he was someone I had watched grow from a young player into an all-star player and coach. No one would ever question his character or integrity. He, too, was someone I had coached and coached with, and I knew that when you were in the proverbial fight, he was someone you wanted to have in the trenches. He was coaching for Bobby Ross in Detroit at that time and had the well-deserved reputation of being one of the top assistant coaches in the NFL.

Because of my personal background with Sylvester, he was also someone who I felt could and would do a good job of getting us through this difficult situation that we were in. We met with Mike Shula in Miami; and he, too, impressed us as someone who could face the challenge and wanted to face it. Mike's name recognition, football pedigree, his age, 39, and his popularity with the fan base were factors that we considered as extremely positive for him.

All three coaches knew that this certainly wasn't the optimum time to become the head coach of the Crimson Tide. While the program had suffered crippling penalties, the fan base's somewhat unrealistic perception was that we were still a team that should win 10 games every year and compete for the National Championship. I knew whoever got the job would face challenges that weren't of his making and would be extremely difficult to overcome.

I felt that considering all the variables that Sylvester Croom was the best candidate for the job and recommended that he be selected as coach of the Crimson Tide. The Chancellor's Office disagreed and felt strongly it would be in the best interest of the University to go with Mike Shula. The Chancellor's Office pushed his recommendation to the Board and Mike was selected.

It was a difficult time and a difficult decision for many of our former players and Sly's teammates. Ultimately, it was felt Mike would have the best chance to overcome the many obstacles we faced, get us through a difficult transition period, and be successful over the long haul.

Certainly the new coach was going to be in charge of an offense that had been totally re-tooled by Coach Price in the spring. Now there would be another overhaul under Coach Shula. The one constant during this time period was Joe Kines, who Coach Price had hired to run the defense.

When Mike Price had searched for a defensive coordinator, he solicited me to make some calls for him, and the name that kept coming up was Joe Kines. I had known Joe through the years, and he had coached at Florida under Charley Pell, Alabama under Ray Perkins, Arkansas under Danny Ford and Florida State under Bobby Bowden and Mickey Andrews.

One day I called Louis Campbell at Arkansas. Louis had played there but had coached with me at Alabama, and in my opinion, was one of the best defensive coaches around. Louis, at the time, was on the Razorback staff helping Houston Nutt. I asked Louis what kind of coach Joe was, and there was a pause on the line, and he said, "Mal, if I were hiring a defensive coach and choosing between Joe Kines and myself, I'd choose Joe Kines."

To me, that unselfish statement spoke volumes about Joe as a coach and as a person. Ironically, Joe had coached with all three of the candidates for the job, and had actually been on Ray' Perkins' staff when Mike played quarterback for the Crimson Tide. All three were pretty adamant about keeping Joe on board; certainly, we needed that stability.

I guess it was karma or just coincidence that we opened the 2003 season against South Florida, coached by Jim Leavitt. It was a historical day for Alabama because it marked the final time the Crimson Tide played at Legion Field in Birmingham. Justifiably, we left the Old Gray Lady on Graymont with a 40-17 win. It would be one of the few highlights of a trying season.

Times change, and certainly the time had arrived for the University to move all of its football games to Tuscaloosa, but I have to admit I felt quite a bit of nostalgia knowing that the Crimson Tide had played its final game at this historic structure. When I was being recruited to play at Alabama, I had gone to the Auburn game there and seeing that stadium with half the crowd wearing crimson and white and the other in orange and blue was truly a spectacle.

Back then, everyone dressed up for the games and I can remember being in the Bankhead Hotel in downtown Birmingham on the eve of the Iron Bowl, thinking that it really couldn't get any better than this for college football.

Having been to Legion Field so many times as a player, then as a coach and finally as an administrator, this last trip elicited many memories. I can recall those bus trips with the police escorts down old Highway 11 leading us to the hotel in Bessemer and then to Legion Field for a big game. It was a unique experience back then and almost like a holiday in Birmingham when the Crimson Tide rolled into town.

After the NCAA changed the recruiting rules about attending off-campus games, and with the disrepair of Legion Field, it became imperative to continue to renovate and improve Bryant-Denny and make it a showcase for our coaches, players and fans.

Although the season had not gone as well as we would have liked, the good news was that we were on the back half of the penalties of the probation (we could start signing 25 again) and there was a certain element of optimism entering the 2004 season.

All that high confidence level crashed early, though, when Brodie Croyle went down with a knee injury in the third game of the year against Western Carolina. After our starting tailback, Ray Hudson, was lost for the year against Kentucky, we really struggled offensively. We did manage somehow to earn a bowl berth against Minnesota in the Music City game in Nashville.

Being able to sign a full complement of players for the 2005 season was certainly a step forward. Plus, we had most of our key players back from '04. There was a more cautious optimism around the program going into 2005.

From a performance standpoint, both the high and low of the season occurred when we beat Florida, 31-3, at Bryant-Denny. Tyrone Prothro put on a spectacular show for three quarters, including catching an 88-yard TD pass from Brodie Croyle.

Tyrone's gruesome fourth quarter injury, a broken leg, ended the career of one of the most spectacular play makers I had ever seen, and again minimized our offensive effectiveness for the remainder of the year. A few weeks before the injury, he had made perhaps the greatest catch I'd ever seen when he pinned the ball on the back of a Southern Miss defender and held on at the goal line. He was a highlight reel ready to happen on every play, a true game changer.

His injury was devastating, as bad as I've ever seen, and he spent weeks and weeks in DCH Hospital trying to recover. His bone had literally shattered, much like a glass window being shattered by a rock. It wasn't a break that would mend normally. Our biggest concern was for his health and ability to walk again. The odds he would play again seemed impossible.

Despite the crushing loss of Tyrone, our team's defense was among the best in the nation, led by future All Pro Demeco Ryans. Entering the Tennessee game, we were still undefeated, and it was a game that had taken on a special meaning in light of the information that been divulged about Volunteer coach Phil Fulmer being a secret witness in the NCAA investigation against us. We took every precaution to ensure Coach Fulmer's safe arrival and departure from Bryant-Denny.

We also had the privilege of hosting Secretary of State, Condoleezza Rice. Actually, we had gotten a call from Dr. Rice's office asking if she could bring a dignitary, Great Britain's Foreign Secretary, Jack Straw, to the game. As one of many facets of her position, Dr. Rice liked to expose foreign leaders to different aspects of American culture. She had grown up in Birmingham and Tuscaloosa and obviously had a lifelong affinity for Crimson Tide football.

On Saturday morning, one of my assistants, Jon Gilbert, waited for them at the complex. I had my daughter, Heather, and her husband Steve with me in my office. Farid Rafiee, one of our supporters from Huntsville, was also there when they arrived. We gave them a tour of the building, especially the locker room and weight room. Mr. Straw was so amazed by the Alabama football phenomena that he asked if he could put on a helmet and have his picture taken in the equipment area.

Dr. Rice was dressed in red that day, and she flipped the coin before she and Mr. Straw went to Dr. Witt's box to watch the game. Mr. Straw, an avid soccer fan, probably thought he was at a soccer match, because there were no touchdowns this afternoon. Roman Harper made a dramatic stop on the goal line, forcing a fumble and Jamie Christensen kicked a field goal, giving us a 6-3 victory. When it was all said and done, the thing I remember most was becoming friends with Dr. Rice.

In the late spring, we have an annual Joe Namath Celebrity Golf Tournament to raise money for athletic scholarships, and it has turned out to be one of the best events of the year for us. We've had a number of famous non-Crimson Tide athletes to participate, including my good friends Archie Manning, Herschel Walker, Dan Reaves and Barry Switzer.

I sent Dr. Rice a letter and asked her if she would like to attend. I was surprised and really pleased when she accepted. I didn't tell anyone but Dr. Witt because I wasn't sure whether she would actually make it or not, but she did. Kevin Almond, one of my assistants and who oversaw the event, handled the details of her trip, including secretly housing her in one of the suites in Bryant Hall. When she appeared at the Sunday night function in "the Zone" at Bryant-Denny, I think everyone was totally surprised.

She had a great time, too, posing for pictures and signing autographs. She even took a golf lesson from our golf coaches Jay Seawell and Mic Potter before playing in the tournament that Monday. We sent her some photos a few days later, and I got a request from her. She wanted Joe Namath to autograph the picture that she had taken with him. Joe still has that charisma after all these years since he starred on the football field.

She also wanted me to know that one of her highlights was getting to meet John David Crow, the Heisman-winning running back for Coach Bryant at Texas A&M and an All-Pro running back for the Cardinals and 49ers. She told me that John David was her father's favorite all-time player and how happy he would have been to know that she had the opportunity to meet him.

There were also other memorable moments for our department, including Coach Mark Gottfried's basketball team becoming the first Crimson Tide team to advance to the Elite Eight and Sarah Patterson's gymnastics team winning championships.

Personally, I was never more proud than when we opened the renovated Bryant Hall in the spring of 2005. I felt it was the crown jewel of our plan, uniting academics and athletics with one of the finest student service facilities in all of college athletics.

In the fall of 2006, we also opened the north end zone upper deck of Bryant-Denny, and I had immense pride in this particular stadium update. I long felt that this historic stadium needed a walkway that would enable fans to experience our history and traditions while also enabling us to increase our seating capacity to more than 92,000.

The Walk of Champions has become a very special time for our players and coaches on each home weekend as they walk exactly 100 yards down a path that features commemorations of our championship history.

While the opening of the latest phase of Bryant-Denny again brought record crowds to Tuscaloosa, rumblings about the coaching staff began to reach a crescendo late in the season.

After we lost to Tennessee in Knoxville, I began to hear not only the calls of disapproval of Coach Shula, but a fan stoked rumor that former LSU head coach and then Miami Dolphin coach Nick Saban might be interested in the job if there was a change.

Frankly, I felt the only way there would be any consideration for a change would be if we lost our final three conference games against LSU, Mississippi State and Auburn. Those final weeks of the 2006 season would become the most critical of my administration, and that included some very trying days for everyone affiliated with the University, as they waited to see what would happen.

35

THE SEARCH BEGINS

The decision to relieve Mike Shula of his duties was a difficult one for me because I really like Mike as a person and as a coach. Unfortunately, the difficult and persistent question mark that kept popping into my head was whether Mike could take us to a championship level and maintain it. I just didn't think he could.

Frankly, keeping a team in the championship talk every year is extremely hard to do and only a handful of coaches have ever mastered that ability to repeatedly have their teams in contention. Ultimately, that was the principal reason I decided we had to make a change. Sure, there were other variables, including losing the confidence of the fan base. When that happens, it is difficult to reverse that field.

While the clamor to make a change really heated up after we lost to Mississippi State in Tuscaloosa, I did feel that a win over Auburn would certainly be helpful for everyone. The psyche of everyone affiliated with Alabama was about as low as I'd ever seen it. In my mind a loss to Auburn would make it nearly impossible for me to justify bringing Mike and his staff back for another year.

During those days leading up to the Auburn game, I decided if I had to make a change I would rely only on a small team of close associates who I could trust not only to help me in the search, but to keep all of our work completely confidential. I got them in my office and reviewed the situation with them, telling them I didn't want anyone to know they were involved and I would never reveal their identities.

We didn't have an agreement written in blood but it was just as good. My administrative assistant, Judy Tanner, would be my point person through the entire ordeal, ensuring that only a handful of people would ever know what was happening. She was a key component of the team.

I was determined that this was going to be the last football coach I ever hired and I wanted a coach who had a championship pedigree. We discussed the possible candidates and it was unanimous feeling that the best man for the job was Nick Saban, contingent of course on if he would even consider leaving Miami and returning to college football.

That was a big if. I also didn't want any surprises this time around either, so I asked my team to find out everything possible about the list of candidates that I had put together. It would be the first of many lengthy meetings and late night phone calls we would share over the next six weeks.

I was also getting pressure to hire a search firm. I relented on that, but mainly to appease some folks and to create a red herring. We hired Chuck Neinas' firm. Chuck did a great job of reviewing candidates and drew the attention of the media and fans. Chuck gave us room to work on the real search.

I knew the news media and fans would be chasing after me and the search firm and all possible coaching candidates. And, they did, too. I had learned the hard way in earlier searches about the tracking of planes. It's funny now, but there were daily internet and media reports on where the school plane was or where Paul Bryant's plane was or even the planes of some of the local guys who flew our coaches around to recruit. They never knew whose plane I was really using, though.

During those weeks leading up to the hiring of Coach Saban, to say I was on a see-saw ride emotionally would be an understatement. There had never been a doubt in my mind that Nick was the best man for the job at Alabama. I had become quite a fan of his during his tenure at LSU, and watching his teams perform there had reminded me so much of the way we had played during those two runs the Crimson Tide had during the 1960s and 1970s under Coach Bryant.

When I was putting my list together of potential coaches, I certainly had Nick in mind but to think it was a done deal or that he would actually consider an offer after the decision was made to dismiss Coach Shula is just not accurate.

Frankly, I didn't know Nick well at all, but I liked him and his entire approach to college football. I did, however, have one ace in the hole that few people knew about, my nephew, Chuck Moore.

Chuck had become quite successful building and remodeling homes, especially around Lake Burton in north Georgia where Nick and Terry had their lake home. When Nick was coaching at LSU, he had hired Chuck to remodel his home on the lake and the two had developed not only a professional relationship but a friendship as well.

When I'd talk to Chuck, he would always marvel at how hands-on Nick was in the project and that he was always motivating the workers as well. Chuck flat told me that you'd love to have this guy at Alabama because he reminds me of just how I used to describe Coach Bryant.

I never dreamed that one day that I'd even remotely have a chance to hire him at Alabama. The reason I wanted to make darn sure that only a handful of my most trusted friends would be involved in this coaching search was because I knew confidentiality was key if we were going to have an opportunity to hire Nick. And confidentiality isn't easy when you have a fan base like the Crimson Tide has. I knew any leaking of information could damage us achieving the goal of hiring a championship-caliber coach

One of my team members, who I had relied on to confidentially get information for me on a number of projects, told me early on that he was getting information that Nick might be interested but I could forget talking to him until the Dolphins season was completed. I knew that was going to be problematic, because I was under pressure to get a deal done quickly.

I asked another member of the team to find out if there was any solid information that, when the NFL season did end, could Coach Saban possibly be interested.

While the team was working covertly to narrow the list of candidates and complete detailed background checks, I called my nephew again to see how he felt about Nick's situation. Chuck told me, "Uncle Mal, when Nick was at LSU, he and I would talk football all the time. He didn't even know I was your nephew."

"One day I told Coach Saban that you were my uncle, and he asked about your career. I told him how you'd been a part of all those championship teams at Alabama and gone on to Notre Dame and the Cardinals. I asked him if he'd ever be interested in coaching at Alabama and, he said he had a great job, but Alabama would be a place that he would love to coach one day if he were in the job market."

There was one other reminder that Chuck shared with me, one of the people that Nick admired the most in the coaching profession was Gene Stallings. When Nick was a little known coach during his early years at Michigan State, Coach Stallings had gone to speak at one of his clinics and that had made a significant impression.

I guess I kept clinging to a ray of hope and the rumor that he didn't like coaching in the pros and might just consider a move. Although I was getting all kind of pressure to forget Nick and hire someone we knew we could get, I didn't want to give up. However, I didn't have any false illusions about the odds on hiring Nick and I knew I needed to talk to other coaches who I felt could return us to a championship level.

One of the coaches I reached out to was Steve Spurrier, who had just finished his second year at South Carolina. Heck, I had known Steve for years, and had actually helped coach against him when he was a star quarterback at Florida back in 1964.

There was no doubt that Steve had dominated the SEC during the 1990s as the Gator head coach, and anyone who knows anything about football recognizes him as one of the truly most innovative football minds of all time. He's a top-level man in my book, too.

Steve and I talked a few times on the telephone. He was honest as he could be and told me that under different circumstances he might very well be interested in the job, but he was in his early years of trying to lift the Gamecock program to a level it had never experienced. While I told him I understood, I told him I'd still like to visit with him in New York at the Hall of Fame dinner.

While I realistically knew Steve was also a long-shot at best, what was really frustrating to me was that some of our fans somehow got his telephone number and started calling him nonstop. Even more troublesome was that some of the fans started calling Nick Saban's agent, Jimmy Sexton. While I know their intentions were good, they were certainly not helping our cause in attracting a coach. In fact, their ill-conceived efforts to help actually hindered our initial communications with Jimmy when one of our team members did reach out to Jimmy.

I can't tell you the number of times during that first week of December that I received calls from prominent supporters and even Board members telling me that they had seen or been told that chat boards on the internet had reported I had a done deal with Coach Spurrier or Coach Saban.

There was one report that people had seen me dining with Steve Spurrier at the Bright Star Restaurant in Bessemer. There is no doubt someone may have seen me at the Bright Star but I can assure you I was never there with Coach Spurrier. And, quite frankly I found it hard to believe that anyone would think that if I did have Steve in Alabama that I would be so conspicuous to be entertaining him in a restaurant known for its clientele of Alabama fans.

There was another internet report about Nick and I playing golf at some resort in the Miami area. That was probably even more ridiculous. Heck, Nick had turned down a luncheon with the President of the United States one time because it interfered with a practice. You think he would take an afternoon off during the season to play golf with me or anyone else?

For anyone to suggest there was a done deal with Nick in December, 2006, well all I can say is there is nothing farther from the truth.

The New York Trip

On Sunday, December 3rd, one of my associate athletic directors, Jon Gilbert, flew with me to New York for the annual Football Foundation dinner and festivities. I didn't want anyone to know that while in New York to attend the Hall of Fame inductions my primary mission was to talk to three coaches about our opening.

I had, one of my team set up a private suite for me where I could talk to two candidates about the job. In my opinion it wasn't really an interview session but more an opportunity to discuss our job, gauge their interest and get a feel if they would fit into what we wanted and needed at the University.

Also, I really didn't think I would be doing my due diligence if I didn't have one more conversation with Steve Spurrier, so I met with him and his wife Jerri and told him, "Steve, I'm not going to another coach until you give me a definite answer that you aren't interested."

Steve was extremely cordial and he told me that under different circumstances he might be interested but the entire Spurrier family was now in the Columbia area and he felt comfortable with his situation at South Carolina.

One of my team had done an unbelievable job of securing the area where we couldn't be bothered by the media or anyone else, and I was thankful for that, because my first real session in New York was with Jimmy Sexton. Jimmy represented a number of the premier coaches in football, and in particular Nick Saban. My team had done a great job of setting what remained a very secret meeting with Jimmy at the Waldorf Towers in New York.

I hadn't met Jimmy before but was well acquainted with him, his professionalism and his tenacity in representing his clients. A few years earlier, I had talked with Jimmy about Chris Samuels, our former star lineman and one of Jimmy's clients, donating money for a scholarship. At the time Chris was one of the NFL's best linemen. That conversation about Chris had been my only contact with Jimmy until our meeting at the Waldorf Towers.

I really felt I had to sell him on the fact that we were determined to get it right at Alabama and if Coach Saban were interested, he was the one person that I wanted to at least engage in a conversation. I also had to ease the situation about him receiving so many unsolicited phone calls from our fans.

Jimmy didn't mince any words. Nick wasn't going to speak to me or any Alabama employee as long as the NFL season was in progress and the Miami Dolphins were still playing.

During our meeting, I showed Jimmy pictures of our facilities, and he was gracious enough to tell me that everyone was well aware of the advances we had made in upgrading our football facilities and Bryant-Denny Stadium. He also assured us that no high-profile coach would be interested in coming to Alabama if we hadn't joined the 21st Century in facilities.

In our conversation, Jimmy did confirm that it was true that Nick had expressed he wasn't overly enamored with the NFL. Nick had noted at one time that if he did leave the NFL that Alabama would be one of the few jobs that he might consider. Jimmy told me that he was not attending the banquet and was leaving the next day. Jimmy promised he would call me by a certain time on Wednesday and confirm if it might be possible to speak with Nick at the close of his NFL season.

I told Jimmy I had to hear back from him by the time we designated, and he said, "No problem." Let me emphasize, Jimmy wasn't going to call back and say Nick Saban would take the job. He was just going to let me know if he was indeed interested and would meet after the NFL season.

Jimmy's answer certainly was no surprise, so I planned to discuss the job with two other coaches on Tuesday, West Virginia's Rich Rodriguez and Rutgers' Greg Schiano.

That delay presented its own problems because I was feeling immense pressure from the athletic committee of the Board of Trustees as well as prominent people in the power structure to hire someone. Most of those people didn't think Nick would take the job. The prevailing theme from them to me was, "if we don't hire someone quickly then we will fail to hire a championship-caliber coach."

Every year in New York, the local alumni group has its annual Christmas party. For years whoever was serving as athletic director spoke to the group. Before we went to the event, Jon Gilbert and I went for a walk. Jon suddenly mentioned to me that he thought we were being followed by someone.

I had the same eerie feeling that we were being followed by someone as well. Jon told me that he was going to turn around and introduce himself to the person he thought was following us and when he did, it turned out to be Charles Goldberg of the *Birmingham News*. Charles wasn't just a sports writer for the News but the beat writer for Auburn!

When Jon introduced himself, I think it took Charles by surprise and he told us that he had been assigned by the News to try to find out what was going on with our coaching search. I thought it was bizarre on the part of the newspaper but this whole search was turning into quite an ordeal.

That same night when I was back in my room and on the telephone, I thought I heard someone up against the room door trying to listen to the conversation. I walked over to the door, looked through the peephole and saw a large man who appeared to be smoking a cigar or cigarette there, his ears seemingly glued to the wall.

By the time I unhooked the latch to the door, he was running down the hall. I never could tell who it was. I don't know if it was a reporter, some interested fan or a house burglar. I was getting a little paranoid, to put it mildly.

The banquet was Tuesday night. During the day on Tuesday we met in the private suite area of the Towers separately with Coach Rodriguez and his wife and Greg Schiano. I really thought we had productive meetings. Both were very interested in the job.

I thought Coach Rodriguez had a better chance of adapting to Alabama but I was impressed with both of them. Both articulated their plans to re-establish

Alabama as a force in college football and revive the championship spirit that had sadly faded over the years.

I don't remember how long I waited for Jimmy Sexton to call back the next day, but I stared at my phone for a long, long time. I called my team member who was in contact with Jimmy to ask if he had heard from him, and he told me to be patient. That was easy for him to say! When I didn't hear back from Jimmy at the appointed time, I contacted Coach Rodriguez.

My gut feeling as well as the advice of my team and my nephew Chuck was to wait until the NFL finished its season the first weekend in January and go for broke with Nick. Frankly, I should have never wavered from my gut feeling. For a lot of reasons, I ultimately offered the job to Coach Rodriguez, sensing he would not only accept it but could also build a championship program in Tuscaloosa.

About five or ten minutes after Rich had accepted the job, my phone rang. It was Jimmy Sexton. He was apologetic about being late, but his plane had been delayed and he was in the air with no cell phone coverage. My heart sank.

I just stared out my window and told Jimmy that I had offered the job to Rich and he had accepted. There was no turning back the clock.

I told Rich that I really didn't want a word of this to leak until we had a done deal and when I said a done deal, I meant a signed agreement. That wasn't going to be the case at all.

I had hardly gotten home that night before the telephone was ringing and satellite trucks were circling my neighborhood. Somehow the news had broken that Coach Rodriquez had been hired, though no official agreement had been reached and no announcement made.

To say my team was none too happy would be an understatement. I wasn't happy either about all of the media coverage indicating a deal was done but I did feel the University was close to reaching an agreement with Rich.

On Thursday, December 8, I was at my home with executive associate AD Finus Gaston and one of Coach Rodriquez's representatives discussing details of the contract when I heard the doorbell ring. We were in a private session and I didn't want to be bothered but I excused myself, went to the door and one of my team was there, telling me that he had some critical information for me.

We walked away from my house where we wouldn't be seen and he told me that I could forget Rodriguez that he was going to pull out later that night and we needed to focus on Nick Saban and forget the others. When I asked him how reliable his information was, he told me that it was impeccable. He had talked to our other team member who had been working the phones and had assured him the information was accurate.

They had never misled me before, but this was certainly another bizarre twist in the story. Here I am trying to finalize a contract with Rodriguez's agent and I'm being told that he was pulling out in the next few hours. My head was spinning to say the least.

True to form, not long after Rich's advisor had left my home, I received the word that Rich was holding a press briefing announcing he wasn't leaving West Virginia. I knew we had to get to work. I contacted my team and told them to meet me at my house Friday night, to park a block or two away where no one would see their cars, and bring every bit of information they had gathered We were going to have an all-night session, reassess where we were and move forward. It was another long night.

I told my administrative assistant and a critical member of our team, Judy Tanner, that I was going to stay home and work from there. She came to my house to help field the calls. I firmly instructed her that I was only talking to a few people: Dr. Witt and the athletic board. I was determined to have a winning game plan and have it that night.

It would be an all-nighter, too. On a cold December night with a few comical moments among those serious hours, we worked to pull off the coup of hiring Nick Saban.

Like I said, for all those claiming hiring Nick Saban was easy or a cinch, well they were sadly misinformed. It's easy to say someone is interested in a position; you have to go to a whole different level to actually get it done.

It would be a long three and a half weeks.

36

THE HIRING OF NICK SABAN

After Coach Rodriguez officially announced he was no longer a candidate for the job, I was determined that I was going to wait until the end of the NFL season and make an offer to Nick Saban. The piece of advice I would give whoever hires the next coach at Alabama is make sure you have the right man, no matter how long it takes.

At all schools, it seems, there is tremendous pressure to hire someone quickly to salvage a recruiting class. In reality, the only solution is to hire the best person for the job. It should be duly noted that the last two national championship coaches at Alabama weren't hired until January. The ensuing results on the playing field proved that hiring Gene Stallings and Nick Saban after the start of a new year paid dividends on the playing field as well as uniting our fan base.

Like I said, for anyone to suggest the hiring of Nick was easy or that it was a done deal early on, all I can say is they don't know what they are talking about. My confidential team members met me at my house in Tuscaloosa on December 9, 2006, a very cold Friday night. It would turn into an all-night meeting, too, as we prepared a game plan to hire Coach Saban.

I didn't want anyone to know that we were meeting, and as I mentioned, the media and fans were everywhere. I didn't want the team parking near my house, so they parked separately several blocks away, and then endured the frigid night walking them through several back yards to arrive for our meeting. I don't know if we would have finished earlier than past the midnight hour when we did finally call it a night, but we had several interruptions.

A couple of my associate ADs showed up unexpectedly to bring some information from the office. I quickly ushered the team members into the laundry room and told them to stay put until my visitors left. Frankly, I thought they wouldn't stay long but they didn't seem eager to leave. I finally told them I had had a long day and they shuffled off.

Finally, the team came out of the laundry room, and we had a good laugh when they joked about inhaling all the detergent fumes in there and I asked them why they didn't finish my laundry. I'm just glad they weren't claustrophobic because that room was the size of a closet.

Our conversation centered on Coach Saban and making sure we could afford to hire him. We didn't know a specific number but we knew what he was making in Miami. Frankly, Alabama had never been at the top of the list in paying salaries, at least dating back as far as I could remember.

When I was an assistant for Coach Bryant, we had one of the lowest paid staffs in the SEC. I knew I had to do a selling job to persuade everyone in power at the University that we were making the right decision in making Coach Saban the highest paid coach in college football.

And, he was going to have to take a pay decrease to accept the job, because he was making more than $5 million a year as the Miami Dolphins' head coach. My confidants brought financial documents from a number of different schools. I didn't ask them how they managed to obtain the detailed information, but the data was eye-opening and helpful, particularly the documents from other universities.

Significantly, Oklahoma's revenues had almost quadrupled from the time the Sooners hired Bob Stoops to two years later when he led them to the National Championship. At the time, Coach Stoops was the highest paid coach in the nation. Obviously, Oklahoma, a school with such a rich tradition, had struggled after Barry Switzer left there in the late 1980s. Their investment had paid off not only on the playing field but in the revenue department as well.

If we could hire Nick Saban for four million a year, I thought it, too, would ultimately pay dividends, because I knew, and had known for a long time, that he was the perfect coach for the Crimson Tide. We reviewed other possible candidates, too, but it always came back to Nick Saban.

While my telephone rang incessantly over the weekend, I didn't want to divulge much information to anyone until I had an opportunity to visit with Dr. Witt and Paul Bryant, Jr. Without their blessing on making a financial commitment that far exceeded what we had talked about in previous conversations, there would be little reason to continue conversations with Jimmy Sexton.

The next week I met with Dr. Witt and Paul, Jr., respectively to make sure I had their blessings before I made contact with Jimmy Sexton, and he agreed to come to Tuscaloosa and meet privately with me and one of my team. No one else was informed that Jimmy would be driving from Memphis a few days before Christmas, 2006.

My team met Jimmy outside of town and left his car with Memphis plates in a shopping center lot in Northport. The team drove him to my house to review all the information on the coaching job. Near the end of the meeting, I asked Jimmy does this mean we have a deal. He just laughed and said, "Mal, this is a deal contingent on Nick Saban deciding to meet with you!"

I replied, "You are either going to make me a hero or get me fired."

Throughout the entire process, Jimmy was a straight shooter and never misled me or my team at any time. Jimmy constantly stressed that Nick Saban was his own man and made his own decisions. Jimmy duly noted that while Coach Saban had expressed he really didn't like coaching in the NFL that much, there certainly was no guarantee that Nick was going to leave the Dolphins and its owner Wayne Huizenga.

When Jimmy and my team left, I called Dr. Witt to inform him of the meeting, and at least, we knew that our financial package would make him the highest paid coach in college football and was at least competitive with his contract with Miami. Naturally, I continued to receive numerous phone calls, and when I would tell the powers-to-be that Nick refused to talk to me or anyone employed by the University, I could sense the proverbial air leave the balloon. While I was encouraged by my meeting with Jimmy Sexton and I knew we had a good plan for follow up communication in place, I certainly knew that I had to start working on a back-up plan.

Our football team was preparing to play Oklahoma State in the Independence Bowl, and thankfully, my associate athletic director, Dr. Finus Gaston, handled all the details in his usual great fashion. Before I went to Shreveport on Christmas Day, I flew to Houston to visit with Mike Sherman, the former head coach of the

Green Bay Packers. At the time, Coach Sherman was the associate head coach of the Houston Texans.

I wanted to gauge Mike's interest in the position and came away impressed by him. Another coach who I visited with on two occasions was David Cutcliffe. We met in Birmingham and there was no doubt David was interested in the job. David had worked in our department back in the 1970s, and I always thought he had a brilliant football mind. He was always eager to learn and helped me out on offense and Coach Donahue on defense.

There is no doubt that David had done a superb job at Ole Miss, becoming the Rebels first coach to beat us twice since the legendary Johnny Vaught was coaching there. One thing that concerned me about David was his health, because he had to sit out a year because of some heart issues. He assured me he had a clean bill of health. I also knew that the top-ranked high school quarterback had told David he would sign with Alabama if he became the head coach.

While I was trying to solidify backup plans, I also had my responsibilities with the team during the week in Shreveport. It wasn't easy either. Thankfully, our interim coach, Joe Kines, helped ease the situation as much as possible.

While Joe by anyone's measure was an outstanding coach, I think anyone who has dealt with him would tell you that he's even a better person. Although he knew he wasn't going to be the head coach and the odds of him remaining on a new coaching staff were small, he not only prepared the team to compete but he went out of his way to call all of our recruits. He told the ones who were committed to us to stick to the Crimson Tide, and the ones who were still undecided, he asked them to meet with the new staff before they committed elsewhere.

The game was played on December 28, and we lost on a last minute field goal. Under the circumstances, I thought we played about as well as we could. While I was happy with the performance, I was eager to get back to Tuscaloosa and prepare for my trip to Miami. I still had not talked directly to Nick Saban. Jimmy Sexton and my team encouraged me to give it my best shot and my best recruiting spiel and bring Nick home to Tuscaloosa.

One of my team drove me back from Shreveport to Tuscaloosa and we re-hashed everything, making sure that every base was covered. I even called Lance Thompson, who had been on our staff under Coach DuBose and then with Nick at LSU, to see if he had any feel as to whether Nick would accept my offer. Lance

– who was coaching at Central Florida then – could only tell me, "Nick is his own man but I wish you well, Coach."

While Miami was playing its final game of the year on Sunday, December 31, at Indianapolis, I was on the phone planning my trip to Miami the next day. I don't know how many times my team and I called Jimmy Sexton to make sure Nick would see me, but I'm sure he probably got tired of his phone ringing.

I had made arrangements with my good friend in Huntsville, Farid Rafiee, to use his airplane for the trip. The good thing about Farid's plane was no one knew I was using it and I knew all the trackers would be keying in on other airplanes. Farid told me to use the plane as long as I needed it, but not to come back without the coach! That was a mantra I would hear from all of the few people who knew of my trip to Miami.

Interestingly, Farid's pilot is Bud Darby, the brother-in-law of my old quarterback Richard Todd. Bud reported to Farid that I had a worried look. That's probably the biggest understatement ever made. It was sleeting and cold when we quietly left Tuscaloosa on New Year's Day, 2007.

One of my team had set up a hotel near where Nick lived and had set me up with a driver he knew, Fancisco Rengifo or "Frankie," who had a Mercedes sedan. Frankie had been a top executive limousine driver and there wasn't a spot in the Miami area that he wasn't familiar with, including the Fort Lauderdale area where the Sabans lived. He stayed with me for the next two days and was a great help.

That night I was in constant contact with my team that was talking to Jimmy and the Sabans. True to his word, Nick still would not talk to me directly until he had a chance to talk to his team and his owner. To be honest, I almost gave up and came home.

That Tuesday morning, I actually checked out of the hotel and decided to go back to the airport and tell Bud to take me back to Tuscaloosa. I decided I'd make one last attempt to see Nick. Frankie drove me to the neighborhood where Nick and Terry lived and Jimmy got Terry to buzz me into the neighborhood.

Terry was the gracious lady she always is and was nice enough to invite me into their home. I like to think that she and I hit it off that day. At least that's the way, I remember it. She served me lunch and we chatted amicably, and she told me that Nick was still at his office, having his year-end meeting with the players. Thankfully, she invited me back that night for dinner, and I felt I would at least have a chance to try to sell Nick on coming to Alabama.

While Frankie and I were going back to the hotel, I learned later that Nick called Terry to tell her that he had decided not to visit with me that he was committed to staying with the Dolphins. Terry told me she told Nick that she had already invited me back that night and she wanted him to at least visit with me.

We had dinner and a productive give-and-take session, but I knew he was torn between coming back to college football or staying with Miami. When I left the house after dinner that night, I really thought it could go either way.

Fortunately, my team had been in constant contact with Jimmy who was also talking to Terry and Nick. Our team had also organized two very important calls with Nick and two of our Alabama legends. Both had a great deal of credibility with Nick and both were Alabama greats that knew how important getting Nick to Alabama would be for the program.

One, Ozzie Newsome had been a friend of Nick's since their NFL days with the Browns. The other, who has to be unnamed, had a long-standing relationship with Nick. Both did a great service to Alabama by discussing our program in coaching terminologies and why Nick would be a great fit, and why he and Terry should make the move.

No one will ever say Nick Saban doesn't do his homework or isn't totally prepared. I was told both were persuasive in easing any concerns Nick may have had about the Alabama job. Both Ozzie and our other caller were keenly aware of our problems and knew that only a person like Nick Saban could re-establish the Crimson Tide as a perennial challenger for championships.

Over the course of that Tuesday night and into Wednesday morning, I think Nick struggled making a decision, probably feeling he had a commitment to Miami but wanting to coach at the college level. Only he can answer that. I don't think it hurt that I believed Terry wanted to come back to college football. Terry was a major reason that Alabama was lucky enough to hire her husband.

When Nick went to meet with Mr. Huizenga that Wednesday morning, it is my understanding the Miami Dolphin owner made it easier by telling Nick to do what was in his best interest and what was in his heart. College football and Alabama, won out.

Now, the trick was getting Nick and his family to Tuscaloosa. That was not as easy as everyone thinks either. Nick called Terry and told her to start packing their bags, and I told Frankie that it would be Coach Saban, Terry and their daughter Kristen riding with me in the car to the hangar and Farid's plane. I knew it was going to be crowded, but when Kristen's friend, Nicole Francois, joined us I realized she was also going with us!

Frankie didn't know how we were going to get everyone in the car, much less where he was going to put everyone's bags. Let me interject this: Frankie didn't know anything about football and didn't have a clue that I was an athletic director much less how important Nick Saban was. I can only imagine what was going through his mind when he saw satellite trucks gathering around the house and helicopters hovering above.

After he backed into the garage area so we could load the car without the media glare, the three ladies crammed in the back seat, holding luggage, while I sat on the console and gear box and Nick squeezed in beside me with the window seat. I told Frankie to get us to the airport as fast as possible, and off we went, with the helicopters chasing us. We made quite a scene and must have truly looked like we were making some kind of *Escape From Miami* movie.

When we arrived at the airport, there were some smiles, especially from me. One of the workers there came running up to me and said, "Roll Tide, Coach Moore. You got us the man." He told me he was originally from Anniston and knew better days were ahead for us.

I had been in constant telephone contact with my team and Jimmy Sexton, and I think they felt as relieved as me that this seemingly endless chase for a coach was over. I had to call my nephew, Chuck, to tell him the news. Without his friendship with the Sabans, I'm not sure we could have ever pulled it off.

I joked with Chuck, and told him that Nick and I were just getting off the 18th green. He laughed and said, "Uncle Mal, I know you might have been playing golf, but there is no way Coach Saban would have been out there with you."

Our team continued the hard work during our flight to Tuscaloosa and got the word out. When we arrived at the Tuscaloosa airport there were literally thousands of people gathered to welcome the Sabans to Tuscaloosa. It was an unbelievable scene, particularly on such short notice. It meant a lot to the Sabans and even more to me. It was a great day for Alabama football to say the least.

Jimmy Sexton probably summed it up best. All the stars and planets had to be aligned perfectly for this hiring to take place. It had never been a cinch. On

Thursday, I officially introduced Nick Saban as the new football coach. For the first time, I felt relieved, because I knew we had the man who would restore Alabama football to its rightful spot in the college football hierarchy.

37

REVIVING THE PROGRAM

On our flight back to Tuscaloosa from Miami, Coach Saban looked at me and said, "Mal, you must think I'm a helluva good football coach, don't you?"

I said, "Damn, Nick, I wouldn't have spent so many sleepless nights if I didn't think you were the man for this job."

I'll never forget him saying, "There are a lot of good coaches out there, but I know how to recruit and get difference-makers. I can't coach without great players."

I answered back, "Nick that's the best thing I've heard you say."

If I ever had any lingering doubts about Coach Saban, that one statement erased them, because I knew we had some good players on campus, but we didn't have enough of them to fight every SEC Saturday against the endless row of heavyweights.

It didn't take long for Nick to leave his imprint on the program. I heard Coach Bryant say a million times, "You gotta have a plan." Great leaders have a plan of action, and Nick had one, too.

Nick had built championship programs before and his determination and demands for excellence had certainly upset some, but only brought a smile to my face. Frankly, it brought back memories of those days so long ago when I was a player and heard another coach change the expectation level of the players and staff members.

Certainly, I'm not going to speak for Coach Saban but I know he didn't feel some of the players bought into his program that spring. That would be a short-term problem but wouldn't be resolved overnight either.

If there was any doubt that our fans were eager for the Saban Era to begin, they erased any concerns at the annual A-Day game that April. I thought we would have a really nice crowd, mainly because our supporters love football, and they wanted to show their thanks to Nick for coming to Tuscaloosa from Miami.

Coach had also made a personal plea with them to attend the game because a big crowd could be the difference in selling a recruit on becoming a member of our program.

Well, Good Lord. I never in my wildest imagination dreamed we'd have a packed Bryant-Denny Stadium with over 90,000 there, plus have thousands more turned away by the fire marshals. It certainly opened some eyes, including mine. It was a statement to the college football world that the sleeping giant had been awakened.

Nick's first season had the expected see-saw results on the field with dramatic wins against Arkansas and Tennessee mixed with heartbreakers to Georgia and LSU. The final month proved much more difficult due to the unexpected textbook issue that would ultimately put us back on probation and erase a number of victories we had earned on the field.

On the eve of the Tennessee game, I was informed of the possibility that some of our athletes, particularly some football players and track athletes, had received free textbooks from the bookstore, which forced us to suspend five players, including center Antoine Caldwell, guard Marlon Davis and running back Glen Coffee.

Although we played a nearly perfect game in a 41-17 rout of Tennessee, the loss of the players certainly contributed to our late season collapse which led to a 7-6 season, including a win over Colorado in the Independence Bowl.

I'll never forget the utter joy in Nick's face after we had beaten Tennessee that October afternoon. We were standing there and I don't know who was happier, him or me, but he took time to say, "This is what Alabama football is supposed to be like."

I couldn't have said it better.

Then, Nick introduced me to a star recruit from Memphis who was also being courted heavily by Tennessee. I really didn't need an introduction to his dad because he had played basketball for us, and his grandfather had been a great basketball coach at North Alabama. The recruit was Barrett Jones and his dad Rex seemed awfully happy, too.

I don't know if that win played any role in Barrett choosing to be a member of the Crimson Tide, but I think that game showed we were definitely going to be back a lot sooner than a lot of our rivals would have liked.

I want to say this about the textbook situation. Our associate athletic director for compliance at the time, Chris King, did a superb job of sifting through a maze of paperwork, finding out exactly what the problem had been and setting the course to correct it. The gist of the issue was a worker in the bookstore who was friendly with the athletes, was giving the athletes textbooks, which was an extra benefit.

The players did repay the full amount of the costs of the books and had their eligibility restored after sitting out four games.

Despite the disappointment of that particular situation and mixed results on the field, I had no doubt that we were in for a run in college football that would again make the Crimson Tide name one to respect and envy.

I had no doubt whatsoever that Nick Saban was the right man for the job when we hired him. Watching him work only enhanced my feeling about him both personally and as a coach. He was A-plus in my book.

He has been called a "relentless recruiter" by analysts but I think that only covers part of his pursuit for excellence. Nick works at recruiting just like he does coaching. He has his own unique style, in which he measures the potential of an athlete not only by his accomplishments on the field but a range of qualities from academics to personal background.

One thing that has changed dramatically in recruiting since I was an assistant is that many of the players' primary goal now is to make it to the NFL. Frankly, back when I was playing, and certainly when I was coaching in those early years, there wasn't much money in pro football. The NFL was a goal of only a few elite players.

Nick has many selling points about the University, including our heritage, facilities and academic excellence. Just as important, he also has a resume replete with a list of players who have excelled at his respective stops in college football and gone on to the pros to earn life-changing money.

I also feel strongly that Nick Saban has his strongest ally and supporter in his wife, Terry. Together they form a team that bonds with the recruits and their families. No one can understate the importance of a coach and his family finding that common link with a recruit.

When all the recruiting gurus finished grading Alabama's 2008 class, most had it ranked among the best in all of college football. As far as I'm concerned the work that Nick and his staff did in recruiting that class elevated Alabama to a status that we hadn't enjoyed in nearly two decades. It was probably the best group of young players I had ever seen on the practice field, and that is saying something.

With young men like Julio Jones and Mark Ingram, I knew our offense would be on a different level, and I'll never forget visiting with long-time practice official Eddie Conyers after a scrimmage in August of 2008.

Eddie started officiating practices back in the early 1960s, and he has had a first-hand look at some bad and an awful lot of very good football players over the years.

When I asked him what he thought, Eddie said, "They are going to win at least 10 games and the reason why is they have the big nose guard, Terrence Cody, who is just going to stuff the run and nobody knows about him."

Our opening game was going to be against Clemson in the Georgia Dome, and we knew it was one of those games that could forever change the psyche of the program.

Nick and I had discussed scheduling philosophies and he felt strongly that he wanted to play a nationally ranked opponent in one of the non-conference games. The concept of playing at a neutral site had an appeal to him because he felt gaining exposure nationally would help us in the recruiting wars, too.

I don't think you can understate the importance of winning a game to boost the energy and confidence not only in the team but the fan base as well. When I hear announcers talk about signature wins I know what they mean, but I'm talking about something even deeper than that. I'm talking about changing the course of the program, not for a few weeks or a season, but for a generation.

That happened when we beat Southern California in 1971. It re-established in the minds of the nation that Alabama was indeed back. I think the same thing happened in 1990 when we went to Knoxville and beat Tennessee. The players began to believe and the result was a remarkable seven-year run under Coach Stallings.

When we finalized the game with Clemson, I know there were some naysayers among our fans who thought if we lost the season opener, the lingering effects could impact the whole season. One thing I knew, though, was Nick Saban loves the challenge and his intensity and will to win certainly convinced me that there was soon to be a lot of winning going on in Tuscaloosa.

I felt deeply that 2008 was about to be a special year for the Crimson Tide and Alabama would return to its rightful spot in the college football hierarchy.

38

RETURN TO GLORY

I'd be disingenuous if I didn't say I felt immense personal pride, not only in the transformation of our football team, but I was also overwhelmed by a call I received from Dr. Witt and the Board of Trustees even before Coach Saban began to work his magic. The University was going to honor me, and my family, by naming the football complex in my honor.

I certainly felt there were many other individuals, who were more deserving, but I told him that no one would be more humbled than I to receive such a recognition. I meant that, too.

Having my daughter Heather come in from Arizona with her husband Steve and my grandchildren Anna Lee and Cannon at the ceremony was very special to me. Equally important was having nearly 70 family members there, including all my surviving siblings as well as a host of nephews, nieces and cousins.

There were so many friends there, too. It was a very humbling experience for me, in such a way by the University I loved. It meant so much to me and my family to be honored in March, 2007.

One day I was watching practice from my office window and someone asked me how it felt to watch the team from "my" building. It didn't register with me at first. I thought this building may have my name but it belongs to every player and coach who sweated and bled to make Alabama the special place it is.

There were some awfully sad moments for me, too. I got a call one morning from Coach Stallings telling me that his beloved son, John Mark, had passed away. I could only imagine the grief that Gene and Ruth Ann felt.

I had been a player at the University when Johnny was born back in 1962 and I had been one of Coach Stallings' graduate coaches when I rejoined the University in 1964, so I knew first-hand the commitment and loyalty the Stallings family had for their son. Back when Johnny was born, a lot of folks tried to encourage Coach and Ruth Ann to put their newborn, who had been diagnosed with Down Syndrome, under special care.

There was no doubt the Stallings family felt they could do a better job in their own home, and they did.

When I was hired by Gene in 1986 to work for the Cardinals, I really got to know Johnny well. He had grown into a man who had a unique quality of making everyone around him feel better. He was a special person who bonded with everyone who was lucky enough to cross his path.

I'll always remember Johnny helping our trainer Bill McDonald or Ken Gaddy and his folks at the Bryant Museum. He always brought a smile to my face and I'll never forget the final time I saw him.

Coach Stallings hosts an annual golf tournament in Tuscaloosa to raise money for RISE, a special school for youngsters afflicted with learning disorders, and the building on campus is named after Johnny.

Johnny would always make that trip back to Tuscaloosa for the tournament, and I was visiting with him on that last trip he made. He asked about my family, because he always remembered people and their names. I told him Heather and her family were doing great.

When he said, "Mal, how is Charlotte doing?" I wanted to cry. I just told him she was doing okay, even though she had long been in the LaRocca Nursing Home and I couldn't even remember the last time she said my name.

I just wished she had been there with me, to visit with Johnny and see the football complex named after me and be part of the revival of Alabama football. Johnny died in the summer of 2008 and I joined a long list of mourners who traveled to Paris, Texas to pay respects to a man who truly made a difference in so many lives. Johnny had loved the Crimson Tide, and I only wish he could have been there with me to watch what was about to take place.

Watching our football team return to glory days was thrilling to me. It had been my most sincere wish when I became Athletic Director, to watch Alabama regain its rightful spot in the college football hierarchy and it happened during those two unforgettable seasons.

When I walked into the Georgia Dome to watch us compete against nationally-ranked Clemson, I felt some of that old adrenalin rush I'd felt so many times when I watched the Crimson Tide roll on the field for its pre-game warm-ups. I just knew in my soul that Alabama was on the brink of something special, and it happened that night as we dominated the Tigers.

That 2008 team had one of the best offensive lines I'd ever seen with All-American players like center Antoine Caldwell, guard Mike Johnson and tackle Andre Smith. They could just dominate like few lines I'd seen and their coach Joe Pendry had the ability to make them play at a high level.

John Parker Wilson blossomed as a quarterback under Coach Jim McElwain and there was no doubt that those players I'd been so impressed with in practice, Julio Jones and Mark Ingram, were indeed difference makers. My old buddy Eddie Conyers had been right: "Mount Cody" completely shut down the middle of the field against the run.

While I am sure there were still a lot of doubters after our win over Clemson, I wasn't one of them. I knew 2008 would be much like our 1971 season. For once I was right.

There were so many magnificent wins that year, including going over to Athens and beating a Bulldog team with its superb quarterback Matthew Stafford. Georgia wore black that night and the crowd responded as well in "Black out Alabama Night." It didn't do them much good. It was more like a "black and blue" night for the Bulldogs.

I think the game that really reinforced the idea that we were a contender was the overtime win over LSU in Baton Rouge. It was one of the most hostile football environments I'd ever seen, mainly because the intensity of the rivalry had escalated to a heightened level with Coach Saban now coaching for Alabama.

After Rashad Johnson intercepted a pass in overtime to stop LSU's attempt to score and quarterback John Parker Wilson sneaked over for the winning touchdown, Alabama was Champion of the SEC West for the first time since 1999. It was a milestone win, but so was the 36-0 romp over Auburn that finally ended the Tigers' six-game winning streak over us.

Our chance to play in the National Championship game ended a week later when we lost a heartbreaker to Florida in the SEC Championship game. Like all big games, it came down to a few plays and the Gators made one or two more than we did.

While it was disappointing to miss such an opportunity and then to play without much intensity in the Sugar Bowl, neither of the final two games should diminish what that team did. It pointed the spotlight back on Alabama and showed the way for the 2009 season, probably one of the best, if not the best season, in Crimson Tide football history.

I'm not sure if any team in the history of college football could surpass what the 2009 team accomplished, especially considering its 14-0 run to the National Championship. It vanquished unbeaten and defending champion Florida in the SEC Championship game and then finished off unbeaten and No. 2 Texas in the BCS Championship in Pasadena at the historic Rose Bowl Stadium.

There were a lot of memorable Saturdays before the final game that proved this team had the heart of a champion. Sometimes I wonder if football experts really appreciate how difficult it is to go through a season unbeaten and how many land mines you have to step over in order to do it.

No team plays at its peak every week. It's impossible, no matter how well coached a team may be. Coach Bryant once told me that you're lucky if you get a team to play at its highest level three times a year. I think that's pretty much accurate. He also used to warn the staff and the players about becoming complacent and taking on the same attitude as the fans, because that's when upsets usually occur. When the fan base doesn't think the opposing team has a chance, you really have to get the attention of your team not to fall into that trap.

Nick Saban does a superb job of teaching that particular football axiom; and he also drives his players to compete within themselves and at their highest level no matter the opponent.

Well, in 2009 Nick did about as good a coaching job as you'll ever see. He also had to find some magic to win when our team didn't respond with their A game, especially the 12-10 win over Tennessee in Tuscaloosa.

In that game "Mount" Cody blocked two fourth quarter field goals, including one on the final play of the game, to clinch the win and keep us alive in the championship race. Players making plays. You have to have that dynamic, especially in a game when the odds seem stacked against you.

We also trailed LSU midway in the fourth quarter when Greg McElroy hit

Julio Jones on a perfectly designed screen pass that went the distance for the winning score. Then there was that drive at Auburn that brought back memories of one that Steadman Shealy engineered against the Tigers in our drive to the 1979 championship.

When McElroy hit Roy Upchurch for the winning touchdown in Auburn, I felt that we had not only escaped the ultimate trap game but we were indeed destined to return to the Championship, even though Florida would be the foremost challenge. Quite simply, the Gator team with Tim Tebow and a cast of future NFLers posed a challenge of epic proportions.

On road games, I'd ride on one of the team buses next to Terry Saban. I don't know which one of us would get more nervous, her or me. I told her one time that I think when I was coaching I never got as nervous because I had to concentrate so much on the game. Her understanding of the game is on the highest level, and she coaches just about every play, just about as intensely as Nick.

As I mentioned earlier, I love poetry, reciting it, too. I started quoting poems to her on the bus. I don't think it calmed either one of us very much, but we both got a good laugh out of it. I got a big laugh when I found out she told Nick I recited poems to her and asked him why he didn't do that for her.

You can imagine his response to Terry on that one.

I admit I was somewhat uptight when I walked on the field during the warm-ups before the 2009 SEC Championship game, but I also had a calming feeling that we were going to win. I knew our team was coiled and ready. They were also eager to erase that year-long memory of losing to Florida in the Georgia Dome.

I'm not sure if I've ever seen a team play so well. That was definitely one of those peak performances that coaches strive so hard to help their team achieve. Greg McElroy probably played the best game of his career. So did Mark Ingram. The defensive play was simply brilliant. When Javier Arenas intercepted Tebow in the fourth quarter, the victory was pretty much iced and Alabama was back on its way to the National Championship. It had been a long time coming since that trip to New Orleans to take on Miami in the Sugar Bowl in 1992.

The week after the 32-13 win over Florida, Mark Ingram became Alabama's first-ever Heisman Trophy winner. Being there to see this exceptional young man and player accept the award made the ending of 2009 about as good as it can get. There were Alabama fans everywhere in New York. When we walked into the awards ceremony, you would have thought you were at a pep rally in Tuscaloosa. Fans clad in crimson were everywhere, yelling "Roll Tide." Alabama was indeed back.

Maybe, I'm old school and feel the bowl games are special because, in most cases, it is the one time every year players have the opportunity to enjoy themselves and celebrate their accomplishments of the season. However, being in the Championship Game is different. It becomes business because of the high stakes at hand. I know; I felt it as a player and as a coach.

This was my first experience as an administrator and I had complete confidence in the preparation of the team and the emphasis Nick instilled in our team that we were in California to beat Texas and win a Championship. There was little doubt that Nick had to get the attention of the team because Texas had a great team and there was always that concern of a letdown after being at such a peak against Florida.

Being at the Rose Bowl really brought back memories. I thought about 1961 when Alabama almost received an invitation but was rebuffed. I also thought about those early teams of Wallace Wade and Frank Thomas and how they had traveled by train from Tuscaloosa to Pasadena and brought back Championships. How I could not think about our fight song an those inspiring words, "Remember the Rose Bowl!"

One day I was in the hotel lobby visiting with some of our fans who stopped by to say hello, and we talked about the legacy of the Rose Bowl and how the Crimson Tide had forever changed Southern football with its trips to California. I told them when I was a kid growing up in Dozier, Alabama, I had gone to those cowboy movies downtown and became enthralled with Johnny Mack Brown, not knowing at the time that he'd been a star on the 1925 team that beat Washington and won Alabama the National Championship.

I think these particular fans got a pretty good laugh when I told them I had met six Presidents, foreign dignitaries, renowned entertainers and some of the most memorable athletes in history, but the one person I was most in awe of was Johnny Mack Brown.

He came to one of our games at Legion Field back in the late 1960s or early 1970s and he came by the locker room. Now that was special!

Beating Texas (37-21) that night was especially gratifying for everyone who cheers for the Crimson Tide, not just because they were a time-honored opponent, but because we had lost so many excruciating games to them, including a few that involved a controversial non-call or two.

By Nick Saban's standards, I don't think it was one of the team's best games, but it certainly had some highlight reel moments, including Trent Richardson's long TD run and Mark Ingram's clincher. Defensively, it couldn't get much better than Marcel Dareus's TD run on the interception of the "whoopee pass" or Eryk Anders' sack causing a fumble on the goal line.

When I was coaching, we used the "whoopee pass," also known as the Utah pass, because it is about a safe a play as you can run. That's the only time I ever saw it result in a turnover, let alone a touchdown.

Finishing 14-0 and returning to the pinnacle of college football was especially gratifying to me because the joy I saw in the eyes of the coaches, players and our fans was irreplaceable. After 17 years, Alabama was again the king of college football.

39

DEALING WITH LIFE'S
TRAGIC MOMENTS

When we returned home to Tuscaloosa the day after our victory over Texas, my first stop was to visit Charlotte at her nursing home. Although she had been there for nearly a decade, I made a daily trip to see her when I was home.

Friends would ask me why I would go to see her so frequently when her condition had debilitated to a point where all she really did was lie in her bed, unaware of her surroundings. Well, I felt it was my responsibility and I felt in her soul she knew I was there. I know if our situations had been reversed, she would have been there for me, too.

While I would be dishonest to say that her condition didn't depress me, I always felt an inner peace and serenity after one of my visits. In my heart, I think she felt the same way.

A week after the National Championship game, I was getting ready to go to work and I had a sinking feeling that was only enhanced when I got a call from an attendant at the LaRocca Nursing Home. The attendant told me that Charlotte had taken a turn for the worse. They didn't think she was going to make it.

I drove about as fast as I could to get there to be with her in her final moments, but I was too late. I was crushed because I felt I needed to be there with her. That was Monday, January 18, 2010. After 41 years of marriage that included all those years that I watched her drift away as a result of her fight with Alzheimer's. I was

242

devastated.

Keith Pugh, who had been our go-to receiver on our 1979 National Championship team, had gone on to become a minister and I asked him to deliver his message of faith at her funeral, which was held at Calvary Baptist Church, the same chapel where we'd been married in the summer of 1968. It was a difficult day.

Charlotte always had a great concern for others and had been the best coach's wife imaginable. She had been the parent for our daughter Heather while I was either in the office breaking down film or on the practice field preparing for another game or on the road recruiting.

I'll always remember our coming back to Tuscaloosa in 1990. She was already exhibiting signs of a memory disorder, but despite her lapses, she had some magical moments as a human being.

In the early 1990s, we came to know a little man who was physically and mentally afflicted about as badly as anyone I'd ever known. His name was Don Fuller, but we all called him Squeaky because he couldn't talk but just kind of squeaked. Apparently, his family had dropped him off at Bryce Hospital when he was a little boy and left him in Tuscaloosa. During the ensuing years, he had managed to survive and learn to take care of himself about as well as he possibly could.

He had become a symbol in our department, even having a desk in the old sports information office in Coleman Coliseum. He loved the Crimson Tide and Coach Stallings had a particular affection for him. I don't think it was any coincidence that he started hanging out around the coaches.

One day after practice, I was the last one to leave and it was raining and Squeaky was there by himself. I asked him if he needed a ride and he hopped in my car. He was trying to point me to where he lived but I couldn't find his little apartment.

I told him that I was going to take him home with me for the night and Charlotte made the biggest fuss over him, taking care of him like a little boy. She cleaned him up, fed him, and even got up several times during the night to check on him, bringing him some extra cover when she thought he was getting too cold. That might sound like a corny story to some, but to me, it just showed what a wonderful, kind heart she had. I feel blessed to have been wedded to her. I miss her every day.

After her burial in Dozier, I knew I needed to get back to work. I returned to Tuscaloosa and prepared for yet another phase in the completion of the football stadium. My primary mission was overseeing the south end zone expansion at Bryant-Denny Stadium. Coach Saban had come to me during the 2007 season and suggested we start looking at completing the stadium and making it a 100,000-plus structure.

There was no doubt that the record crowd at A-Day for Coach Saban's first spring game and subsequent sellouts and long waiting lists for tickets certainly made that suggestion a sensible one. We began work and by early 2010, we were nearing the completion of the structure that would make the stadium one of the best in all of college football.

I could only think back to the first time I walked in what was then Denny Stadium as a recruit back in 1957. There were probably about 20,000 fans in a stadium that seated 31,000. We officially dedicated the renovation the night before we opened the 2010 season with a 48-3 win over San Jose State. A week later we beat Penn State in what was the first major game that year in the newest edition of Bryant-Denny.

The rest of the season didn't go nearly as well as we struggled in the back half, losing to South Carolina, LSU and Auburn. Even though all three of those schools had excellent teams, especially Auburn, which won it all, I know Nick didn't feel like the team had responded to the challenges in the manner he expected.

There was a prevailing sentiment the next spring that the 2011 team would be special. That school year would be one of the greatest in Crimson Tide history when we won National Championships in four sports. I know as Athletic Director, you couldn't ask for much better than that.

However, all of those magnificent championship moments certainly were secondary in everyone's thoughts when a devastating tornado ripped through Tuscaloosa and other Alabama towns that April 27.

I was sitting in my office, literally watching the tornado on the horizon. It appeared to be headed straight toward Bryant-Denny so I and other staffers headed down to the training room on the bottom level of the football complex.

Although the path of the tornado missed the stadium and the other athletic complexes, its destruction near the campus was indescribable. Not only were buildings leveled but, more importantly, lives were lost. Among our athletes there were no fatalities, but two who lost their lives off-campus really stung me.

Our long snapper, Carson Tinker, survived but tragically, his girlfriend Ashley Harrison didn't. And I was really hurt by the death of Loryn Brown. She was the daughter of one of our former star players, Shannon Brown, who had gone on to become a successful high school coach.

I had recruited Shannon back in 1992 and he had developed into an outstanding defensive lineman for us during the 1992-95 seasons. Loryn was a little girl when Shannon was playing, and I could see her running around the practice field waiting for her dad to come hug her after we finished a session.

Shannon was living up in Madison, Alabama, and he drove frantically to Tuscaloosa to try to find her when he learned the storm had hit and he wasn't able to get her on the phone. When he finally found what remained of her residence, the coroner asked Shannon if he could identify his own daughter.

My heart ached for him when he told me the story. I can't imagine the pain he felt that day. When we played Vanderbilt for homecoming that fall, the city and university honored all of the responders who helped during this tragic time and the families who endured the tragedy. I thought it only fitting that we have Shannon serve as the honorary captain that night.

I know it hardly alleviated his personal pain, but I hoped he knew that his Alabama family members shared in his anguish.

Despite those difficult days, there would be some moments on the athletic fields that helped reunite the community and boost its morale.

Although a lot of the focus was on the football team, I was just as proud of the efforts of Sarah Patterson's gymnasts, Mic Potter's women's golf team and Patrick Murphy's softball squad. About the only disappointment was the men's golf team losing on the final hole for the national title. Under the format used in men's golf, I think it might be the toughest championship of them all to win. I felt badly for Jay Seawell and his team because I know they felt like I did. They were the best team in the country.

Winning the second national championship in football in three years wasn't easy either. Not only did we have to overcome an early November loss to LSU at Bryant-Denny, but we were competing in the toughest division of college football. Late in the season, LSU, Alabama and Arkansas were all ranked among the top-four in the polls, an absolutely amazing situation.

I really felt throughout the season that we had the best team but the LSU game was a downer. We lost 9-6 in overtime in a game of field goals, although I thought we had controlled the game and missed a number of opportunities to win. To LSU's credit, the Tigers never backed down to our challenges and stopped us repeatedly when we got within the shadows of their goal posts.

Regardless of the outcome, that was a special night for college football. CBS aired the game at prime time and the demand for tickets was unimaginable. Dignitaries from all over the country wanted to be there.

Robert Kraft, the owner of the New England Patriots, was among the many guests in attendance. He told me that this was not only football at its very best but what he had witnessed made him proud to be an American. The spirit of competition between the two schools and the classy manner in which they competed made a lasting impression on Mr. Kraft, who went on to tell me that he wished it was like this in the NFL.

I wish I could remember everyone we helped get tickets to this game. I do remember meeting baseball star Derek Jeter of the New York Yankees, basketball legend LeBron James of the Miami Heat, and renewing my friendship with one of our former cheerleaders and now movie star Sela Ward.

Because of the BCS structure, we knew we had to have a lot of luck sneaking through the backdoor into the Championship game. We received a lot of help when Iowa State beat Oklahoma State and Stanford upset Oregon to move us back to No. 2 in the polls and set up the rematch with LSU.

Playing LSU again was certainly a challenge, especially in their backyard at the Louisiana Superdome but I think all the coaches and players relished that challenge, especially since they felt we had the better team.

One morning I got up early in New Orleans and decided to take a solo walk and reminisce about all those other memorable games the Crimson Tide had played in the "Crescent City". We were staying at the Marriott on Canal and I wanted to go visit the Roosevelt where we had stayed back in 1961. I never thought I would be in such a grand hotel.

We had also stayed there when we lost that heartbreaker to Notre Dame and again when we won the last championship for Coach Bryant against Arkansas. Talk about memories flooding though me. Although this technically wasn't the Sugar Bowl, it was still that to me and I always felt that New Orleans was kind of our second home.

I took time to visit with Billy Neighbors, my close friend and old teammate. His grandson Connor (whose dad Wes was a great center for the Crimson Tide) was a fullback on the LSU team and we shared a laugh about who he was going to pull for in the championship game. I was more concerned, though, that Billy wasn't feeling well, and that wasn't anything to laugh about.

That night in the Dome, the Alabama defense played about as dominating a game as you'd ever see, allowing LSU to cross the 50-yard line only one time. A.J. McCarron was the game's MVP and deservedly so. He played the quarterback position flawlessly and continually pushed the ball down the field against LSU's great defense.

Our kicker Jeremy Shelley hit five straight field goals to virtually cinch the win, but I was still glad to see Trent Richardson break free for a touchdown in the fourth quarter, mainly because the two teams had played seven quarters and one overtime period without either one of them being able to cross the goal line.

There was a lot of jubilation that night and in the ensuing months, the gymnasts, women golfers and softball team would bring home championship hardware as well. Watching those teams compete to become champions was special, too.

Amidst all those championship moments, though, I was asked to deliver eulogies at the funerals of two of my old teammates, Bobby Skelton and Billy Neighbors. My concern about Billy in New Orleans, I guess, was prophetic. A few months later a heart attack claimed his life.

I couldn't help think about sitting around the dorm as a freshman and hearing Billy tell us he had read up on Coach Bryant in the library and he might be the meanest man alive, or having Billy tell me that Coach Bryant had passed away and we both cried. Losing Billy touched me deeply.

Friends are forever, and I had lost one of the best.

40

HALL OF FAME YEAR

B ack in December of 2011, I had received a call from my good friend Edgar Weldon telling me that I had been elected as a member of the State of Alabama Sports Hall of Fame and would be enshrined in May. Frankly, I was stunned to receive such recognition, and during the enshrinement dinner, I duly noted that there were a lot of folks more deserving, but none more appreciative than I was.

Having grown up in the state and having had the unique opportunity to have become friends with so many of the great athletes and coaches who forever impacted Alabamians was a treasure to me, but to be enshrined with them, now that was indeed special.

Among the class of inductees in 2012 were my old teammate Charley Pell, who went on to be the head coach at Jacksonville State, Clemson and Florida; and E.J. Junior, our great defensive end back in 1978-80. Sadly, Charley was inducted posthumously, but it was great to renew my friendship with E.J.

Actually, E.J. was a member of the team in St. Louis when I coached the Cardinals. He was one great player, too, and I tell you he was the master of the big play. I'll never forget him blocking a punt at Missouri in 1978. Rickey Gilliland picked it up and ran it for a touchdown, and that kind of flipped the whole game. In 1979, he scored our first touchdown when he intercepted a pass against Georgia Tech, returning it for a touchdown.

After about a dozen years in the NFL, he got into coaching and became the head coach at Central State University in Ohio. Being enshrined with the entire group was humbling but especially being commemorated with E.J. and Charley.

I'll never forget when Ozzie Newsome was chosen to the Hall of Fame and he made the statement that there are ought to be two Halls of Fame, one for Coach Bryant and one for the rest of us. Probably no one could relate to Ozzie's statement better than I could. Frankly, being included with Ozzie and all those others was something I wasn't sure I deserved either.

During that same week of the state's ceremony, we hosted our annual scholarship golf tournament in Tuscaloosa. One of our celebrity guests was Archie Manning, who had become a good friend of mine through those many years that had passed since he was such a great player at Ole Miss. He is an even a better representative for college football as a spokesperson and a key member of the National Football Foundation's Hall of Fame.

One year when we were in New York for the Hall of Fame function, Archie brought his youngest son Eli to lunch at the 21 Club, where a group of us would congregate every December. Eli had helped the New York Football Giants win the Super Bowl earlier that year. I told Eli as good as he and his brother were, they still weren't as good in college as their Dad.

Eli smiled and said something to the effect that a lot of people had told him and Peyton that over the years, but Archie never once had.

Anyway, I was so appreciative of Archie taking time from his schedule to come to Tuscaloosa and participate in our fund-raiser. Archie pulled me aside and told me he wanted to make a special announcement. He stood before the gathering and announced that the National Football Foundation and Hall of Fame had chosen me as the 2012 recipient of the John Toner Award, which goes annually to the best athletic director in the nation. I was shocked, thrilled and appreciative of winning this recognition.

That was quite an honor for me, but I want to say this and I mean it. Awards may be given to individuals, but they are always won by teams. I had a great group working with me, and there's little doubt any accolades I received were related to the University's hiring of Nick Saban and the Championships he helped bring home to Tuscaloosa.

While being recognized by my state and by the National Hall of Fame were special, so was having the Tuscaloosa Caring Days Center named in honor of Charlotte and me. Caring Days is a facility where individuals with memory afflictions are cared for, and the new facility in Tuscaloosa was a state-of-the-art center in which everyone in the community should take great pride.

The 2012 football season would really be memorable as we marched toward another National Championship, the 10th for me as a player, coach and administrator.

That August, I wasn't feeling very well and checked into DCH to have a few tests run on my heart. I received a good report and was back at work in a few days, readying for a football season that would result in our run to play Notre Dame in the championship game in Miami.

Again, it was a remarkable season, including that dramatic win at Tiger Stadium against LSU when A.J. McCarron connected with T.J. Yeldon on a screen pass in the final seconds to secure a 21-17 victory. The next week we suffered a tough lost at home to Texas A&M and its dynamic quarterback, Johnny Manziel.

The Sunday after the game against the Aggies, I went down to Nick's office and let him know I understood how he felt and encouraged him to keep the faith. While we chatted, he said he'd never coached against a better player than Manziel and he was almost impossible to defend. I told him that he reminded me of David Palmer when we used him at quarterback during some special moments in the 1993 season.

I don't know if anyone realistically thought that teams above us in the polls would drop like they had the previous year, but that's exactly what happened. There was a lot of celebrating down on the Strip near campus when Stanford beat Oregon in overtime and set up a very meaningful SEC championship game. In essence, it was a playoff game.

Whoever won our game with Georgia would play Notre Dame for the title in January, and I don't think there's ever been a better SEC Championship game than that one. Eddie Lacy was the game's MVP and I want to say this about Eddie. I've been around football for an awfully long time and I don't think I ever saw a back play like he did those final games of his career. He was simply amazing, just unstoppable.

After we beat Georgia at the final whistle, I think everyone in crimson felt like we had survived a heavyweight championship bout in which both sides had left everything on the field. It was a sense of relief more than euphoria. While I was so proud and happy for our coaches and team, I felt for Mark Richt, the Georgia staff and players. I've been on both sides of games like that and you never forget the agony of defeat.

Now it was time for the annual trip to New York and the Hall of Fame ceremonies. Being recognized by the Football Foundation certainly was a high point but I'd be remiss in not mentioning that another honoree that night was Barrett Jones, our great offensive lineman who had been chosen as the nation's top student-athlete for 2012.

Barrett started at three different positions for three National Championship teams, an accomplishment that will likely never be duplicated. His courage on the football field during the SEC Championship and Notre Dame games was inspiring. Few people knew how badly he was injured, and the difficult surgery he faced after the BCS game. That type of courage on the field coupled with his athletic and academic achievements make him one of the most remarkable players in the history of college football.

Our win over Notre Dame capped a most memorable year for me. There haven't been many individuals fortunate enough to work for both of these tradition-rich universities, and being a member of that select fraternity is especially meaningful to me.

I can't tell you the number of interviews I had with national as well as local media members leading up to the game. When I was asked how I thought the game would end, I told them I just hoped the best team would win. Deep down inside, I felt we were better and had a distinct edge in our passing game.

A.J. McCarron was nearly flawless. So was Eddie Lacy, who set the tone of our 42-14 win with his touchdown on the first drive.

When we had our National Championship celebration and I was asked to say a few words, I mumbled something to the effect that I was sure glad Nick Saban was on our side, and I meant it, too. He had certainly restored the pride in everyone who has ever worn those jerseys but all of those who cheer on the Crimson Tide.

One thing we all share is our legacy of winning and the pride we have for Alabama in our crimson hearts.

THE EPILOGUE

Ronny Robertson was a standout linebacker for the Crimson Tide from 1972-74. He joined the athletic staff in 2005, serving as Senior Associate Athletic Director. He was one of Mal Moore's closest friends and confidants.

By Ronny Robertson

I first met Mal Moore in August of 1970 when I reported as a freshman to play football for Alabama. Since Mal was an offensive coach and I was playing linebacker, I didn't have much interaction with him during my five years as a player for the Crimson Tide.

Yet, during my time at the University, my teammates and I considered Mal as a "straight-shooter" and a player's coach who was respected, I repeat, respected by all. Little did I realize, or know then, that some 35 years later, I would receive a phone call from him that would change my life and create a chapter for which I will be forever indebted to him.

That phone call came in January of 2005. Mal asked if I would come to Tuscaloosa to spend the day with him. I had been briefed by the friend from whom Mal had gotten my number that he wanted me to visit with him regarding raising money for the athletic department. Frankly, I had no interest in the job.

However, out of respect for Mal Moore, I made what I thought was merely an obligatory trip from New Orleans to Tuscaloosa to spend some time with Mal, a man I had seen only a handful of times since I finished my playing career in 1974. Mal and I spent that entire January day together. He took me on a tour of every single athletic facility, showing me the improvements that had been made, and his vision of those that would be made in the future -- provided the money could be raised.

The rest is history. I accepted his job offer to return to the University and help him raise $50 million, the goal he had set for his campaign to improve the athletic facilities at the University of Alabama. He named it the Crimson Tradition Campaign and it was the first capital campaign ever undertaken by the athletic department at the University.

Through the love, dedication and financial support of thousands of Crimson Tide faithful we exceeded our $50 million goal in 2007 with over $70 million in private gifts and pledges.

Beginning with this campaign Mal was at first my boss, then my mentor as we continued to raise money for the future well-being of Crimson Tide athletics. In our last years together we became friends, very close friends, and it pained me so to see what was beginning to happen to him during the latter part of 2012.

During the football season -- at least to me -- Mal seemed to be doing well, but I noticed he'd developed a nagging cough that slowly seemed to become more bothersome. After we beat Georgia in the SEC Championship game in Atlanta, a small group of us from the University went to New York City to be with Mal when he was honored at the National Football Foundation and Hall of Fame as its 2012 recipient of the John Toner Award. It's an award that goes annually to the best director of athletics in the NCAA.

It was a significant recognition and obviously well deserved. The award's dinner was on Tuesday night, so our official party attended an annual dinner hosted by Mal's attorney and friend Kirk Wood, at Peter Luger's Steak House in Brooklyn.

Mal usually loved these get-togethers because he had the opportunity to regale us with stories of his days growing up in Dozier or coaching, but it was easy to see he wasn't feeling that well.

Our dinner group included my wife Sue, Mal's daughter Heather and her husband Steve, his administrative aide Judy Tanner, executive AD Finus Gaston and his wife Martha, our business manager Carol Park, our photographer Kent Gidley, Kit Morris, and Mal's friend Mary Reyner along with Kirk, Joe Whatley and Edith Kallas. After dinner, Kirk had arranged for us to go to the area where the Twin Towers had been destroyed and they had begun rebuilding.

A former New York policeman gave us a tour and explained to us in detail about what had happened that day and about the rebuilding project. Mal was coughing noticeably, and Sue turned to him and said, "Mal, you need to see a doctor about that cough."

Sue would later say that Mal gave her "that look" which simply meant end of conversation. I knew what she meant because he gave that same look to everyone who suggested he have a doctor check on his cough.

I think Mal actually willed himself to be at his best at the different events those days in New York and I don't know if I ever saw him look any better than he did that night at the Waldorf when he was honored.

A few weeks later, we were invited to go on a hunting trip with Garry Neil Drummond, who is one of our supporters, at his Oaks Plantation near Albany, Georgia. Paul Bryant, Jr., was also invited and we were going to drive together to Birmingham to meet at the Drummond hangar to fly down.

While we were waiting on Paul in Mal's carport, he told me that he didn't know if he could hunt and that he wanted me to hunt for him. I was taken aback and I asked "Why?" He replied, pointing toward his mailbox 20 steps away, "Ronny, I can't walk that far."

When you quail hunt, you do it in pairs and after you flush the covey and shoot, then you hunt the singles. During our first hunt at the Oaks, I did walk alongside of Mal each time he went to flush a covey of birds, but after he shot he handed me his gun and told me to hunt the singles for him. He simply couldn't walk the distance to hunt the single birds.

My heart saddened to see my friend, with whom I had enjoyed many a day hunting, was no longer was able to enjoy the quail hunt that he loved so much. I didn't know what was wrong with his health, but I had that sickening feeling in my gut that it was not good.

After we returned to Tuscaloosa, his cough worsened. I know several other staff members had asked him to go to a doctor about it. One morning Judy Tanner called and asked me to talk to him and get him to a doctor.

I went by to see Mal and we visited on some department matters and then I said, "Mal, I came here with my employee hat on", as I gestured like I was removing a hat, "but now I'm going to put on my friend hat" and I gestured as if putting on a different hat.

"I want to take you to see Dr. Allen Yeilding in Birmingham and let him check you out." There was a long pause, as Mal looked out over the practice field. He finally turned back toward me and said, 'I think I'll take you up on that.'"

Allen had played golf at Alabama and is a supporter of our program. I drove Mal to Birmingham early one morning in February, and Allen ushered us in through a side door so no one would know Mal was there.

He checked him out and told him that everything other than a couple of problems that they already knew about was okay, but he said he wanted to do a chest x-ray before we left. On our drive back to Tuscaloosa, Allen called me after reviewing Mal's x-ray and told me that Mal needed to see a pulmonary specialist as soon as possible.

I told Mal and he asked me to get back with Allen and get an appointment. On February 19, I drove him back to Birmingham for his appointment with Dr. Christopher Roney at Brookwood Hospital.

When Dr. Roney came back in the room after Mal's MRI, I said that I would wait outside, but Mal strongly said, "No, I want you here with me." I knew at that moment our coach/player/boss/employee/mentor/ relationship of the past was extinguished. We were now close friends, and I would be there for him for whatever lies ahead.

The news wasn't good. Dr. Roney told Mal that he had idiopathic pulmonary fibrosis or IPF. When Mal asked him exactly what it meant, the doctor told him a well-functioning lung was like a sponge and soaked up oxygen like a sponge does water. However, his lungs were now like sheetrock and oxygen couldn't enter them.

There are three stages and from all indications, Mal was in the moderate level, which wasn't good; however, if he were in either the aggressive or super aggressive stage he would only have a few months to live.

At that point Dr. Roney told Mal that he needed to make a bucket list of things he still wanted to do because regardless of the stage he didn't have a lot of time left. Talk about a heartrending, emotional moment for me. I could only imagine what Mal was thinking.

I know when he got back, he confided in a few people including Judy Tanner and Mary Reyner, and he called Steve Townsend and they began the process of working on his exit strategy as Athletic Director. He also got in touch with Kirk Wood about his estate and his retirement from the University.

During those last couple of weeks in Tuscaloosa, Mal's primary focuses were working on his exit plan and watching the completion of the new weight room. He actually prepared two resignation letters, one for the end of the fiscal year and the one for the end of 2013.

On Friday, March 8, Mal was in his office for the final time. It was probably only fitting that his final lunch was at Rama Jama's, right across the street from Bryant-Denny Stadium. That Sunday he called me while Sue and I were on our way to church and he told me he needed to see the doctor again, and I didn't realize he meant right away.

By the time I got out of church, I received a call that an ambulance was on its way to his house. Immediately, I headed to Brookwood Hospital in Birmingham. For the next couple of days, a small cadre of his friends stayed with him. Coach Saban and Terry came up on that Wednesday as did Paul Bryant, Jr., and Dr. Robert Witt.

His only hope was to qualify for a lung transplant at Duke University. Steve Tisch, one of the owners of the New York Giants and a friend of Mal's, made arrangements with the medical center in Durham to accept Mal as a patient. He was flown there on an AirEvac plane that Wednesday night with the understanding that a transplant was a long-shot at best. Heather was with him every minute.

One person who really deserves special mention is Duke football coach David Cutcliffe, who was a classmate of mine at Alabama. Not only did he frequently visit Mal, but he set it up so that his football trainers took care of those of us who were in Durham during this time. Mary Reyner and Tricia Stone also maintained a daily vigil at the hospital with Mal and his family.

Although I had stayed part of the time with Mal, I was back home in Tuscaloosa that Saturday morning, March 30, when Judy Tanner called to tell me Mal had passed away. Actually, Judy along with Steve Townsend, Kirk Wood and

Bill McDonald were scheduled to fly up to see him that morning.

After I called Steve to tell him the news, I simply said, "Steve, he's gone." Nothing else was said. We both knew an era of Alabama athletics like none other was also gone. I had lost a great boss, but an even greater friend.

I know of no one, who loved not only Crimson Tide Athletics, but the entire University of Alabama more than Mal Moore. He was the Great Ambassador, the Elder Statesman for the University.

He was so proud of the University and all it stood for. He took great, great pride in all that it and all its students, and not just our athletes, accomplished. He loved the beauty of the campus. He loved Homecoming, especially the Friday night pep rally on the quadrangle. He loved hearing the Million Dollar band play "Yea Alabama." The University of Alabama was in his soul.

My last day with Mal was at Duke University Hospital in Durham, N.C. on Thursday, March 28, two days before he died. Judy Tanner asked me to read him press accounts about his retirement as A.D. I sat on the side of his bed and began to read.

When I got to the line where it said, "I've decided it is in the best interest of the athletic department that I resign my position as ..." I choked up and had to stop. I looked at him sitting up in his hospital bed and he looked at me. I know I showed a look of bewilderment and heartbreak and he looked the same.

I hated seeing my friend with that look. I eventually gathered myself and finished reading the release. I looked at him and he stuck out his hand. As weak as he was he gave me one of his characteristic firm Mal Moore handshakes. He then spoke and said, "Ronny, it's been a helluva ride."

If everyone could only know what a ride it was. National Champions, scotch and waters. Quail hunts and countless nights of Mal's stories on late night drives back to Tuscaloosa after his speaking engagements of selling Alabama athletics. Lunches at Gus' Hot Dogs, and representing the Crimson Tide with Mal while attending the College Football Hall of Fame ceremonies at the Waldorf in New York.

Meetings with the political figures, turkey hunts, and appointments with the state's successful business leaders asking for financial support for the Crimson Tide Foundation. Dove hunts, lunches at the 21 Club, representing Crimson Tide Athletics at the funerals of former athletes, and celebrating a Tide victory with cigars on his screened porch. It was without a doubt one helluva a ride.

At the time of his death it had been eight years since Mal had brought me into his life with a phone call and allowed me to live in his hip pocket until his death. For this I consider myself a blessed man, a very blessed man and my life will forever be richer because of what Mal Moore did for me.

Thank you my friend, you were the best.

Final Notes

By Steve Townsend

In November, 2012, Mal asked Kent Gidley, Judy Tanner and me to go to his house and start an inventory of all his championship memorabilia, including his rings and watches. He was determined they would be permanently displayed in the Mal M. Moore Building.

Many of his rings and watches were still in their original boxes, stashed in various drawers in his house. He got a good laugh when we uncovered his 1959 Liberty Bowl gift, a transistor radio, saying, "I doubt whether any current player would have a clue what the radio was."

During that same time period, he contacted attorneys Kirk Wood and Greg Hyde to review his will and estate plan. He also talked about buying a vacation home in a resort near Flagstaff, Arizona, where the Cardinals train. He wanted to have a place there, not only to visit but to leave for his daughter, Heather.

While we worked on his memoirs and retirement plan in January and February, he waited to visit Dr. Judy Bonner, Paul Bryant, Jr. and Dr. Witt until he felt it was time to retire and they could begin to search for a replacement. I'm not sure he even communicated to them the severity of his illness, not wanting to burden them.

That was the Mal way.

Coach Moore's Last Public Speech
Honoring the 2012 National Champions at Bryant-Denny Stadium

Winning a championship is always a team effort and it can only be accomplished by everyone from the Board of Trustees to the student managers working as one to achieve the ultimate team goal, being the national champion.

And, I wish I could stand here and thank each person who played a role in returning the championship trophy to Tuscaloosa.

Obviously, I can't do that but I would be remiss in not recognizing our Board of Trustees. Dr. Robert Witt, our Chancellor, is a magnificent leader for all the campuses within the University system.

Dr. Judy Bonner, whose vision continues to elevate all aspects on our campus, including athletics and our football program.

I don't know what else can be said about Coach Nick Saban that hasn't already been said or written. He's the best coach in America and we are proud of what he has accomplished at the University not only on the athletic field but his impeccable academic record as well.

All I can say is I'm sure as hell glad he's on our side.

And, I know how much I appreciate not only what he has accomplished for the Crimson Tide but what he and Terry have done for the University and the Tuscaloosa community. They have been leaders in helping rebuild this city and I know every Alabama fan is grateful for what you have done.

I certainly want to thank our fans for their support, not only in the games played at Bryant-Denny but wherever the Crimson Tide plays, your presence and enthusiasm play an important role in inspiring our team.

I know Coach Saban will talk about the team but I just want them to know how much I have enjoyed watching them compete not only this year but in their remarkable achievement of winning three national titles in four years.

That has only been done three times in the history of college football. I'm also proud to say that the University of Alabama became the first team ever to repeat as champions for the fourth time.

Sometimes statistics can be skewed but I'd be remiss in not noting that over the last four seasons, including SEC Championship games and bowl events, our teams have posted a record of 6-0 against teams with a combined record of 60-2.

No doubt, you have earned the right to be called champions.

No matter where you go in your personal life and career, you will always be a champion and a representative of your school, teammates and coaches. I encourage you to never forget what you have achieved, not as individuals, but as a team. I'm so proud of you.

Thank you.

Mal Moore's Retirement

Below is a copy of Coach Moore's final letter to his staff, officially announcing his retirement. He passed away nine days later.

Thursday, March 21

From the Desk of Mal Moore

Dear Coaches and Staff:
Dear Alabama Alumni and All Crimson Tide Fans:

It is with great sadness and a tremendous amount of emotion that I write this letter. As many of you may know, due to factors related to my health, I am at a point that I can no longer fulfill my duties as Athletics Director in the true championship manner the position requires.

One of Coach Paul Bryant's guiding principles was that you have to have a plan: a plan when you are ahead by three touchdowns and a plan for when you are behind in the fourth quarter.

I believe we have a great plan to move forward that allows this great institution to continue on the path of academic excellence and championship athletics. We have developed a plan that also allows me to focus on my health while maintaining an on-going working relationship with this great University as Athletics Director Emeritus. I know I can count on each of you to continue your unequaled support for me and the University of Alabama as we move forward with this plan.

I cannot put in to words what this institution that I have been a part of for over 50 years means to me. It is where I arrived when I first left my home in Dozier, Alabama; it is where I was educated; where I met and married my wife; and where my daughter was born and grew up. It is the place I have called home and with people I identified as my family for over 50 years.

I cannot adequately express what this institution and the people that have made it great means to me and my family and what it means to have a truly crimson heart. Coach Bryant always told us to show our class. I hope you will allow me to complete this great journey and move to the side of the stage with love and class for an institution and a fan base that is nothing but a winner.

There is no way humanly possible for me to convey my appreciation to each one of you for your loyalty to me personally and to the University as a whole during my tenure as director. While I would personally like to be able to visit with each of you personally to thank you for your service, I hope I can convey through this letter how proud I am to have worked with you.

Let me close by saying always represent the Crimson Tide with dignity, whether it's in your moments of exhilaration or when you suffer a momentary setback. Roll Tide.

Kindest Regards,
Mal

Notes On Mal Moore's Career

• During his years as a coach at Alabama, the Crimson compiled a record of 222-41-5, won six National Championships, 16 SEC Championships, and appeared in 23 bowl games. Against Alabama's chief rivals, Moore was on staffs that compiled records of 18-3 vs. LSU, 17-4 vs. Auburn and 16-5-1 vs. Tennessee.

• As a player, coach and administrator at the University, Alabama football teams won 10 National Championships, 17 SEC Championships, participated in 39 bowl games and won 428 games.

• While a member of the offensive staff, Alabama led the SEC in scoring offense 10 times, rushing offense nine times, and passing efficiency five times.

• During Moore's tenure as Director of Athletics, Alabama produced national championship teams in football, gymnastics, softball, men's golf and women's golf as well as Southeastern Conference championships in football, basketball, baseball, gymnastics, men's and women's golf, men's cross country and softball. Alabama athletes earned some of the highest honors the SEC and NCAA have to offer, including SEC Athlete of the Year, SEC Scholar-Athlete of the Year, NCAA Top VIII, NCAA Postgraduate Scholarships and NCAA Sportsperson of the Year.

• Moore directed more than $240 million of capital improvements to University of Alabama athletic facilities. Those projects encompassed the entire scope of all Crimson Tide athletic programs and benefitted every Alabama student-athlete, coach, and administrator.

• During his 1999-2013 tenure as Athletics Director, he oversaw the north end zone and south end zone expansions of Bryant-Denny Stadium that increased the capacity to more than 101,000. The Walk of Champions, his vision for a gateway to campus and the stadium, features the statues of the five National Championship coaches and plagues commemorating all of the championship football teams.

- Coach Moore spearheaded the Crimson Tradition Campaign for facilities, which included building new complexes for soccer, golf and tennis, the renovation of Bryant Hall, Coleman Coliseum, Foster Auditorium and the Sam Bailey Track Stadium.

- Coach Moore initiated plans to rebuild Sewell-Thomas Baseball Stadium and the new rowing facility.

- In 2007, the football complex was named in his honor, and the Mal M. Moore building underwent extensive changes during his administration tenure, including a totally new area for the football coaches that feature state-of-the-art dressing and meeting rooms and a players' lounge.

- In his final week, the new weight room in the indoor football facility was completed, and groundwork had commenced on the Sarah Patterson Championship Plaza, featuring the heritage of all Crimson Tide sports.

- In 2008, the State of Alabama Sports Hall of Fame named Moore as its recipient of the Distinguished Sportsman of the Year.

- In 2011, he was elected to the State of Alabama Sports Hall of Fame for his accomplishments as a coach and an administrator. After the completion of the 2011-12 academic and athletic seasons, Moore was named the winner of the John L. Toner Award, given to the nation's best athletic director.

- In 2012, the City of Tuscaloosa honored him and his late wife Charlotte by naming the new facility the "Mal and Charlotte Moore Caring Days Center," a facility that serves as a daycare program for adults with Alzheimer's and other memory disorders.

- In 2013, Coach Moore was honored posthumously as the winner of the College Athletic Director of the Year Award presented by the *Street & Smith's Sports Business Journal* and *Sports Business Daily*.